EKBERT FAAS

TED HUGHES: THE UNACCOMMODATED UNIVERSE

With Selected

Critical Writings

by Ted Hughes

& Two

Interviews

Santa Barbara
BLACK SPARROW PRESS
1980

For information concerning the subsidiary rights solely to the material
by Ted Hughes quoted in this book please address Olwyn Hughes,
Literary Agent, 100 Chetwynd Road, London NW5 1DH, England.

Thanks to the following publishers whose books are quoted in this
study: Agathon Press, Carcanet New Press, Doubleday, Faber and
Faber, Harper & Row, Hutchinson, Rainbow Press and Turret Books.

Thanks to the following magazines in which some of the excerpts
from Ted Hughes' critical writings as printed in Appendix I originally appeared: Leonard Baskin, Children's Literature in Education,
Critical Quarterly, Guardian, Listener, London Magazine, New Statesman, New York Review of Books, Poetry Book Society Bulletin, Tri-
Quarterly, Vogue and Your Environment.

LIBRARY OF CONGRESS CATALOGING IN PUBLICATION DATA

Faas, Ekbert.
    Ted Hughes: the unaccommodated universe.

    Includes index.
    1. Hughes, Ted, 1930-   —Criticism and interpretation.
PR6058.U37Z68   821'.914   79-27434
ISBN 0-87685-460-9
ISBN 0-87685-461-7 lim. ed.
ISBN 0-87685-459-5 pbk.

For My Parents

Contents

TED HUGHES: THE UNACCOMMODATED UNIVERSE

A Personal Pre-Preface

My personal contacts with Hughes over the last ten years have been little more than sporadic. Yet even our first three-hour discussion in March 1970 was enough to turn me from an admirer of his poetry into a witness of an interior saga whose gradual unfolding in his writing has held my interest ever since. During this talk, Hughes merely alluded to Sylvia Plath's suicide in February 1963. But the main focus of our discussion—the story of a quester's descent to save his desecrated bride from the underworld through his self-sacrifice—bore the obvious imprint of this event. Even in private, Hughes is a confessional poet only at the level of transmuting autobiographical details into mythic symbols, and until the publication of *Gaudete* in 1977, this transmutation kept the poems at a near unrecognizable distance from their hidden source. For good reason, Hughes asked me to omit his detailed account of the story from our published interview of January 1971.[1]

In the meantime, bits and pieces of this story have been made public in various places, and when I first encountered the underworld "baboon woman" with her "crudely stitched patchwork of faces" (G,104)* in *Gaudete*, the right moment seemed to have come to give my own account of Hughes' work and development. To this attempt the poet again lent his support in correspondence and further discussion. One major directive for the following study thus derives from Hughes' own comments on his work in private and, more indirectly, in his wide-ranging critical essays which provide a more rationally articulated counterpoint to his poetic vision. Yet another stems from my own ongoing effort to graph the emergence of a new aesthetic to which Hughes' work presents a major contribution. In some ways a loner in the British poetry scene and a distinctly original voice in contemporary poetry generally, Hughes nevertheless finds his company in an international artistic context characterized, to use the most general terms, by its departure from the mainstream Western tradition. To

---

*For an alphabetical list of the bibliographical abbreviations used in this study and in Appendix I, see ABBREVIATED REFERENCES FOR WRITINGS BY TED HUGHES on page 147-50 below.

11

quote from a previous study, Hughes, like a number of his contemporaries, no longer views creativity "as an imitation of reality in stasis" but "as a reenactment of nature in process, achieved by projective empathy and psycho-physiological spontaneity."[2] His individual talent, not unlike that of peers like Stockhausen, Olson or Grotowski, defines itself in relation to a multicultural and interdisciplinary hybrid ranging from shamanism to quantum mechanics rather than with regard to any specific literary tradition.

My first two chapters then deal with Hughes' own sense of this new global tradition and aesthetic, while the remaining ones go on to trace his artistic development within this wider framework. Here, the aim is neither to give isolated New Critical analyses of Hughes' major poems nor a reader's guide to his poetry in general—although with the help of its index the book may partly fulfill such needs. Hughes' greatest poems, as in the case of Yeats or Rilke, are best appreciated if seen as single efflorescences of the poet's spiritual growth, and it is this semi-biographical perspective which will guide us through his work. The chapters dealing with Hughes' poetry, in other words, mark the chapters of his interior development, and it is no accident that only the final ones should carry the titles of his recent collections. Hughes' absorption in his quest, in which Sylvia Plath, in life and more decisively in death, played the role of an initiator, has deepened over the years. As a result, his successive volumes of poetry, at first loosely grouped around certain themes, as *The Hawk in the Rain* and *Lupercal*, more and more patently point to a specific phase in his development, though without ever spelling out the full story. What Hughes described as the "single adventure" of *Wodwo* (W,9) clearly perplexed rather than enlightened the readers of that volume. To those of *Crow* and *Gaudete*, the same announcement would have seemed less implausible generally but equally difficult to figure out in detail. These alone, it seems to me, are sufficient reasons for looking at the several adventures of Hughes' works as parts of the hidden saga from which they sprang and to thereby retrace his poetic development from its beginnings.

My thanks are due to Ted Hughes for allowing me to include excerpts from my forthcoming edition of his critical writings as well as for the openness with which he answered my questions, to Barbara Lecker, who first suggested that I write this book, for her indispensable advice throughout its various stages, to Seamus Cooney who helped me give it its final shape, and to John Blazina who did most of the checking.

Thou wert better in a grave than to answer with thy uncovered body this extremity of the skies. Is man no more than this? Consider him well: thou owest the worm no silk, the beast no hide, the sheep no wool, the cat no perfume. Ha! here's three on's are sophisticated. Thou art the thing itself; unaccommodated man is no more but such a poor bare, forked animal as thou art. Off, off, you lendings! Come, unbutton here.

(*King Lear* III, iv, 103-111)

In a way their world reminds one of Beckett's world. Only theirs seems braver, more human, and so more real . . . Their poetic themes revolve around the living suffering spirit, capable of happiness, much deluded, too frail, with doubtful and provisional senses, so undefinable as to be almost silly, but palpably existing, and wanting to go on existing—and this is not, as in Beckett's world, absurd . . . They have managed to grow up to a view of the unaccommodated Universe, but it has not made them cynical, they still like it and keep all their sympathies intact. They have gone back to the simple animal courage of accepting the odds and have rediscovered the frontier.

(Ted Hughes, 67,P,201-2)

PREFACE

It is impossible not to recognize what looks more and more like a simple fact: whenever [he] wrote at top intensity . . . he was almost invariably hammering at the same thing—a particular knot of obsessions . . . [His] poetry has its taproot in a sexual dilemma of a peculiarly black and ugly sort . . . It was his great recurrent dream . . . lust, this boar of blackness, emerging to do murder, accompanied—as a rule—by various signs of a hellish apparition, and leagued with everything forbidden,

> 'Perjured, murderous, bloody, full of blame,
> Savage, extreme, rude, cruel, not to trust. . . .'

combines with the puritan mind—a mind desensitized to the true nature of nature—and produced . . . men of chaos.

The poet Hughes has singled out for such criticism has little in common with the traditional image of the "gentle Shakespeare." Instead, Hughes describes him as a man who in play after play shed his own sickness in posing "a chronic sexual dilemma . . . The arguments are the same, and carried on with the same almost repulsively obsessive zest." But however narrow its focus, Shakespeare's obsession managed to reflect the major psychic conflict of his time, the struggle between Calvinist witch-hunt

13

misogyny and the Celtic pre-Christian Mother worship surviving in the cult of the Queen. "It was a gigantic all-inclusive trial" resulting "in an upheaval of Civil War and an epidemic of murders of women" (71,S,181ff.).

If diagnosed in his own language, Hughes, particularly since *The Wound* (1962), seems to be writing from a similar knot of obsessions. But, as in Shakespeare's case, it is hardly enough to merely graph the manifest content of this great recurrent dream. What if *Crow*, as one reviewer noted disapprovingly, has dozens of images involving blood, death and disease or if "stabbing, smashing, screaming, writhing, and so on" are "the book's key violent verbs" (*TLS*, January 8, 1971)? Many great works of literature would, as we know, yield similar results, and even if Hughes' concern with violence and suffering should exceed that of his predecessors, there is little in that to surprise us. Considering the millions of people killed during the poet's lifetime, it would need a madness of its own to be left unaffected by violence in our time. Even during childhood, Hughes, as his father's "luckless double," heard of "blown-off boots, tree-stumps, shell-cases and craters" (W,155), and whatever reinforced these memories during adulthood has come to inform his poetry like an ongoing nightmare of a peculiarly black and ugly sort. Our concern then will be not only to follow this mythopoeic dream but to unravel its hidden motivation wherever possible, an attempt in which Hughes' critical writings on Shakespeare as well as other poets and subjects provide an invaluable source of information.

Negative responses to Hughes' work markedly resemble what critics for a long time thought of some of Shakespeare's plays. Even when the Romantics began to include the demonic and irrational in their art, poets and critics still considered *King Lear* as transgressing "beyond the . . . *ne plus ultra* of the dramatic" (Coleridge), as simply "painful and disgusting" (Lamb) or as anticipating the modern "dissolution of everything spiritual."[1] Of course, it is this very "humour of the abominable thing" (Hegel)[2] which has fascinated *King Lear's* more recent audiences. Sensitized by the endgame despair of a Beckett or Ionesco, many among them now see the play as reflecting "the decay and fall" of their own world,—a *Book of Job* performed by clowns making a "mockery of all eschatologies: of the heaven promised on earth, and the heaven promised after death . . . [and] of man made in the 'image and likeness' " (Jan Kott).[3]

No wonder that Hughes included Lear's speech about "unaccommodated man" in his 1971 *Choice of Shakespeare's Verse*. For, like the world of several Eastern European poets which he summed up in Shakespeare's phrase, his own is that of unaccommodated man in an unaccommodated universe, "humanity stripped of everything but the biological persistence of cells . . . waiting in empty eternity" (76,P,9). And even before Jan Kott described Shakespeare as "Our Contemporary," Hughes had made him his own in *Eat Crow*, a play written in 1964. Here Morgan Producer explains to his alter ego how to articulate Lear's "Never, never, never, never, never!" His advice takes us into the very center of Hughes' universe. The words, he suggests, should be pronounced as if by a man who is "losing the world":

> the king is using this word NEVER like a knife, to carve up his own insides
> . . . He's forcing it down into the last, deepest cellars and underground
> resistance of his life-illusion, murdering himself.

Lear's dying words deny us the reconciling spectacle of a hero who is ennobled by his suffering or able to turn it into a boon to others, but to Hughes there is something else. "He's cracked open the foundations—the light floods in" (EC,15,16). However, *King Lear* was only a stage in a long career, and though Shakespeare may have been plagued by a "particular knot of obsessions" for most of his life, it seems wrong to claim, as Hughes does, that he never solved his "cruel riddle" or that he began to cheat in the romances (71,S,181,182,195). On the contrary, his mockery and eventual transcendence of all eschatologies was to lead him to a new existential understanding of life beyond despair not dissimilar to, yet, in my mind, more far-reaching than Hughes' own.

What both poets share is the "experience of disintegration and renewal" (66,P,81) which is the major theme of both Shakespeare's post-apocalyptic world since *King Lear* and of Hughes' unaccommodated universe since the early sixties. Not surprisingly, we find Hughes describing this death and rebirth process in an essay on Sylvia Plath whose suicide on February 11, 1963 more than anything else was to launch him on this journey—"the central experience of a shattering of the self, and the labour of fitting it together again or finding a new one" (66,P,81). The poet was quick to recognize the wider mythopoeic dimensions of this personal destiny, and his 1964 review of Mircea Eliade's *Shamanism* mapped the area of world poetry to which his own has been contributing ever since:

> The initiation dreams, the general schema of the shamanic flight, and the
> figures and adventures they [i.e., the shamans] encounter, are not a sha-
> man monopoly: they are, in fact, the basic experience of the poetic tem-
> perament we call "romantic." In a shamanizing society, "Venus and
> Adonis," some of Keats' longer poems, "The Wanderings of Oisin," "Ash
> Wednesday," would all qualify their authors for the magic drum; while
> the actual flight lies perceptibly behind many of the best fairy tales, and
> behind myths such as those of Orpheus and Herakles, and behind the
> epics of Gilgamesh and Odysseus. It is the outline, in fact, of the Heroic
> Quest. The shamans seem to undergo, at will and at phenomenal inten-
> sity, and with practical results, one of the main regenerating dramas of
> the human psyche: the fundamental poetic event. (64,E,677-8)

Here again, the poet's major precedent is Shakespeare, and to a further extent, perhaps, than Hughes himself has been aware of. For nothing in Western literature besides Goethe's *Faust*, it seems to me, presents a fuller account of the shamanizing experience than the Shakespearean spectrum: from the call in "Venus and Adonis," through "magical death [and] dismemberment" in the tragedies, towards resurrection in the late plays—and all of it "full of [the] buffoonery, mimicry . . . and magical contortions" (64,E,677) typical of primitive ritual. Yet given Hughes' idiosyncratic understanding of this development, his own has taken a major impulse from the half-conscious attempt to retrieve Nature from the desecration in which he thinks Shakespeare had left her. Where the playwright "banished Venus, as Sycorax, the blue-eyed hag" and "humbled Tarquin as Caliban, the poetry crammed half-beast" (71,S,198), Hughes makes Caliban reappear in his half animal-like quester heroes like Gog and Wodwo who eventually, in the figures of Crow and the seal-like Lumb, set out to rescue the banished, desecrated and demonized Earth Mother from the underworld.

In a review of Dylan Thomas's letters, Hughes takes issue with the New Critical separation of poetry from the poet. This may work with writers "who set their poetic selves . . . into the third person" but fails with poets like Yeats or Thomas whose lives, "letters and legends belong to [their] poetry" (66,T,783). Hughes himself belongs to this second group, and just as his poems, as he says, resemble "ragged dirty undated letters from remote battles and weddings" (71,F,15), his critical writings represent the richest source for shedding light on these remote events. This is particularly true of what he has written about Sylvia Plath with whom, as he once said, he shared an all-absorbing working partnership and "an unspoken unanimity in every criticism or judgment" (65,H). Her idea "of the great civilised crime of intelligence that . . . has turned on its mother" (66,P,84), for instance, not only provides the subject of "Logos," one of Hughes' earliest mythopoeic poems, but also pervades the later apocalyptic visions of world destruction preceding the birth of Crow and the new creation. With Sylvia Plath he also shares the basic "experience of disintegration and renewal" and, like her poems, his own can be considered as "chapters in a mythology where the plot, seen as a whole and in retrospect, is strong and clear—even if the origins of it and the *dramatis personae*, are at bottom enigmatic" (66,P,81).[4]

The opening chapters of the Hughes mythology, as traced in the early volumes of poetry up to the "single adventure" of *Wodwo*, tell of the "split personality of modern man" (65,H), of his self-exile from Mother Nature and of his last ditch effort to recapture some of her lost elemental forces by a poetic invocation of plants and animals. Their author is the "modern mediumistic artist" characterized in a later statement of his:

Sure enough, when [he] looks into his crystal, he . . . sees the last nightmare of mental disintegration and spiritual emptiness, under the superego of Moses . . . and the self-anaesthetising schizophrenia of St. Paul. . . . But he may see something else. He may see a vision of the real Eden, "excellent as at the first day," the draughty radiant Paradise of the animals, which is the actual earth, in the actual Universe. (70,N,81)

At this point, a few more hints must suffice to indicate the extent to which Hughes' critical writings can be shown to elucidate his further poetic development. Whereas an early poem like "The Thought-Fox" evoked "the vital, somewhat terrible spirit of natural life" (70,N,81) by summoning what is "both a fox and a spirit" (P,20), the Crow poems reflect a more direct mythopoeic apprehension of the spirit world. Suddenly erupting in poems such as "Logos" or "The Bear" (both 1966), this development was heralded by several reviews of books on primitive literature. The reviews reveal the frustrated mood of a poet searching for the unearthed treasures of an art which, unlike primitive music, painting and sculpture, had never had the chance to exert its full impact on the modern imagination.

By remedying this deficiency, Hughes' *From the Life and Songs of the Crow* (1970), a volume written between 1966 and 1969, represent a landmark in the history of Anglo-American poetry. Many of its poems seem like prototype versions of those "little fable[s]" and "visionary anecdote[s]" made by a "primitive, gnomic spellmaker" which Hughes, in 1967, had come to see in the lyrics of Vasko Popa. To be sure, Popa's "folktale surrealism" (67,P,204) with its odd but sophisticated arabesques is further removed from primitive poetry than Hughes', while the resemblance between *Crow* and the verse of the original *Technicians of the Sacred* (1968), as anthologized by American poet Jerome Rothenberg, is all the more striking for being fortuitous. No wonder if that collection, as friends report, became Hughes' constant companion for a time after he first discovered it in 1970

The Crow poems also seem to draw on the poet's previous concern with such diverse phenomena as Sufism, the tricksters, non-Western mythology and in particular Shamanism. Of special importance here is the shamanistic *Tibetan Book of the Dead*. Such "folklore hieroglyphs and magical monsters" (67,P,204) as the "Womb Door" or "King of Carrion," for instance, seem directly inspired by the *Bardo Thödol* while the latter's basic shamanistic quest pattern of death and rebirth, "together with the principal terrific events, and the flying accompaniment of descriptive songs," provide a general analogue to the *Life and Songs of the Crow*. Crow's capacity to survive despite the ordeals and mutilations he is exposed to also resembles the shaman's rebirth after his "magical death [and] dismemberment . . . with all possible variants of boiling, devouring, burning, stripping to the bones" (64,E,677).

Hughes' evolution into a "primitive, gnomic spellmaker" meant a simultaneous change in the language and the structure of his poetry. Whereas the early poems often seem like bravado feats in the "art of explosive compression" (63,H,11), those in *Wodwo*, in trying to portray the "single adventure" of a repeated descent into disintegration, develop a new strategy reminiscent of the loose "constellation[s] of statements" (63,D,47) that Hughes had noted in the later poetry of Keith Douglas. They often turn into "free poem[s] of sorts where grammar, sentence structure etc, are all sacrificed in an attempt to break fresh and accurate perceptions and words out of the reality of the subject chosen" (P,23). And though Hughes remains convinced "that formal patterning of the actual movement of verse somehow includes a mathematical and a musically deeper world than free verse can easily hope to enter" (71,F,20), his poetry since *Lupercal* has all but for a few exceptions been cast in the free verse mode. For the advantages won in exchange seem to be more than a greater "freedom of the voice" which Hughes remarked in the later verse of Sylvia Plath,—"the more free it gets, the more musically exact it gets . . . Every one of its casual free lines is like a sudden new melody—surprising and inevitable" (71,P,170).

Animal sounds sometimes manage to evoke what human words, even those of the poet, more often than not tend to obscure, and then, as Hughes writes, "you hear the whole desolate, final actuality of existence in a voice, a tone" (71,0). As if to emulate such magic, Hughes' poems have gradually acquired an ever more powerful suggestiveness through their sheer onomatopoeic impact. *Orghast*, a mythic play in a language of pure sound, scripted for the 1971 performance in Shiraz directed by Peter Brook, carried this tendency to its *ne plus ultra*. By contrast, Hughes' more recent poetry, in its search for shamanistic rebirth in a new mythic world, combines vibrational magic of sound and imagistic concision with an unprecedented lucidity of statement, of the kind he noted in the poetry of Popa—"making audible meanings without disturbing the silence . . . making no mistakes, but with no hope of finality, continuing to explore" (67,P,202).

In analysing these and other relations between Hughes' criticism and his poetic development we shall, of course, try to avoid the pitfalls of the intentional fallacy and, what is more, explore the puzzling contrast between Hughes, the poet of apocalyptic doom, and Hughes, the essayist searching for and suggesting ways out of the spiritual dilemma of our time. To take one example: In 1970, only a year after the death of his companion Assia and their child Shura, Hughes felt hopeful enough to testify to a phenomenon "unthinkable only ten years ago, except as a poetic dream: the re-emergence of Nature as the Great Goddess of mankind, and the Mother of all life" (70,N,83). Yet as any reader of the more recent

Gaudete (1977) can tell, the poetic realization of this dream met with unexpected difficulties. Asked if the fatefully preordained victimization and murder of women caused by Lumb's dabbling attempts to resurrect the Great Mother reflected his own growing pessimism concerning the task, Hughes replied in a letter: "The pessimism of the theme is an inevitable part of the working out of the theme." The more optimistic bent of Hughes' critical thinking may well point up the eventual goal he will reach in his poetic development. In the meantime, his role as a poet remains that of the visionary witness who, as Carl Jung put it, "can only obey the apparently alien impulse within him and follow where it leads, sensing that his work is greater than himself, and wields a power which is not his and which he cannot command."[5] Commenting on his Jaguar poems in our interview of March, 1970, Hughes said: "In a perfectly cultured society one imagines that jaguar-like elementals would be invoked only by self-disciplinarians of a very advanced grade. I am not one and I'm sure few readers are, so maybe in our corrupt condition we have to regard poems about jaguars as ethically dangerous" (71,F,9). More recently, I asked Hughes if, implicit in this statement, was a sense of irresponsibility for having failed to control the energies he had invoked. His written reply was:

> No I don't feel any bad conscience for what appears in what I write. It's more a case I think of being a witness. When the present quiet civil war in England has played itself out, I imagine my poems about Jaguars will look very tame.

I.

Origins

Poetry at its most primitive seems first to occur as a one-line chant of nonsense syllables in accompaniment to the rhythm of a stamping dance. Chimpanzees have got this far, and with them there is evidently not much before it. (62,B,781)

Looking at this image of global unity, so prehistoric and yet so actually present, we see how far ahead of its time Conservation has been. While Politicians, Sociologists, Economists, Theologians, Philosophers and the rest pick over the stucco rubble of a collapsed civilisation, the Conservationists are nursing a new global era. (70,N,83)

I. ORIGINS

Ted Hughes is nothing if not an English poet. Yet there is more to his Englishness than the literary debt he may owe to Hopkins, Owen, Donne and others who are commonly cited as his models. What set him off writing, in fact, were some "odd pieces by Shapiro, Lowell, Merwin, Wilbur and Crowe Ransom" in a "Penguin of American poets that came out in about 1955" (71,F,14). And the English poets that contributed to this early outburst of creativity did so by helping him retrieve what had dwelt in the dungeons rather than the amphitheatres of the post-Restoration Academy of English Letters—that "radical Englishness" (71,S,198) defunct since 1660, gradually reemerging in Blake, Yeats, Lawrence and Thomas, yet permanently alive in the West Yorkshire dialect the poet has spoken since childhood. "Without it," Hughes stated in 1970, "I doubt if I would ever have written verse" (71,F,11).

As it is, "the terrible, suffocating, maternal octopus of ancient English poetic tradition" (64,D,23) clung closely enough, and there are several poems in the early collections which suggests that Hughes himself was quite unable to follow his own advice, addressed to younger poets, to "ignore all influences" and instead "mine [their] way back to the source of poetry inside [their] head[s]."[1] For in the very effort to shed the "frivolous system of vocal team-calls which we inherit as Queen's English" (71,S,198), he found himself following poets like Owen, Hopkins and Yeats who had fought a similar battle before him. Nor did his drive for a radical Englishness take its impetus from the so-called modernist poets. "Up to the age of twenty-five," Hughes recalls, "I read no contemporary poetry whatsoever except Eliot, Thomas and some Auden" (71,F,13-14).

1. The New Global Tradition.

The roots of Hughes' true Englishness go far deeper than all this. "After all the campaigns to make it new," he stated in 1970, "you're stuck with the fact that some of the Scots ballads still cut a deeper groove than anything written in the last forty years" (71,F,14). For here, as in Chaucer or Shakespeare, the English tradition that Hughes is ready to acknowledge as his own breaks open into regions beyond its Judaeo-Christian and classicist encrustations. One such area is the as yet largely unavailable treasure of our own mythologies. "A full unwatered collection of this material, coming into the museum desolation of modern English imaginative life," Hughes augured in 1964, "could alter certain individuals profoundly, especially just at this time, when the dead crust of the over-latinate intelligence is beginning to show cracks."

Yet even this lore of the "deities of our instinct and ancestral memory," told in the Anglo-Saxon-Norse-Celtic language "where our real mental life has its roots" (64,T,464), is only part of a much larger network, mankind's universal literatures and myths. Hughes' critical writings alone testify to a truly polyhistoric grasp of this material from Eskimo songs to Chilean folktales and from the *Nibelungenlied* to the *Bardo Thödol*. And he reveals more than a mere dilettante's approach to it when he calls Turville-Petre's *Myth and Religion of the North* the successor to Grimm's *Teutonic Mythology* (64,T,484) or praises R. K. Narayan's collection of tales from the *Ramayana, Mahabharata* and other sources "in the immense Indian reserves" as the "best retellings of Indian tales" from among the "some hundreds" he has read (64,S,7).

There is little in this global attitude to remind us of T. S. Eliot's claustrophobic belief that only a "continued veneration of our ancestors . . . in the literatures of Greece, Rome and Israel"[2] could prevent the decline of the West. Instead, Hughes' more radical conservativism is that of a worldwide new poetics in progress which, in the wake of pioneers like Pound, Lawrence and others, is gradually replacing its post-Aristotelean antecedent. In the terms of American poet Robert Duncan, "we are coming from what were once national traditions . . . into . . . a community of meanings [where a] psyche will be formed having roots in all the old cultures."[3] In Hughes' similar view, Eliot, Joyce and possibly Beckett still belong to the last phase of Christian civilization and are suffering its disintegration.

> But there are now quite a few writers about who do not seem to belong spiritually to the Christian civilization at all. In their world Christianity is just another provisional myth of man's relationship with the creator and the world of spirit. Their world is a continuation or a re-emergence of the pre-Christian world . . . it is the world of the little pagan religions and cults, the primitive religions from which of course Christianity itself grew. (71,F,15-16)

Paradoxically it was this neolithic conservativism which turned Hughes into his country's major spokesman for mankind's sudden and unprecedented evolution into a new global culture. His collaborations with Peter Brook's International Center of Theatre Research, and their joint production of *Orghast*, a compound of multi-cultural myths in a language using root syllables from Anglo-Saxon, Greek, Avesta etc., was but one demonstration of this fact. For the excitement of belonging to a generation which in Gary Snyder's words is the first ever to have "all of man's culture available to our study"[4] seems to inform his every activity, interest, and more recent poetic creativity. Crow, for instance, is made to escape through a Tibetan Buddhist Womb Door into primordial worlds of Biblical myth turned comic book parody, sings Eskimo songs, parodies Sophocles' Oedipus, gives idiosyncratic accounts of St. George's battle with the dragon or tears open apocalyptic vistas of imminent nuclear holocaust.

Such eclectic fantasizings, cutting across all the boundaries of space, time, and consciousness, are fed by a restless pursuit of knowledge which via his Cambridge studies of archaeology and anthropology can be traced back to the twelve-year-old boy's precocious interest in his native folklore. The latter led him to Yeats who in the late forties held the young poet spellbound by his mythopoeic phantasmagoria fusing Irish folklore with Hermetic magic and Rosicrucian theosophy while opening into the whole body of Indian mythological and religious texts. When the Chinese composer Chou Wen-chung in 1959 invited Hughes to write a libretto for a musical presentation of *The Tibetan Book of the Dead*, he found a poet well prepared for his task. Their plans never materialized, but Hughes rewrote the entire *Bardo Thödol* several times while Chou Wen-chung had "the most wonderful plans . . . Gigantic orchestra, massed choirs, projected illuminated mandalas, soul-dancers and the rest." "We had no idea," the poet recalled in 1970, that "we were riding the zeitgeist so closely . . . and now of course we've lost the whole idea to the psychedelics" (71,F,16).

In the sixties, a period of trial and error, particularly after the death of Sylvia Plath, the poet's search for a new spiritual basis began to diversify its perspectives. Paralleling similar pursuits among his contemporaries, the inquiries into non-Western and primitive culture now gained additional momentum from kindred forays into those borderline areas of modern scientific research which suggest the need for a new understanding of man and nature. Here physics, anthropology, ecology, ethology and parapsychology have held Hughes' consistent interest while his search amongst the rare texts of primitive myth, poetry and folklore intensified as his poetry turned more and more mythical. In an often exasperated tone, several reviews written between 1962 and 1968 plead with the scholars to provide unbowdlerized translations of their source materials instead of pouring out further Ph.D. type analyses obsessed with "the Universal folktale motif index" and more often than not the mere products of a mentality "dry-rotten with comparison, analysis, boredom . . . [and] fed only by print and anxiety" (68,L,699). In 1965, "the explosive transformation Radin's African collection worked on the poetry of Sylvia Plath" (65,G,35) was the only instance Hughes could adduce of how modern poetry had absorbed the direct impact of the primitive. Yet such deficiencies were soon to be remedied by American poets like Snyder and Rothenberg, Vasko Popa's "folktale surrealism" of the "primitive, gnomic spellmaker" (67,P,204) and, of course, Hughes' own poetry.

Wherever his own vocation was called upon, the poet's discontent with scholars and translators erupted into constructive activity. Launched by Ted Hughes and Daniel Weissbort, *Modern Poetry in Translation*, now in its sixteenth year, is the most fruitful British enterprise of its kind to date. Its opening statement of editorial policy wards off purist opponents of poetry translation who speak "as though 'the poetry' were some separable ingredient, some additive like the whitening agent in a detergent," and pleads for a new English poetry benefiting from a "closer acquaintance with what is being written elsewhere." To the editors, the first issue's poetry by Israeli Amichai, Russian Voznesensky, Czech Holub, Poles Herbert and Milosz, Yugoslavs Lalic and Popa, for instance, seemed "more universal than ours. It deals in issues, universally comprehensible. It does not fight shy of philosophy. It does not hide behind perverse imagery. As compared with our poetry it comes out into the open."[5]

Despite the apparent grimness of his vision, Hughes' general drive as a writer, as Peter Brook put it in '71, "is from dark to light, sunset to sunrise."[6] What distinguishes him from, say, his American fellow poets is not a lack of future-oriented optimism but the fact that Hughes, as European and adolescent witness of World War II, feels a greater need than they do to test and retest his global vision against the acid memory of mankind's recent historical collapse. Hence his deep attraction to the Central European poets speaking from that "disaster-centre of the modern world" (76,P,9) which has been a staple of Hughes' nightmare fantasies ever since, as a four-year-old boy, he started to hear of battles in Flanders and Gallipoli while turning into his father's "luckless double . . ./ Among jawbones and blown-off boots, tree-stumps, shell-cases and craters" (W,155). His admiration for these poets and the more recent ties of friendship have, since the launching of *Modern Poetry in Translation*, brought forth three collections of poems by Popa, Pilinszky and Amichai, which the English poet translated with the help of native speakers. Hughes' extensive introductions to these volumes make no secret of the kinship he feels with their authors, and more often than not they read like passionately shared manifestos rather than critical commentaries. Thus Popa and Pilinszky, in Hughes' view, give first-hand accounts of what we usually see only "clutter of our civilised liberal confusion" (67,P,201): the vision, so akin to Hughes' own, of modern man as " 'a gasping, limbless trunk' savaged by primal hungers, among the odds and ends of a destroyed culture"(76,P,9). In this they spontaneously rejoin the primitive, especially in the "pre-creation atmosphere" of Popa's work (67,P,203). And just as Kafka, in Hughes' reading experience, can come as an anticlimax after the "cruelty and obscenity and 'absurdity'" of certain primitive folktales (63,S), so their vision of the unaccommodated universe represents a definite step beyond Beckett's world of the absurd.

Hughes' vision of contemporary civilization finds its deepest affinities amongst Central European poets. By contrast, his neo-primitivist speculations about a way out of the present impasse have their analogues elsewhere. Originally inspired by "Yeats's whole-hearted attempt to recover the pre-Christian imagination of Ireland" (64,T,485), they have come to encompass a scope far beyond the ken of Hughes' Irish predecessor, while coming closer and closer to many science-inspired insights of his American fellow poets. Just as Heisenberg's Uncertainty Principle, according to Charles Olson, has reclaimed the Heraclitean *panta rhei*,[7] so nuclear physics, in Hughes' view, has reinstated the "wild Heraclitean/ Buddhist notion that the entire Universe is basically made of fire" (64,M,500). Or like Gary Snyder who invokes "the most archaic values on earth" describing the evolution of man as a regression in general attentiveness and brain size,[8] Hughes extends his image of man far beyond the history of human culture. To him civilization "is comparatively new [and] still a bit of a strain on our nerves," breeding a multitude of swarming neuroses while teaching us "lazy habits of not really listening and not really looking." An experiment with modern Americans and African tribesmen both watching a submarine underwater manoeuvre in a movie (as discussed in *Poetry in the Making*) reveals an atrophy of attentiveness and memory on the part of civilized man when compared with the all-absorbing photographic vision of his primitive counterpart (P,76,88-9). While for the most part unaware of such common interests, Hughes and his American peers often drew upon the same sources. One of these is modern ethology.

After World War I, the founder of psychoanalysis began to evolve his gloomy picture of man "beyond the pleasure principle" harassed by death instinct and civilized discontents. Perhaps it needed an even greater ordeal of mass psychosis and destruction to strip philosophers of the last trappings of their humanitarian pretensions before science, after World War II, developed a less anthropocentric but at the same time more hopeful etiology of social behavior. This often misrepresented refutation of Freud's *Civilization and Its Discontents* was provided by the newly established biology of *homo sapiens*. According to Konrad Lorenz, the ritual behavior patterns of our Darwinian ancestors, which manage to deflect intra-specific aggression into bonds of loyalty and love, can teach us a lesson of civilized behavior while at the same time refuting Freud's hypothesis about a death instinct existing "as an opposite pole to all instincts of self-preservation."[9] Although Hughes, by November 1962, was familiar with Lorenz's "celebrated account of how he became foster-mother to a brood of ducklings" (62,J,666), the philosophical conclusions derived from such accounts seem to be his own. *Das sogenannte Böse*, the original version of Lorenz's *On Aggression* (1966), did not appear before 1963, yet the general outlook Hughes developed from reviewing a number of related books like R. Froman's *The Nerve of Some Animals* or J. C. Lilly's *Man and Dolphin* during 1961-2,[10] clearly parallels that of the Austrian scientist. Moreover, these reviews reveal a man interested in animals not as a voyeur of violence but as a new species of ethological moralist. By an inversion typical of the new science, Hughes sees the "subtle, civilised understanding" of a lioness, as described in Joy Adamson's *Living Free*, as

> a step not so much in the education of lions as in the civilisation of men. And insofar as it is more important to throw one's energy into forming traditions of kindness and summoning a spirit of sympathetic understanding, even in the smallest things, rather than exercising any further the overdeveloped weapons of the hands and the head, this book is a small gospel. (61,A,712)

Another new science that has strongly influenced Hughes as well as other contemporary poets is ecology. With the help of modern technology, it has recently retrieved "the basic intuition of most primitive theologies": "the idea of nature as a single organism." That, at least, is the conclusion Hughes derived from his reading of Max Nicholson's *The Environmental Revolution*. In sum, the "image of global unity, so prehistoric and yet so actually present," for which Hughes praises ecologists, provides the crucial formula for his own sense of a living tradition rooted in the most archaic values on earth. Like others of today's major poets, Hughes, as he puts it, nurses "a new global era" instead of picking "over the stucco rubble of a collapsed civilisation" (70,N,82-83).

2. A Radical Primitivism.

If in all this Hughes seems to differ from, say, Snyder, it is mainly because of the English poet's more faithful commitment to the primitive. Snyder, an ardent primitivist at first, gradually came to recognize through his Far Eastern studies that "traditional Hinduism and Buddhism have added a great deal onto basic Shamanistic and primitive ritualistic, ceremonial practises and life styles."[11] Thus his major achievement to date rests with poems characterized by the customary thrust of Far Eastern mystical poetry which his own emulates so successfully: from "an absolute foundation of human experience" out "into emptiness and into the formless which is the nature of pure joy."[12] The few comparable examples from Hughes' work have a diametrically opposite drive: away from the ecstatic apprehension of *śūnyatā* or the "objectless radiance of the Self" (63,O,293) towards a re-immersion in reality and an embracing of life in despite of death and suffering. The following lyric, first published in 1968, reads like a credo of this anti-mystical attitude.

> I said goodbye to earth
> I stepped into the wind
> Which entered the tunnel of fire
> Beneath the mountain of water
>
> I arrived at light
> Where I was shadowless
> I saw the snowflake crucified
> Upon the nails of nothing
>
> I heard the atoms praying
> To enter his kingdom
> To be broken like bread
> On a dark sill, and to bleed. (G,186)

According to Hughes there is a "two-way journey toward Reality" which we find him facing as early as 1963—"toward the objectless radiance of the Self, where the world is a composition of benign Holy Powers, and toward the objective reality of the world, where man is a virtuoso bacteria" (63,O,293). There can be no doubt as to which path Hughes came to choose as his own.

Not that he is unfamiliar with Eastern thought or unappreciative of the insights to be reached by the Zen or Sufi masters' "highly refined course of moral self-development." As he notes in a 1964 review of Idries Shah's *The Sufis*, these self-disciplinarians

undergo many years of rigorous mental and spiritual training . . . annihilating themselves without heaven or hell or religious paraphernalia of any kind, and without leaving life in the world, into the living . . . power of Creation.

The Sufis, Hughes concludes, "must be the biggest society of sensible men there has ever been on earth." At times, Hughes may even admit to nostalgic fantasizings about a common cradle of both Eastern and Western culture. For many "forlorn puzzles in the world"—the romance tradition with its natural affinity for "love," the occult, the Druidic culture, the early poets of Ireland as well as the Sufis or other mystics belonging to the school of Vedanta or Zen—all seem to suggest "that some great spiritual age somewhere in the Middle East had long since died and left indecipherable relics and automatisms to trouble our nostalgia" (64,E,678).

Still, Eastern thought has only had an indirect impact on Hughes. His empathetic insight into the dread vision at the core of Emily Dickinson's poetry—"final reality, her own soul, the soul within the Universe . . . almost a final revelation of horrible Nothingness" (68,D,13)—seems to apply to his own vision as much as to the notion of an "empty eternity" he has discerned in János Pilinszky's world (76,P,9). Unlike the Hungarian poet's more passive stance towards this dread emptiness, Hughes' attitude is one either of stoical defiance or of pragmatic, instinct-directed adjustment to the odds of the unalterably unaccommodated universe. Yet nowhere do we find an equivalent to the cosmic dance of joy (lilā)[13] with which Indian or Far Eastern poets have expressed their experience of the ultimate "void of inexhaustible contents."[14] One of the most joyful poems in Hughes' entire œuvre, "Gnat-Psalm," whose very title implies a poetical credo involving a similar symbolism, still reads like a dance of death rather than of life:

> The little bearded faces
> Weaving and bobbing on the nothing
> Shaken in the air, shaken, shaken
> And their feet dangling like the feet of victims
>
> O little Hasids
> Ridden to death by your own bodies
> Riding your bodies to death
> You are the angels of the only heaven!
> And God is an Almighty Gnat!
> . . . . . .
> Your dancing
>
> Your dancing
>
> Rolls my staring skull slowly away into outer space.
>
> (W,180-1)

Like Nietzsche and Lawrence before him, Hughes is as dubious of what he sees as the "quietism" of Eastern philosophy as he is wary of any direct appropriation of non-Western sources. His basically non-Western stance thus, for the most part, results in inversions of classical or Judaeo-Christian models, inversions for which Blake's works provide the closest analogue. Hughes' recent introduction to Pilinszky reads like a summing up of this attitude. What speech, he asks, "is adequate for this moment, when the iron nails remain fixed in the wounds, with an eternal iron fixity, and neither hands nor feet can move." Hughes' answer inverts the Christian symbol implicit in the question. For to him the crucifixion is a symbol of what "Christianity has managed to cover only with a loud chord of faith" (76,P,10-11) or the Greeks with their Promethean myths of rationalist and technological progress: creation's unalterable duality of life and destruction, which Artaud summed up in the word "cruauté" in the sense of "life-appetite, cosmic rigor and implacable necessity." "For it is understood," as the Frenchman wrote, "that life always means death to someone else."[15]

A direct offshoot of Peter Brook's "Theatre of Cruelty" season at the National Theatre in London and its biggest success beside Weiss' *Marat/Sade*, Hughes' adaptation of Seneca's *Oedipus* almost reads as if the poet had translated a work by Artaud rather than by Seneca. The chorus' opening description of Thebes—

> streets homes temples gutted with the
> plague   it is one huge plague pit   the new heaps
> of dead spewed up everywhere   hardening in the
> sickly daylight—

or Oedipus' ever more torrential outbursts of grief find closer parallels in "The Theatre and the Plague" than in Seneca. A similar intensification of the direct source turns one of Jocasta's speeches into a "théâtre de la cruauté" manifesto:

> I carried him for this
> for pain and for fear
> for hard sharp metal   for the cruelty of other men
> and his own cruelty. (O,17,23)

Orghast, the sequel to *Oedipus* in Hughes' collaborations with Peter Brook, seems to take a step beyond a mere protrayal of cruelty. Although the manuscript has been lost, we know from the poet's comments that the mythic draft plan of *Orghast* involved a "cure of the universe." What has been corrupted by materialist rationalism and puritanical repression is restored to the primordial "bliss of the divine harmony . . . of making and unmaking."[16] Similarly, Hughes' *Orpheus* and *Prometheus on His Crag* seem like Nietzschean recastings of Greek tragedy with the attempt to unearth the

> Greek of the ecstatic mystery religions, the primitive savage under the tragic Drama, the Greek of the early myths [who] lived in a world which we still find alarming—too open in every direction, too dominated by supernatural beings who use men like playthings, too insanely violent.

For if cleansed of its later philosophical misinterpretations, early Greek mythology can still present us with "a working anatomy of our psychic life in a very complete and profound way."[17]

In this way, Hughes' Prometheus is at best an anti-hero to the Aeschylean prophet-champion of human progress and freedom. His freedom is an empty dream from which he awakens "to the old chains/and the old agony," "all his preparations/For his humanity/Were disablements." He "had already invented too much" and so has "bitten his prophetic tongue off." Where his speech used to "hold/Pieces of the wordy earth together," his mouth now "shuts/Savagely on a mouthful/Of space-fright which makes the ears ring." The secret, held by Aeschylus' Prometheus, which guaranteed his ultimate triumph over Zeus and, along with it, the triumph of Prometheus' protégé, man, has passed on to the vulture who becomes the story's real hero:

> Prometheus on his crag
> Began to admire the vulture
> It knew what it was doing
>
> It went on doing it
> Swallowing not only his liver
> But managing also to digest its guilt. (Pr,6,7,9,13,15,19)

The only triumph left to this anti-Prometheus is a "passivity of transfiguration" (76,P,13) in the acceptance of eternal suffering without apotheosizing the sickness. He is made to understand that the vulture is a necessary "Death In Life" (Pr,16), causing the "eternally repeated death in pain" of man's manifestation in time.[18] This "post-apocalyptic silence, where the nail remains in the hand, and the wound cannot speak" (76,P,11), rather than the somewhat artificially tagged on last poem suggesting Prometheus' rebirth into a new "gleaming man," gives the sequence its powerful impact. Prometheus' songs are like those of Hughes' Orpheus after recognizing that Persephone's "flower-face" of life conceals a maggot's "pointed, eyeless face" of death. Orpheus henceforth ceased to make music of either mindless happiness or mad despair, and only sang "of growing and withering . . . of birth and of death."[19]

In this way, Hughes' transformations of Orpheus, Oedipus and Prometheus into emblem figures of his own creeds result from the general effort to unearth the primitive savage under their classical representations. Yet Hughes goes even further. His search for "the features of our own literature's embryonic stage" (62,B,781) extends the concept of the primitive into the very realm of the half- or non-human, and his most appropriate spokesmen also stem from here. There are the songs of skylarks, owls and gnats or the poetic mutterings of *homo sapiens*-type beings like Wodwo. "Just discovering that it is alive" (P,62), this goblin creature tries to posit its identity, both in relation to an alien world that keeps it imprisoned and to the emptiness from whence it came.

> Do these weeds
> know me and name me to each other have they
> seen me before, do I fit in their world? I seem
> separate from the ground and not rooted but dropped
> out of nothing casually . . . (W,183)

The earliest exponent of this rock bottom primitivism is Gog, another Caliban-like "poetry crammed half-beast" (71,S,198) inspired by both *Revelations* (12:4) and *The Tempest:*

My great bones are massed in me.
They pound on the earth, my song excites them.
I do not look at the rocks and stones, I am frightened of what they see,

I listen to the song jarring my mouth
Where the skull-rooted teeth are in possession. (W,150)

Crow, as we shall see, is of the same lineage and the most powerful emblem figure to date of Hughes' overall attempt to evolve his own poetic biology of *homo sapiens* as well as a new idiom appropriate to this task.

II.

Poetics

So what we need, evidently, is a faculty . . . which keeps faith, as Goethe says, with the world of things and the world of spirits equally.

   This really is imagination. This is the faculty we mean when we talk about the imagination of the great artists. The character of great works is exactly this: that in them the full presence of the inner world combines with and is reconciled to the full presence of the outer world. And in them we see that the laws of these two worlds are not contradictory at all . . . We recognize these works because we are all struggling to find those laws, as a man on a tightrope struggles for balance, because they are the formula that reconciles everything, and balances every imbalance. (76,M,91-2)

Yes, I met Jung early, and though I think I have read all the translated volumes, I've avoided knowing them too well, which no doubt frees me to use them all the more. [1]

II. POETICS

Looking back over Hughes' career since 1957, one finds little in the young poet's surroundings that might have inspired the startling new vision he developed within little over a decade. The results have obvious analogues in today's avant-garde art. Yet what to the American poets of the late fifties, for instance, had already turned into a common quest within several clearly defined movements was a solitary path of single-handed experimentation to an English poet of the same decade. As if to add to this task, Hughes, while addressing an audience recently trained on the civilized sensibility of Robert Conquest's *New Lines* poets, had been inspired to write his first poems of adulthood by an anthology of American poets dominated by the New Critical school of a Richard Wilbur and John Crowe Ransom.[2] The impact of a style largely derivative of Eliot's metaphysical period is apparent in the grimly backhanded wit, the elaborate conceits and contorted syntax of early poems such as "A Modest Proposal" or "The Decay of Vanity."

Ironically, this indebtedness may have helped the poet gain his first acceptances in predominantly American magazines, and win a contest sponsored by the New York YMHA, giving *The Hawk in the Rain* immediate publication by Harper. What the influence meant to his development is obvious from its almost total disappearance in *Lupercal* (1960). Yet even this second volume, which by a careful pruning of previous stylistic excesses established Hughes as "a poet of the first importance" (A. Alvarez),[3] gave small indication of what was ahead.

Analogously, Hughes' comments on poetry before 1962 sound more or less conventional. In a *Poetry Book Society Bulletin* statement of 1957 he introduced himself as dealing with the "war between vitality and death" and celebrating "the exploits of the warriors of either side" (57,H). Despite its rebellious invectives against "the soots and verdigris and corrosive deposits of our poetry industry," his 1962 essay on Keith Douglas strikes a similarly conservative note. A general understanding of poetry as in one sense "the eternal's view of the temporal" and the qualities to be admired in Douglas's work—an "aggressive nimbleness of mind," an "obsession to get the facts down clear and straight," the "thoroughness of his artistic conscience" refining a "style that combines a colloquial prose readiness and variety with a poetic breadth" (62,D,1069-70)—are documented by poems as strongly influenced by a Donne or Marvell as several in *The Hawk in the Rain*. Except for a brief description of Douglas' later poems as loose "constellation[s] of statements" (63,D,47)—a phrase characteristically added to the essay in '63 before it became the introduction to Douglas' *Selected Poems* (1964)—there is little here to reflect Hughes' ongoing change from an empathetic miniaturist of plants, animals and men into a visionary spellmaker of polyhistoric dimensions and sweeping vatic gestures. What the essay praises "is not a mind trained in philosophy, or privileged by visions" but "common life, recounting what it has had to undergo" (62,D,1069). Ironically, it was this very privilege of vision which the poet was secretly searching out in his deeper self.

1. "Flash Vision" Creativity.

The critical acclaim that Hughes, hardly turned thirty, enjoyed after the publication of *Lupercal* might have been enough to make him end, like other poets before him, in either lifelong poet laureate self-complacency or dead-end suicidal inability to resurrect the early achievement. As if alive to these dangers, we find Hughes, early in 1962, pondering the fate of some of his predecessors. Yeats, for instance, being alert to his true genius, went on "developing as a poet" and "pursuing those adventures, mental, spiritual and physical . . . that his gift want[ed]." By contrast, Wordsworth at first trusted his gift, "producing the real thing," but subsequently became "absorbed by the impersonal dead lumber of matters in which his gift ha[d] no interest." Yet as Hughes was well aware, chance plays an important role in such destinies, and his obsessive concern with the elusiveness of inspiration reveals some of his own fears at the time—"it visits [the poet] when he is only half suspecting it, and he is not sure it has visited him until some days or months afterwards and perhaps he never can be sure." No craft, education, professional dedication and experimental ingenuity, not even the most thorough artistic conscience, will produce great poetry in default of this inspiration.

What emerged from such fears was a new poetic credo setting the parameters for Hughes' future creativity. Here also, the poet begins to join a new multicultural æsthetics shared by a number of his contemporaries in both America and Europe. The poet, Hughes concludes,

> can study his art, experiment, and apply his mind and live as he pleases. But the moment of writing is too late for further improvements or adjustments. Certain memories, images, sounds, feelings, thoughts, and relationships between these, have for some reason become luminous at the core of his mind: it is in his attempt to bring them out, without impairment, into a comparatively dark world that he makes poems. At the moment of writing, the poetry is a combination, or a resultant, of all that he is, unimpeachable evidence of itself and, indirectly, of himself, and for the time of writing he can do nothing but accept it. If he doesn't approve of what is appearing, there are always plenty of ways to falsify and "improve" it, there are always plenty of fashions as to how it should look, how it can be made more acceptable, more "interesting," his other faculties are only too ready to load it with their business, whereon he ceases to be a poet producing what poetry he can and becomes a cheat producing confusion. (62,C,44-5)

Artistic creativity should spring with unimpeded spontaneity from the deepest core of the human mind, and no revision should be allowed to falsify this primal impulse. Such notions are shared not only by Hughes' twentieth century peers and such isolated forerunners as Blake, Keats, Whitman or Rimbaud but by numerous artist literati from non-Western cultures. The poet, according to Chinese æsthetician Lu Chi (ca. 300 A.D.), for instance, simply has to accept the volcanic uncontrollable outbursts of his imagination—

> When it comes, it cannot be checked;
> When it goes, it cannot be stopped.[4]

According to Arthur Rimbaud, he should give free expression to the collective soul ("l'âme universelle") in which he immerses himself—"if what he brings back from *down there* has form, he gives form; if it is formless, he gives formlessness."[5] For whatever forms the poem will assume organically as an expression of this impulse, must, as Tung Yu wrote, emerge "like the unfolding and blooming of leaves and flowers."[6] Or if poetry, in Keats' words, "comes not as naturally as the Leaves to a tree it had better not come at all."[7] Rather than plan and revise, the poet should catch the sudden "flash of insight," as Bashō says, and "put it into words before it fades away in [his] mind."

> Composition of a poem must be done in an instant, like a woodcutter
> felling a huge tree or a swordsman leaping at a dangerous enemy. It is
> also like cutting a ripe watermelon with a sharp knife or like taking a large
> bite at a pear.[8]

This concept of a "first flash vision" (71,O), "a single 1,000-volt shock,
that [lights] up everything" (P,120), as the true source of great poetry, has
become more and more prominent in Hughes' poetics. Without it, he
wrote in his 1971 *Orghast* commentary, a man might write "a heart-
searching book of poems every two or three years for thirty years without
setting down one live or true word" about his "real life." His "huge suffering lump of vital shut-away truths," the "luminous spirit" or "crowd of
spirits" in which our individual selves find their real homeground through
self-annihilation, remain incommunicado (71,O). Only by an infinite
alertness to this flash vision will the poet's words, so classical Chinese
æstheticians put it in a crucial formula, turn into a "resonance or vibration
of the vitalizing spirit and movement of life" (*ch'i-yün shêng-tung*),[9] or as
D. H. Lawrence wrote, be like "life surging itself into utterance at its very
well-head."[10]

Yet, what are the concrete strategies by which such visions can find
embodiment in words and hence be transferred to the reader? The
psycho-physiological model which Hughes, like others of his contemporaries, proposes as an answer, again finds crucial analogues among the
classical writings of Eastern artist literati rather than among the predominantly ideational art theories of the West. Thus Bashō advised his disci-
ples to learn "about pines from pines, and about bamboos from bamboos,"
meaning that they should immerse themselves "within an object . . . perceive its delicate life and feel its feeling, out of which a poem forms itself."[11] Hughes seems to emulate such Zen Buddhist empathy when he
claims that the poet, before writing about something, should imagina-
tively "touch it, smell it, listen to it, turn [himself] into it" (P,18).

Though such notions have become predominantly associated with the
name of Charles Olson in modern Anglo-American poetics, Hughes' life
ironically provides a better illustration of them than the writing desk
habits of the American poet. Long before Olson's 1950 "Projective Verse"
essay could have taught the younger poet how to "cause the thing he
makes to try to take its place alongside the things of nature,"[12] Hughes'
childhood hunting around Mytholmroyd and Mexborough taught him a
more natural lesson. Thus, beginning to write poems at about fifteen was
"partly a continuation of [this] earlier pursuit":

> The special kind of excitement, the slightly mesmerized and quite in-
> voluntary concentration with which you make out the stirrings of a new
> poem in your mind, then the outline, the mass and colour and clean final
> form of it, the unique living reality of it in the midst of the general

lifelessness, all that is too familiar to mistake. This is hunting and the poem is a new species of creature, a new specimen of the life outside your own. (P,17)

The way Hughes talks about the poem itself or its impact on the reader has remained equally indebted to this early impulse. The images, rhythms and words of a poem should be an "assembly of living parts ruled by a single spirit," all "jump[ing] to life as you read them." And just as poetry ought to be made "out of experiences which change our bodies, and spirits," so the words employed in it should belong directly to one or several of the five senses. For words can be like little goblins, "as if each one had eyes, ears and tongue, or ears and fingers and a body to move with." And if the poet knows how to control them, they "can so affect you that delicate instruments can easily detect the changes in your skin perspiration, the rate of your pulse and so on" (P,17-18,32).

2. Exercises in Meditation and Invocation.

Apparently unfamiliar with similar creeds held by American poets, Sylvia Plath for a time became the disciple of her husband. Her letters abound with praise of all the things she learned in this all-absorbing working partnership: how she sharpened her impressionistic perceptions according to Hughes' photographic vision, how she enriched her imagination by reading not only novels and poems but "books on folklore, fiddler crabs and meteorites," or how she learned to break through a writing block by just pouring out "a few pages of drivel until the juice came back." Yet the major impact on her poetic development derived from the psychic powers of her "hypnotizing husband," a subject which, as early as July 1956, she had planned to explore in a short story of that title. Ted would often hypnotize Sylvia to sleep, a practice which also, as he recalls, made her focus and concentrate on work in certain ways. One of the possible results, as recorded in a letter of June 1958, was that Sylvia decided to dispense with the conscious use of "symbols, irony, archetypal images and all that" as favored by the climate of the New Criticism. We will try, she wrote, "to get along without such conscious and contrived machinery. We write and wake up with symbols on our pages, but do not begin with them."[13] In late 1959, while staying in a lonely artists' colony at Yaddo, Ted and Sylvia devised "exercises of meditation and invocation" (66,P,85) which Hughes, aided by handbooks of Cabalistic and Hermetic magic, had been pursuing for some time. The main technique was to invoke and hold composite images with the aim of unlocking hidden sources of imaginative energy. Franz Bardon's *Initiation into Hermetics* describes a more advanced form of such "Concentration of thoughts with two or three senses at once" by imagining, say, a gong

> of which you must hear not only the sound but also see the person sounding it . . . If you have reached this degree of concentration, try to do the same exercises, with your eyes open, whether fixing your look at one definite point, or staring into vacancy. The physical surroundings, then, must no longer exist for you, and the imagery you chose is to appear before your eyes floating in the air like a fata-morgana.[14]

The aim of these exercises of meditation and invocation was "to break down the tyranny, the fixed focus and public persona which descriptive or discursive poems take as a norm" (66,P,85). With similar intent Sylvia devised "a deliberate exercise in experimental improvisation on set themes" which, as Hughes recalls, allowed her "to let herself drop, rather than inch over bridges of concepts." Her final, most accomplished work, starting with "Tulips," composed in hospital during March 1961, was the fulfilment of this magically liberated imagination. As Hughes recalls, she wrote "Tulips" "without her usual studies over the Thesaurus, and at top speed, as one might write an urgent letter. From then on, all her poems were written in this way" (66,P,85-6).

Hughes' own development along similar lines was gradually reinforced by modern depth psychology and its analogues in Eastern thought. As early as 1960, the poet had had ample opportunity to explore this connection in trying to turn Evans-Wentz' translation of the *Bardo Thödol*, complete with Carl Jung's "Psychological Commentary," into an oratorio for his Chinese friend from Yaddo. Yet there is more than the evidence of such direct influence that points to the deep affinity existing between basic concepts of Hughes' post-1962 poetics and those of the East as seen through the eyes of Jung.

Post-Freudian psychiatry has tried to carry its searchlights into the ghost-ridden psychic realms of what Buddhists call the huge memory storehouse of the "universal Mind" in which "discriminations, desires, attachments and deeds" have been collecting "since beginningless time" and which "like a magician . . . causes phantom things and people to appear and move about."[15] Partly with the help of such insights, Carl Jung managed to render a detailed account of these realms. A major step along this way was his 1938 introduction to *The Tibetan Book of the Dead*. What the *Bardo Thödol* describes as the dead man's journey through mystical enlightenment (*dharma-kāya*), the phantasmagoria of the "Universal Mind" (*sambhoga-kāya*), and the ego-inspired fantasies of the personal "mind-system" (*nirmāna-kāya*) back through the "Womb Door" into reincarnation, serves Jung as an inverse model for our ongoing reinitiation into the collective unconscious.[16] By 1954 the same Sanskrit terminology had come to provide him with the central concepts for describing the human psyche.

The unconscious is the root of all experience of oneness (*dharma-kāya*), the matrix of all archetypes or structural patterns (*sambhoga-kāya*), and the *conditio sine qua non* of the phenomenal world (*nirmāna-kāya*).[17]

Jung's model of the human psyche, as Sino-Japanese scholars are ready to acknowledge before our own,[18] opens a badly needed new access to the basic notions of Eastern æsthetics, and by extension, to their present-day analogues in the West. For long before Romantics and Surrealists began to explore their troubled egos, or isolated mystics managed to safeguard their visions from religious persecutors and doctrinaire rationalists, Eastern artists had ranged freely through the entire human psyche, from the personal mind, through the collective unconscious, towards mystical enlightenment. Traditional translators, much like the early missionaries who emasculated primitive literature, are to be blamed for the one-sided image we still have, for instance, of Chinese poetry as abounding with self-complacent serenity and pathetic fallacies. More recent renderings such as A. C. Graham's of Late T'ang poetry or Gary Snyder's of Han-shan's afford us glimpses both of the unrelentingly de-anthropomorphized vision of Eastern mystics and a world of nightmare phantasmagoria beside which most surrealist art looks like the horror chamber of a charmingly obsolete country fair.

Theoretical treatises, again brought to light by more recent scholarship, fill in the picture. In classical Chinese æsthetics, for instance, it is an assumption so common as to go almost without saying that art springs from an immersion into the innermost core of the mind. Yet enough artists have left hair-raisingly firsthand accounts of what it means to follow their two most basic precepts of creativity, that poetry, for instance, should be "a vehicle of the Way" (*wen yi tsai Tao*) by "express[ing] in words the intent of the . . . mind" (*shih yen chih*).[19] After nine years of meditative exercise, one of them writes, his self "both within and without, has been transformed . . . My eye becomes my ear, my ear becomes my nose, my nose my mouth."[20] Prescribing an immersion into the subconscious through "Meditation before Writing," Lu Chi, down to the very images he employs, anticipates Hughes' similar plea from *Poetry in the Making* by over one and a half millennia: "All external vision and sound are suspended." And the mind is "as a diver into a secret world, lost in subterranean currents. Hence,/Arduously sought expressions, hitherto evasive, hidden,/Will be like stray fishes out of the ocean bottom to emerge on the angler's hook."[21] Or as Hughes puts it:

There is the inner life, which is the world of final reality, the world of memory, emotion, imagination, intelligence, and natural common sense, and which goes on all the time, consciously or unconsciously, like the heart beat. There is also the thinking process by which we break into that inner life and capture answers and evidence to support the answers out of it. That process of raid, or persuasion, or ambush, or dogged hunting, or

surrender, is the kind of thinking we have to learn and if we do not
somehow learn it, then our minds lie in us like the fish in the pond of a
man who cannot fish. (P,57-8)

Although familiar with Eastern thought practices, Hughes, with his
natural antipathy against today's mail-order Buddhism, is an unlikely person to have borrowed these notions from such sources. Instead, an entirely
natural impulse, prior even to his interest in Hermetic and Cabalistic
magic, had opened an access to the meditation and concentration rituals of
Eastern sages. Just as hunting led him to write poetry at fifteen and from
there to evolve a whole new body poetics of the neo-*"primitive-abstract,"*[22]
so another childhood passion taught him the "trick or skill" to "catch those
elusive or shadowy thoughts, . . . and [to] hold them still so [he could] get
a really good look at them." Certainly, none of this was learnt at school.
Here, on the contrary, he was often unable to articulate what might be no
more than a "numb blank feeling" although it seemed so much more fas-
cinating than the ideas he was made to write about in essays. The "mental
exercise in concentration on a small point" which finally revealed some of
these hidden interior treasures was acquired while fishing. Despite
Hughes' disclaimers about trying to turn "English lessons into Yoga ses-
sions," his account of this childhood pursuit, as given in *Poetry in the Making*, is close enough to what one might find in a Buddhist primer of meditation:

> I fished in still water, with a float. As you know, all a fisherman does is
> stare at his float for hours on end. I have spent hundreds and hundreds of
> hours staring at a float—a dot of red or yellow the size of a lentil, ten
> yards away . . . All the little nagging impulses, that are normally dis-
> tracting your mind, dissolve . . . If they do not, then you cannot settle
> down: you get bored and pack up in a bad temper. But once they have
> dissolved, you enter one of the orders of bliss. (P,57-8,60-3)

3. Concept of Language.

But how can such insight into "the world of final reality" be embodied
in human language, a medium so much of conscious reasoning and
purpose-oriented communication? A deep distrust of its cognitive potential, which is as old as the teachings of Lao Tzu, the Buddha or the Up-
anishads, has protected the East from what Wittgenstein called the over
two thousand year long "bewitchment of our intelligence by means of
language."[23] Metaphysical claims for language as a secret code of the Absolute, which have haunted poets and philosophers since the days of Socrates, are as alien to their Eastern peers as our present-day despair over
language. In all areas of mental activity, language was considered no more

than a means to those ends which are ultimately inaccessible to any form of human communication. As Chuang Tzu's often repeated parable from the third century B.C. puts it:

> The fishing net is used to catch fish. Let us take the fish and forget the net . . . The word is used to convey ideas. When ideas are apprehended, let us forget the words. How delightful to be able to talk with such a man, who has forgotten the words![24]

The schoolboy poet's classroom experience of being unable to articulate the tantalizing stirrings of his innermost self, implanted a similar scepticism in Hughes. Hence his later conviction that "the meaning of our experience is finally unfathomable," and language a mere tool, an indicator or general directive towards it. Words, "learned late and laboriously and easily forgotten . . . are unnatural, in a way, and far from . . . ideal for their job" (P,119). Such insight, like Chuang Tzu's, is at once more radical and hopeful than the despair of many poets who like Hugo von Hofmannsthal have felt words disintegrate in their mouths like "mouldy mushrooms,"[25] and have been driven to creative or real suicide by this language crisis. Against the critics who in their wake have been announcing the death of literature or a new æsthetics of silence, Hughes seems to propose a future poetry beyond silence which at the same time may be man's oldest,—a poetry of "truly primitive speech, a medicine bag of provisional magic and rough improvisations—childlike, playful, bizarre, in a perpetual restless state of dissolution and re-invention."[26] To Hughes, the strategies developed by East European poets like Popa, Holub or Herbert "of making audible meanings without disturbing the silence" (67,P,202) are the best refutation of Adorno's famous dictum that writing poetry has become impossible under the shadow of the death camps. It may be true that such memories have totally devalued an already debased currency of ideational and humanitarian concepts to which Western languages have been subjected for so long. As Hughes himself is prepared to admit:

> The silence of artistic integrity "after Auschwitz" is a real thing. The mass of the human evidence of the camps, and of similar situations since, has screwed up the price of "truth" and "reality" and "understanding" beyond what common words seem able to pay.

Yet though poets may now want to write "as if [they] had remained silent," their task of making this silence audible, even if by no more than "a seasoned despair, a minimal, much-examined hope, a special irony" (76,P,10), is a more challenging one than ever. All the less justifiable seems to be the real silence of those who, like Laura Riding, gave up poetry by despairing over language as such. For to "respect words more than the truths which are perpetually trying to find and correct words is the death of poetry."[27] Behind such respect is no more than the unwarrantable claim with which language has been charged by post-Platonic ideational philo-

sophy or by the Biblical creed that all creation is ruled by an underlying
"Logos."

Hughes' 1966 poem of that title, which also marks the beginning of his
mythopoeic period, is the first to reveal in what esteem the poet holds such
philosophizing. In ways that are typical for many poems from then on it
reverses the biblical doctrine:

> Creation convulses in nightmare. And awaking
> Suddenly tastes the nightmare moving
> Still in its mouth
> And spits it kicking out, with a swinish cry—
> > which is God's first cry.

> Like that cry within the sea,
> A mumbling over and over
> Of ancient law, the phrasing falling to pieces
> Garbled among shell-shards and gravels,
> > the truths falling to pieces. (W,34)

Numerous poems since "Logos" in which the emergence, destructiveness and recent collapse of language are the central concerns of a socio-
historical critique are more than obvious and have been amply discussed.[28] More innovative than their negative message, is Hughes' search for
man's original language uncorrupted by our Judaeo-Christian and Greek
ways of thinking. There were others before him who were dissatisfied
with the reason-, time- and space-dominated patterns of Standard Average
European when compared, say, with the situational immediacy of Hopi
(B. L. Whorf),[29] or who have speculated about non- or pre-Western languages as resembling "vivid shorthand pictures of actions and processes in
nature" (E. Fenollosa)[30] or expressing an archaic form of "rotary image-
thought" (D. H. Lawrence).[31] Olson, by way of illustrating his conviction
that the original "phonetic and ideographic" potential is "still present and
available for use as impetus and explosion in our alphabetic speech,"[32]
uses examples (in their turn derived from Fenollosa) closely resembling
those of Hughes. Where the latter discovered a relationship between
HOAN, his Orghast word for "light," and the forms of the verb "to be"
("You can't say 'is' without saying 'light,'" Hughes observed),[33] Olson
found that our abstract "is," for instance, "comes from the Aryan root, *as*,
to breathe," just as "be" is from "*bhu*, to grow."[34] Yet despite such similar
pursuits in theory, there is little to parallel Hughes' attempts towards their
realization in practise. Whatever else they might suggest, lines like

clun alclun hoandaclun	closed all closed heaven closed
urdboltabullorgaclun	clayrockdarkness closed
deyool omclun	worse woman closed[35]

certainly bear out the author's belief that the actors in true poetic drama should speak in anything but discursive language. Instead they should use "every muscle, every inflection, every position," their utterances consisting of mere "tones and sounds, without specific conceptual or perceptual meaning" and the whole spectacle turning into a luminous sound image of the poet's "flash vision" that "makes the spirits listen" (71,O). Again, the basic concept is hardly a new one. As early as 1933 the author of "Le théâtre de la cruauté" had demanded that words, if the theatre is to allow them at all, should first be reattached "to the physical movements which gave them birth, so that the logical and discursive aspect of language may disappear under its physical and affective one."[36] Yet only after 1971, when Peter Brook commissioned Hughes to provide his actors with a "subtext for improvisation" for a play to be performed at the Fifth Arts Festival of Shiraz, were such speculations ever put into practice. It has been amply documented how Hughes discarded an early attempt to write the script in his own language ("English was hopeless. It could never have come near it"),[37] and then worked his way from early Orghast, a rigidly hieroglyphic language threatened with premature ossification, towards the final version, a free sound sequence retaining hieroglyphic elements but at the same time resembling "an electrocardiogram and encephalogram combined."[38] Although Hughes holds that similar experiments remain meaningless in poetry,[39] their final result recalls Ginsberg's attempts to explore the relations "between poetry and mantra chanting by means of the yoga of breath."[40] "The ideal Orghast," Hughes concluded after the work was done, "would be a language with a fairly fixed system that opened it to a magical, mantra way of speaking it."[41]

4. Myth, Parapsychology and the Poetic Imagination.

Of course, an "animal" instead of a "mantra" way of speaking would be the more appropriate formula for what Hughes has in mind here. For to him, the supreme gift of flash vision is not so much as it is, say, to Bashō, a matter of human spiritual enlightenment, but of an experience which on its deepest level is shared by all living beings.

> It is human, of course, but it is also everything else that lives. . . Some animals and birds express [it] pure and without effort, and then you hear the whole desolate, final actuality of existence in a voice, a tone. . . Far beyond human words. And the startling quality of this "truth" is that it is terrible. It is for some reason harrowing, as well as being the utterly beautiful thing.

A little anecdote related in the same context vividly illustrates Hughes' belief that the imagination should be at home amongst the "crowd of spirits" surrounding us:

> Once when his spirits were dictating poetic material to Yeats, an owl cried outside the house, and the spirits paused. After a while one said: "We like that sort of sound." And that is it: "That sort of sound" makes the spirits listen. It opens our deepest and innermost ghost to sudden attention. It is a spirit, and it speaks to spirit. (71,O)

Via immediate predecessors like Yeats, Goethe or Blake, this concept of the imagination, like his pre-creative exercises of meditation and invocation, places Hughes in the mainstream of the Hermetic tradition. Just as Hughes, echoing Goethe, believes that the imagination should keep faith "with the world of things and the world of spirits equally" (76, M, 92), so Pico della Mirandola claimed that the poet should have "familiarity with the race of demons, knowing that he is issued from the same origin," or Giordano Bruno that the imagination is "the sole gate to all internal affections and the link of links."[42] Also like his Hermetic predecessors, Hughes believes in the concrete reality of myths. To him they are more than idle fantasies from mankind's adolescence, secret subliminal scripts recording man's civilized discontents, or archetypal projections of a collective unconscious.

It is true that Jung's 1912 discovery of this ancestral memory with its common traces in ancient religious scrolls as well as modern schizophrenics' dossiers, meant a major breakthrough in the ongoing rehabilitation of myth. Its basic model, however, remains that of a slide-projector in which the actual presence of the mythic numen (or image on the screen) remains an illusion, always ready to vanish with the repository of archetypes in the individual's unconscious (or the carousel of slides in the projector). Although most parapsychologists embrace the same model, their evidence seems to speak against it. For what are we to make of psychic feats performed by men like Raudive and Ted Serios, for instance, who under conditions of strictest scientific supervision are able to conjure up voices and images so that they register on Polaroid cameras and tape recorders?[43] Are their brains the storehouse projectors of these images and voices or do they simply relay them in the way that television sets register and transmit images and sounds floating through space? Perhaps it is time to recognize that this dichotomy should be solved not by one of Western logic's customary "either or" verdicts but by the "both and" acceptance of a duality such as modern nuclear physics has had to acknowledge in comparable issues. One such "lesson of atomic theory" resulted in Niels Bohr's "law of complementarity." As the physicist points out, this law tries to resolve a problem already confronted by thinkers like the Buddha and Lao Tzu "when trying to harmonize our position as spectators and actors in the great drama of existence."[44]

In the light of similar considerations, Hughes asserts that myth is both real and imaginary, just as the imagination is at once spiritual and concretely physical. The two are connected not by a one-way system of projective or receptive dependence but by interchangeable correlations. In one of his typical sweeps of polyhistoric eclecticism Hughes points out how physicists have verified supernatural phenomena while at the same time reinstating "the wild Heraclitean/Buddhist notion that the entire Universe is basically made of fire." Thus

> they've landed themselves, and us, in a delicately balanced, purely electrical Creation, at the backdoor of the house of activities formerly called "supernatural." For a purely electrical Creation is one without walls, where everything, being an electrical power, can have an electrical effect on every other thing, and where electrical effects are vital effects. (64,M,500)

As early as 1958, Hughes made light of "our science" and "small psychology" which try to debunk the supernatural as mere dream fantasies while unable to escape its thrall.

> Did they dream it?
> Oh, our science says they did.
> It was all wishfully dreamed in bed.
> Small psychology would unseam it.
>
> Bitches still sulk, rosebuds blow,
> And we are devilled. And though these weep
> Over our harms, who's to know
> Where their feet dance while their heads sleep? (L,48)

His 1964 review of T. C. Lethbridge's *Ghost and Divining-rod* allowed the poet to present these versified convictions in a more explicit manner. Besides apparitions which are indeed mere projections of a diseased imagination there are, Hughes points out, "ghosts or 'presences' which haunt one spot, where different people, and animals, react to them." To be sure, even Lethbridge's explanation—a ghost being an electrical field created by "some individual in a state of intense emotion," stored in the "Ge-field of the earth" and finally discharged into or registered by the awareness of another individual in a low state of electrical potential—leaves much to be answered. Yet to Hughes there is proof enough that such things are evidently part of the the logic of the earth and may soon be verified "by some spectacular development of sensitive recording equipment." His own response to such speculations makes no secret of the world the poet feels most at home in:

> What an entertaining place the world would become again! What a chaos!
> The only respectable sanities to survive undiscredited in all that would be
> physics and art. (64,M,500)

In other words, what physics' scientific credentials have recently managed to rehabilitate, art has—or at least ought to have—treated as its domain throughout history. How then can the imagination be a mere projector of repressed subliminal fantasies or archetypal images? Even Shakespeare's notion that it gives a local habitation and a name to airy nothing hardly describes the concrete magical potential which Hughes attributes to the human mind. With the possible exception of Jerome Rothenberg, none of his contemporaries seems to come closer than Hughes to rejoining the primitive shamanistic belief that it is possible to acquire the "technique for moving in a state of ecstasy among the various spiritual realms, and for generally dealing with souls and spirits, in a practical way, in some practical crisis." Whether primitive shaman or modern mythographer poet, the experiences and techniques are common ones pointing to "something closer to biological inevitability [rather] than to any merely cultural tradition" (64,E,677). In modern society these are also shared by the depth psychiatrist, and Hughes, by way of introducing such notions, is fond of quoting the anecdote from Jung's autobiography in which the Swiss doctor, while trying to illustrate some general point in conversation with a patient, gave a "detailed circumstantial account of that man's own private life" (P,122,cf.64,M,500).

To Hughes, such feats as well as the psychometrist's gift to conjure up, from the sight of a "weapon or tool used in a crime" (P,12), an image of the criminal, are potentials dormant in all of us. And modern parapsychologists seem to agree with him in acknowledging some kind of negative or positive psychic power in everybody. Where the two tend to disagree is as to how such phenomena should be explained. In the same way that ghosts are presences to Hughes, while to most parapsychologists they are psychic projections, so the imagination to him is a concrete physiological or magical power while to the majority of scientists its potential is limited to an ill defined realm of the psychological. In sum, the poet considers both as "common propert[ies] of life's electrical constitution" (64,M,500). The imagination is "simply one of the characteristics of being alive in these mysterious electrical bodies of ours, and the difficult thing is not to pick up the information but to recognize it—to accept it into our consciousness" (P,123).

As this pedagogical afterthought for the school readership of *Poetry in the Making* may suggest, Hughes, after all is said, is far from being a poet of the occult. His insistence on ghosts or on the imagination's conjuring powers is the natural reaction of a poet exasperated by our customary rejection of entire realms of psychic and mythic experience simply "because they inhabit a gulf where our careful civilisation would disintegrate" (64,M,500). Apart from that, there is little in a piece such as the recent "Myth and Education" that a man as worldly-wise as Goethe might not have agreed with. And it is in the German poet's demand for an imagination which keeps faith "with the world of things and the world of spirits equally" (76,M,92), that Hughes finds his own ideal formula for man's greatest spiritual potential. If the two poets differ, it is over a fact which Goethe may have foreseen, though hardly to its full extent: that is to say, the sudden outbursts of violence and destructiveness called upon us by the same puritanical rationalism which, since the very beginnings of Western culture, has made us repress or minimize man's potential for evil. In Hughes' words, such repression has turned our whole inner world into a "place of demons" which finally erupted in a spectacle that left the world stage littered with millions of tortured and massacred human bodies in little over fifty years. Ironically, we more than ever refuse to own up to what we see when we catch a glimpse of our inner selves. "[We] recognize it with horror—it is an animal crawling and decomposing in a hell." Yet, as never before, our only hope lies in an acceptance of this inner world.

> Down there, mixed up among all the madness, is everything that once made life worth living. All the lost awareness and powers and allegiances of our biological and spiritual being. The attempt to re-enter that lost inheritance takes many forms, but it is the chief business of the swarming cults. (76,M,90-1)

It is also the business of Hughes' more recent poetry. But a discussion of how the poet approaches it through a new kind of psychological rather than moralistic didacticism belongs to a later chapter.

III.

Beginnings

Perhaps Georgian language wouldn't look nearly so bad if it hadn't been put to such a test. It was the worst equipment they could have had—the language of the very state of mind that belied and concealed the possibility of the nightmare that now had to be expressed. (65,P,208)

I think the fact that I know that my main audience will be an academic audience, in a roundabout way and against my will, influences the kind of thing I write. I tend to build in satisfactions for that audience. I can see it in the verse when I've finished it.[1]

III. BEGINNINGS

In what amounts to an over two hundred year old poetic chronicle of Romantic ecstasy, Victorian defensiveness, and *fin de siècle* apathy, Western man has been trying to confront the reemergence of Nature as her Gorgon head began to rise from the dungeons of rationalist and puritanical repression. Only Blake among the English Romantics seems to have seen and faced her entire: both as the creator and the destroyer as envisioned, say, in the "monstrous serpent" of *The Marriage of Heaven and Hell*, its "mouth & red gills hang[ing] just above the raging foam, tinging the black deep with beams of blood." For "the Prolific," the poem comments, "would cease to be Prolific unless the Devourer, as a sea, recieved the excess of his delights."[2] By contrast, Blake's contemporaries went bounding headlong in the fever of their over-excited minds, to end in premature death or exhaustion, in the artistic suicide of dry rot philosophical speculation or in the poet laureate retreat of reactionary middle age. Nature "red in tooth and claw" (Tennyson, *In Memoriam*, LVI), which "Hath really neither joy, nor love, nor light,/ Nor certitude, nor peace, nor help for pain" (Arnold, "Dover Beach"), became the atrophied vision of their Victorian successors.

Only in our century, after the holocausts of world wars and death camps, have artists and poets learned to accept nature both in her magnificent creativeness and "eternal fierce destruction" (Keats).[3] Transcending Nietzsche's pathos of defiance or the self-reflective bathos of absurdist despair, they have come to acknowledge their position of unaccommodated man in an unaccommodated universe that is "neither meaningful nor absurd" (Alain Robbe-Grillet),[4] but full of the agonies and ecstasies that are nature's eternal gift to man. What they unearthed from the ruins of our civilization is little more than what other cultures reared on books like the *Tao te Ching* or *Bhagavad Gita* have lived with since time immemorial. Yet the cost at which this vision was retrieved has turned the best of present-day art into an unprecedented gospel of survival. And what is more, the prophecy no longer tends to exclude the prophet as it used to in innumerable cases from Rimbaud to Hart Crane. Dylan Thomas, whose *Deaths and Entrances* (1946) became "a holy book" to Hughes (71,F,12), may have served the younger poet as a warning in this. Given his vision of a "morally undetermined, infinitely mothering creation," Thomas had "made a half-conscious attempt to take on all the underground life that the upper-crustish, militant, colonial-suppressive cast of the English intelligence excludes" (66,T,783). Yet lacking Lawrence's largesse of culturo-historical insights as well as Yeats' instinct for survival, he neither fulfilled his task nor was able to protect himself from the demons. A similar case was Sylvia Plath's, whose psychic gifts, as Hughes recalls, gained her "access to depths formerly reserved to the primitive ecstatic priests, shamans and Holy men." But she "had none of the usual guards and remote controls to protect herself from her own reality" (66,P,82).

1. Boyhood, University and Early Poetry.

Perhaps it was the double self he began to develop as an eight year old boy—leading one life with the Mexborough town boys and another in solitary companionship with Nature, never getting the two mixed up "except once or twice disastrously" (P,16)—which saved Hughes from a similar fate. The academic "ordeal for initiation into English society," which the poet underwent as a student at Cambridge, was shattering enough. "It's a most destructive experience," Hughes recalled in 1965,

> and only tough poets like Peter Redgrove ever survive . . . In effect university is a prison from life in your last three or four most formative years. It's a most deadly institution unless you're aiming to be either a scholar or a gentleman.

While this meant escape into interior exile—"I spent most of my time reading folklore and Yeats's poems" (65,H)—his rear guard defenses always seemed up to outfacing society's attempts to track down or ostracize the outsider. Rereading the poems and prose pieces Hughes wrote under the influence of his Cambridge years, one cannot but recall his portrait in the words of a fellow student:

> He lived with such vehemence, and such a perfect absence of self-consciousness, and such a total indifference to the modes of the Establishment. . . . He was unfettered, he was unafraid; he didn't care, in a tidy bourgeois sense, he didn't care a damn for anyone or anything.[5]

There is the direct attack, successful for its satire rather than humor, on student types like the rich Bartholomew Pygge Esq., whose drinking feats and freshman pranks turn him into a "University Personality" (in a story published May 4, 1957 in the college magazine *Granta*); or the caricature of a scholar (first published in 1962):

> dribbling tea
> Onto his tie, straining pipe-gargle
> Through the wharf-weed that ennobles
>
> The mask of his enquiry.
> ("Tutorial," R, 36)

More significant, although shortlived in terms of the poet's career, was a stylistic character armor Hughes developed after 1951 when, upon entering Cambridge, he "began to read occasionally about modern poetry" (62,D,1070). Thus a starkly new vision frequently seems to writhe in a style that in the wake of Eliot's neo-metaphysical period had dominated Anglo-American poetry under the New Critical ægis for several decades: a style of tough-minded intellectualism dense to the point of obscurity, replete with symbols and knotty syntactical contortions, its much praised objectivity often a mask for aggressive arrogance and backhanded cynicism. Such at least, whatever their model, are the stylistic hallmarks of several of Hughes' early poems. Yet even here, the poet's vision already puts him, along with Thomas or Lawrence, into polar opposition to the basically rationalist, neo-Aristotelian literary establishment which his style seems to emulate. In "The Man Seeking Experience Enquires His Way of a Drop of Water" or "Egg-Head" such opposition becomes the poem's central message. The intellectual's "staturing 'I am'" and "Braggart-browed complacency in most calm/Collusion with his own/ Dewdrop frailty" (H,35-6) is placed in ironic contrast with the man whose openness of mind dares take the risk of self-annihilation.

> A leaf's otherness,
> The whaled monstered sea-bottom, eagled peaks
> And stars that hang over hurtling endlessness,
> With manslaughtering shocks
>
> Are let in on his sense:
> So many a one has dared to be struck dead
> Peeping through his fingers at the world's ends,
> Or at an ant's head. (H,35)

At the same time the poet debunks all talk about the insoluble union achieved through love as an "Old Eden commonplace" or of a God-given "universal brotherhood" on earth as wishful fantasies of this "world-shouldering monstrous 'I' " that is unable to face the "square-pupilled yellow-eyed look" of a mountain goat (H,26,38,39,47).

Such fiercely uncompromising ideas had a hard time fitting into their narrow New Critical moulds, and only in two cases did the stylistic model prove strong enough to coerce the poet's vision into some form of disciplined control. Each poem forms a single, enlarged conceit, "The Dove Breeder" likening love's destructive powers to a hawk striking into a dovecote, and "A Modest Proposal" comparing man's latent hatefulness with that between two raging wolves. And the concluding lines in both manage to contain these emotions in powerful symbols of ritualistic control. The dove breeder finally ends up riding "the morning mist/With a big-eyed hawk on his fist" while the two wolves stand overawed at the sudden sight of a near heraldic spectacle:

> Suddenly they duck and peer.
>   And there rides by
> The great lord from hunting. His embroidered
> Cloak floats, the tail of his horse pours,
> And at his stirrup the two great-eyed greyhounds
> That day after day bring down the towering stag
> Leap like one, making delighted sounds. (H,23,25)

2. The Breakthrough of "The Thought-Fox."

There are no poems after "The Dove Breeder" and "A Modest Proposal" that imply a similar belief, as one critic writes, "that violent energies might be controlled and diverted into creative channels by ceremony."[6] Such a belief was never more than a stylistic pose and disappeared as quickly from Hughes' work as the model was alien to his true poetic temperament. Even in the early work, the poet's vision more often than not seems to explode rather than fit into its tight neo-metaphysical armor. As in "Fair Choice" this falling apart of style and content can reach a degree where the poem may be read on two separate levels. The actual statement (or *signifié*) made by the conceit (or *signifiant*) is that the lady would have done better to make a clear-cut choice between her two lovers. But so little does the poet's heart rest with such Petrarchan clichés that the conceit, through a realistic overelaboration of its components, begins to spin out its own story suggesting a woman with twins who is harangued for not, shortly after their birth, having killed one of the two infants.

Yet aside from such unintended double entendres, the reader is spared a poetic display of ambiguities and its several types. Wherever he makes an abstract statement, Hughes, in fact, uses only a few of the most basic rhetorical strategies. The most important one, which in various forms he has retained to date, is that of contrast between animals and men, primitive life and modern civilization or "The Ancient Heroes and the Bomber Pilot," usually made to the latters' disadvantage. As in that poem, dramatic distancing between a persona (the bomber pilot) and his subject matter (the ancient heroes) is one device, used in several poems from *The Hawk in the Rain* as well as *Lupercal*, in order to establish such opposition. A more frequent one, employed in the majority of poems that seem to reason out a specific point, is a simple "but" or its equivalent, introducing the second part of the argument. Though the results may be somewhat facile even in later poems like "Thrushes," it is wrong to measure Hughes' poetry by Eliot's demand for "a direct sensuous apprehension of thought, or a recreation of thought into feeling."[7] Such reasonableness never was nor would be akin to the poet's essentially evocative, visionary and mythopoeic talents, and Hughes did well in ignoring Robert Conquest's complaint that the author of *The Hawk in the Rain* had not as yet "found much to say" but that there was hope for improvement in the future.[8]

Like Robert Conquest, most reviewers could not help acknowledging the aggressive resourcefulness of language with which almost every poem in *The Hawk in the Rain* virtually seems to leap at the reader. Yet none of them isolated the pages on which this talent was first made subservient to Hughes' true poetic genius. In hindsight this may be obvious enough, although even now the poet's erratic growth from these sudden explosions of dead-right artistic accomplishment is as astounding as the outbursts are typical for his entire development. In any case, Hughes was hardly aware of his true gifts himself, or he would probably have chosen "The Thought-Fox" as the title poem of his first volume. Such hindsight evaluation is apparent only in his 1972 *Selected Poems 1957-1967* in which Hughes used the poem as the opening piece to his choices from *The Hawk in the Rain* while omitting the former title poem along with most of his early neo-metaphysical exercises.

Next to "Song," "The Thought-Fox" is probably the earliest poem to be included in *The Hawk in the Rain*. The poet's prison term at Cambridge had stifled all creative impulse, and Hughes published next to nothing during that period. Only after graduation, living alone in dreary London lodgings, did memory suddenly strike the tap root of his future creativity. Buried under the lumber of academic learning, his innermost self, cherished since early schooldays at Mexborough, was still intact and its sudden release brought forth one of the dozen or so most haunting poems Hughes has written to date. Discussing how starting to write poetry was in a way a direct continuation of his childhood hunting and fishing, Hughes recalls the specific circumstances of that crucial moment:

An animal I never succeeded in keeping alive is the fox. I was always frustrated: twice by a farmer, who killed cubs I had caught before I could get to them, and once by a poultry keeper who freed my cub while his dog waited. Years after those events I was sitting up late one snowy night in dreary lodgings in London. I had written nothing for a year or so but that night I got the idea I might write something and I wrote ["The Thought-Fox"] in a few minutes. (P,19)

"The Thought-Fox" already seems to carry the full impulse behind Hughes' gradual evolution into a visionary and mythmaker. The poem, unlike most others in *The Hawk in the Rain*, is neither all rhetoric and conceit nor all narrative and description. What it manages instead, is to embody a psycho-physiological process of imaginative projection and creation both prompted and carried by the poet's subconscious. Nor does it reflect this process by rehearsing emotions "recollected in tranquility." The subtle orchestration of program-music-like sound patterns ("A fox's nose touches twig, leaf") and syntactical rhythms—

> Two eyes serve a movement, that now
> And again now, and now, and now
>
> Sets neat prints into the snow (H,14)—

suggests the magical moment-to-moment incantation of a totem figure rather than a mind mulling pensively over half forgotten memories. Some poems from *The Hawk in the Rain* such as "Wind," "The Jaguar" and "October Dawn" may excel "The Thought-Fox" in their powerful evocations of elemental forces, supernatural dimensions, or primordial worlds. But none reaches the joint complexity of poetic incantation, spontaneous self-revelation and numinous suggestiveness with which its subject is literally brought alive, the thought-fox, like no other creature in Hughes' work before the soliloquizing hawk in *Lupercal*, becoming "both a fox and a spirit" (P,20). And certainly no poem before "Hawk Roosting" was to manage all this with a super-simple language so totally unlike the erudite contortions of several of Hughes' other poems of the same period.

The poems thematically close to "The Thought-Fox" now read as if this pure and single impulse first had to work its way free of academia's stylistic ballast before it could steer its destined course. Despite the impact of individual lines, "The Hawk in the Rain," for instance, hardly rises above a schoolbook exercise in a specific style too obvious to need pointing out. As Hughes once told me, Hopkins' model is the typical windhover of an Oxford don ignorant of the world actually inhabited by birds, so that his own poem turned into a deliberate effort to do the same thing differently. Nevertheless, the stylistic model remains so close that in lines like and I

> Bloodily grabbed dazed last-moment-counting
> Morsel in the earth's mouth, (H,11)

imitation almost turns into unconscious parody.

A different case of overwriting is provided by "Horses." Not before "Stealing Trout on a May Morning" (R,31-4) did the poet, for comparable length, manage to sustain this high pitch in the magical evocation of natural scenery. Drawn in by the lines' somnambulistic sureness of pace and vision, the reader soon finds himself

> Stumbling in the fever of a dream . . .
> .   .   .   .
> There, still they stood,
> But now steaming and glistening under the flow of light,
>
> Their draped stone manes, their tilted hind-hooves
> Stirring under a thaw while all around them
>
> The frost showed its fires. But still they made no sound.
> Not one snorted or stamped,
>
> Their hung heads patient as the horizons,
> High over valleys, in the red levelling rays—(H,16)

To end the poem at this point would have been more than appropriate. But the poet preferred to conclude with a Romantic coda whose indebtedness to "Resolution and Independence" would be recognized by any schoolboy.

> In din of the crowded streets, going among the years, the faces,
> May I still meet my memory in so lonely a place
>
> Between the streams and the red clouds, hearing curlews,
> Hearing the horizons endure. (H,16)

To readers interested in Hughes' development, this little Wordsworthian prayer may sound like the poet's *cri du coeur* at a time when, actually living amidst the din of crowded streets, he suddenly discovered that such memory was to be the mainspring of his future work. To readers simply interested in his poetry it comes as a curious anticlimax.

3. In Search of Lupercalia and "Hawk Roosting."

With the notable exception of "Hawk Roosting," *Lupercal* shows few crucial advances over the earlier volume. Published less than three years after *The Hawk in the Rain*, it mainly junked its predecessor's neo-metaphysical trappings, toned down its hyperboles, eliminated its show-offish rhetorical posturing and, following the impulse of "The Thought-Fox," shifted the emphasis towards animals and nature. Again as in *The Hawk in the Rain* there is caricature ("The Good Life") as well as personal encomium ("Dick Straightup"), poems about the present ("A Woman Unconscious," "Fourth of July") as well as the past ("Nicholas Ferrer"). Recalling "Six Young Men," "Griefs for Dead Soldiers" or "Bayonet Charge" from *The Hawk in the Rain*, one misses poems about war, a genre whose very source in another childhood experience as his father's "luckless double" (W,155) was to resurge in the more confessional vein of *Wodwo*.

Even the new title poem, which like "The Hawk in the Rain" is missing from *Selected Poems*, was basically a step in the wrong direction. A sequence of four sections, each dealing with one of the four participants (dog, woman, goat, athletes) in the actual Lupercalia, an annual Roman fertility ritual for the cure of barren women, it shows the first traces of a long search for symbols and rituals that might still be alive under the debris of present-day civilization. Yet despite the use of the present tense throughout and a lack of direct historical references, there is little to relate these symmetrically patterned and finely drawn miniatures to our present situation.

Indeed, but for several other poems in the same volume, there would be little reason to assume that such an impulse actually inspired "Lupercalia." None of these other pieces tries to actually reclaim the ancient life rituals. But by hinting at how they were destroyed, the poems reveal a more and more overcharged powerhouse of discontent which eventually, from about 1966 onwards, was to pour forth a multitude of ready-made, up-to-date pseudo-biblical parables, fables and commandments as well as neo-primitive icons, riddles, songs, spells and invocations.

Like Shakespeare before him, Hughes, in "Cleopatra to the Asp" bemoans how millennia of Oriental splendor and sensuousness embodied in the cosmically aggrandized self-portrait of the queen, were destroyed by Rome's money-grabbing puritanical imperialism.

> Nile moves in me; my thighs splay
> Into the squalled Mediterranean;
>
> . . . . .
>
> Now let the snake reign.

> A half-deity out of Capricorn,

> This rigid Augustus mounts
> With his sword virginal indeed; and has shorn
> Summarily the moon-horned river
>
> From my bed. May the moon
> Ruin him with virginity! (L,60)

Added to this is Hughes' discontent with the second mainspring of Western culture which the poet vents in a fierce attack on the Savior—

> This six-day abortion of the Absolute—
> No better for the fosterings
> Of fish, reptile and tree-leaper throughout
>
> Their ages of Godforsaken darkness—
> This monstrous-headed difficult child!
> Of such is the kingdom of heaven.
> ("The Perfect Forms," L,51)

Only a year later, in a humorous but crucial sequence of psycho-historical fables entitled "Dully Gumption's College Courses," Hughes was to intuit the fatal link between Roman imperialism and Christian slave morality:

> When Caesar clamped mankind in his money-mould,
> With a cry of pain out flew the effeminate soul
>
> And turned into vengeful Christ—
> The first Romantic raging at the first Formalist.
> ("Humanities")[9]

Just as these lines were written before Hughes read Nietzsche, so his more general attacks on the ongoing destruction of life were far from commonplace before ecology became the rage in the late sixties. There are the repeated references to the "last wolf killed in Britain" (L,13,cf.42) or the "last sturgeon of Thames" (L,42) while "Strawberry Hill" inveighs against Horace Walpole and his associates who made a stoat dance to the tune of their effete neo-gothic nursery games before they killed it. "Fourth of July" turns the general theme into a programmatic attack on our de-spiritualized global village.

> Even the Amazon's taxed and patrolled
>
> To set laws by the few jaws—
> Piranha and jaguar.
> Columbus' huckstering breath
> Blew inland through North America

> Killing the last of the mammoths.
> The right maps have no monsters.
> Now the mind's wandering elementals,
> Ousted from their traveller-told
>
> Unapproachable islands,
> From their heavens and their burning underworld,
> Wait dully at the traffic crossing,
> Or lean over headlines, taking nothing in. (L,20)

Epitaphs for a lost world though these poems may be, they also cele-brate its underground survival. The stoat after disappearing into some grave, "Emerges, thirsting, in far Asia, in Brixton" (L,16), while the wolf, and all the elemental forces it embodies, lives on in our subconscious. The close resemblance to an earlier poem is not fortuitous. For the same incan-tatory techniques that resurrected the thought-fox from childhood mem-ory now manage to summon this nightmare wolf from our collective un-conscious.

> Now it is the dream cries "Wolf!" where these feet
>
> Print the moonlit doorstep, or run and run
> Through the hush of parkland, bodiless, headless;
> With small seeming of inconvenience
> By day, too, pursue, siege all thought. (L,13)

More recently, Hughes has described his early animal poems as little totem texts written in search of the demon god of fertility.[10] For all that, most of them seem to convey a sense of control rather than of religious yearning. The individual line with its downward beat—"Killers from the egg: the malevolent aged grin" (L,56)—seems to grapple with its content like tautly strung wire around some unmanageable bundle. A still-life lan-guage of photographic precision often holds the violence of its subject mat-ter as if under hypnotic control. And the attitude of the speaker—the expository pointing out of certain biological facts all too easily overlooked by the reader ("To Paint a Water Lily"), the didactic eulogies of animal vitality contrasted with man's self-worshipful activities ("Thrushes"), the interpolated anecdotes of animal prowess ("Esther's Tomcat") or the casu-alness of semi-autobiographical digressions ("View of a Pig")—all this be-speaks mastery rather than longing. So the spiritual orientation of *Luper-cal*, as apparent as it may be now, remained a secret to most reviewers to whom the author was simply another animal poet. Hughes' composite self as inherited from childhood resisted personal effusions, especially after the stylistic role-playing in the earlier volume had successfully accomplished its half-conscious aim. In 1963, Peter Orr asked Hughes if he conceived his poetry around a consistent "I" with a clearly defined attitude towards life. Ironically his reply was more self-revelatory than the poems he had published till then:

> I tend to suspect that my poems are written by about three separate spirits or three separate characteristic states of mind . . . if they went under different names it's possible they'd deceive most people as being written by different people.[11]

As if to make the disguise complete, Hughes put the volume's most personal statement into the mouth of a persona. Yet "Crag Jack's Apostasy" is anything but a dramatic monologue. A few more directly autobiographical lines from "Pike" in which the speaker sits by a pond at night—not daring to cast his line, but instead fishing "With the hair frozen on [his] head/For what might move, for what eye might move"—not only seem to unravel its secret, but to relate it to the poet's childhood experience of literally fishing for those "elusive and shadowy thoughts" which in flash visions of sudden revelation opened an access to the "luminous spirit" of life:[12]

> The still splashes on the dark pond,
>
> Owls hushing the floating woods
> Frail on my ear against the dream
> Darkness beneath night's darkness had freed,
> That rose slowly towards me, watching. (L,57)

The new God whom Crag Jack invokes after abjuring the dark churches of his childhood resembles this "Darkness beneath night's darkness." As the divine Eye beneath the pike's eye, He is asked to reveal himself "through/The world under the world."

> Come to my sleeping body through
> The world under the world; pray
> That I may see more than your eyes
>
> In an animal's dreamed head. (L,55)

Hughes' general fascination with the tramp in *Lupercal* confirms the poem's oblique confessionalism. Where Crag Jack has "kicked at the world and slept in ditches" (L,55), the down-and-out protagonist of "Things Present" seems to have reached a here-and-now affirmation of life beyond such rebelliousness. The poet's sympathies for the type are also obvious from "November" whose speaker watches a tramp in the pelting rain, "Face tucked down into beard," wondering "what strong trust/Slept in him." Yet the protagonist of "Things Present" is dreaming while the imagery of "November," if read at its deepest and perhaps unintended level, seems to undercut the poet's musings. For the animals which the speaker, himself frantically escaping from the rain, discovers towards the end— their chins, like the tramp's, lowered "on chests,/Patient to outwait these worst days" (L,49-50)—are dead.

Philip O'Connor's firsthand portrayal of *Vagrancy*, a book Hughes reviewed in September, 1963, may have helped the poet avoid such fallacies in the future. There was little here to leave room for idealization. "Salvation Army hostels, Rowton Houses, demoralisation in six weeks, and so perhaps on to alcoholism, to meths and surgical spirit . . . psychologically dismantled for good, and just scrounging along in despair between vague efforts to get back into society." The impact of these facts was strong enough to make the reviewer quarrel with O'Connor who sanctifies the tramp as a victim of our competitive society. In an unusually argumentative tone, Hughes questions this theory as a basic fallacy of the Christian ethic as it survives in the secularized form of humanitarian socialism. The vehemence here may be partly self-directed, as a consequence of his having, in several poems, indulged in similar fantasies himself. But it also serves to remind us of the neo-Darwinism which is central to Hughes' vision of nature.

> Civilisation is horribly sick, and vagrants undergo the hardest pains of it. But could anything growing as fast and on such a scale as mankind be much better than very sick, and in what kind of society would there be no individuals misfitting to the point of vagrancy? . . . [And] is it true that competition is as thoroughly evil in fact as it is in [O'Connor's] imagination? When non-competition is enforced, what sort of genetic torpor ensues, and worse? (63,O,294)

Even though Hughes was to abandon the mask of the tramp, Crag Jack's longings have continued to determine the route of his poetic development. The first result was that Hughes, calling upon God in "an animal's dreamed head," managed to invoke not God but the devil. "Hawk Roosting," Hughes' most widely anthologized piece to date, is the product of an early morning concentration exercise focussing on the phrase that became the poem's title. It is the first poem before *Crow* in which the impulse that, in "The Thought-Fox," had invoked "both a fox and a spirit," conjured up a creature of mythic dimensions. The result was a grim surprise to the poet himself. Hughes' first impression while writing the poem "was that in this hawk Nature is thinking. Simply Nature." But it soon became apparent that this was more difficult than expected "because Nature is no longer so simple." So finally the hawk came to sound, not "like Isis, mother of the gods, which he is," but "like Hitler's familiar spirit" (71,F,8).

> I kill where I please because it is all mine.
> There is no sophistry in my body:
> My manners are tearing off heads—

The allotment of death.
For the one path of my flight is direct
Through the bones of the living.
No arguments assert my right:

The sun is behind me:
Nothing has changed since I began.
My eye has permitted no change.
I am going to keep things like this. (L,26)

It seems wrong to call the poem a dramatic monologue whose author deliberately manipulates our attitude towards a persona or, worse, celebrates the hawk for being "a fascist" or "some horrible totalitarian genocidal dictator" (71,F,8). To say so would be tantamount to accusing the author of *Job* of irresponsible thinking because he made God describe himself as a Leviathan. In neither case is the poet thinking through a persona. Instead, he seems to have undergone what Jung describes as "a primordial experience which surpasses man's understanding . . . chilling the blood with its strangeness" and bursting "asunder our human standards of value and æsthetic form."[13] This is particularly obvious in "Hawk Roosting" if considered in the context of Hughes' other work. Not unlike "The Thought-Fox," though for different reasons, the poem stands out uniquely from all others in the same volume. While an ongoing invocation is the very subject matter of "The Thought-Fox," "Hawk Roosting" embodies its startlingly autonomous product as its numinous force invades our consciousness. Over twenty personal pronouns all referring to the "I," "me" or "mine" of the hawk, are the most obvious and, in this case, egomaniacal sign of such autonomy. And every line, with its clipped self-sufficiency of madness, seems to pronounce its deadly verdict like an oracle of destruction. Not before "How Water Began to Play" (C,83), although with diametrically opposite results, did a poem by Hughes achieve a similar impact through the very simplicity of its language and craftsmanship.

The potential dangers of such poetry are fully obvious to the author. Yet to Hughes these are due to historical circumstance rather than personal obsession. The Old Testament poet of *Job*, for instance, still had an at least rudimentary sense of the older genuine almighty destroyer and creator combined. But when "Christianity kicked the devil out of Job what they actually kicked out was Nature . . . and Nature became the devil" (71,F,8). Shakespeare's work, in Hughes' view, is the prime example of how Western poetry ever since has in a way been correcting this one-sided misrepresentation of Nature. Like Jung, who believed that art "is constantly at work educating the spirit of the age, conjuring up the forms in which the age is most lacking,"[14] Hughes stands convinced that poetry "is nothing if not . . . the record of just how the forces of the Universe try to redress some balance disturbed by human error" (71,F,7). Shakespeare's final repudiation of Nature in "Sycorax, the blue-eyed hag," anticipates a near schizophrenic deepening of this error, for which T. S. Eliot's "dissociation of sensibility" is a dangerous euphemism. So, the task that Shakespeare, in Hughes' view, failed to accomplish is now more than ever what the poet must confront. "Nature's attempts to recombine, first in love, then in whatever rebuffed love turns into" are the main impulse behind twentieth century poetry as they were "the power-house and torture-chamber" of Shakespeare's complete works (71,S,192,197-8). And the imbalance will only be rectified if we avoid the rationalist and puritanical repression that caused it.

The problem, of course, is more complex than that, and Hughes' oblique self-criticism where he discusses the risks of such openness hints at the strategies by which the poet has tried to solve it. Like his roosting hawk, "The Jaguar," to Hughes, is not only "a beautiful, powerful nature spirit" but also a symbol of what such natural energy has turned into in the course of Western civilization, "a symbol of man's baser nature shoved down into the id and growing cannibal murderous with deprivation." No wonder that poetic releases of such demonized forces are particularly dangerous in an age without the customary controls of ritual and religion.

> The tradition is, that energy of this sort once invoked will destroy an impure nature and serve a pure one. In a perfectly cultured society one imagines that jaguar-like elementals would be invoked only by self-disciplinarians of a very advanced grade. I am not one and I'm sure few readers are, so maybe in our corrupt condition we have to regard poems about jaguars as ethically dangerous. (71,F,8-9)

The statement is from Hughes 1970 interview, given shortly before the publication of *Crow*. Compared with the bravado of his 1962 manifesto which described the poet as little more than a passive recipient of his visions, it recalls both the tragic disasters such risk-taking has spelt in the poet's personal life and the mythic controls he was to search out during its course.

> If you refuse the energy, you are living a kind of death. If you accept the energy, it destroys you. What is the alternative? To accept the energy, and find methods of turning it to good, of keeping it under control— rituals, the machinery of religion. The old method is the only one. (71,F,10)

IV.

Towards *Crow*

[T]he archetypal journey to the bottom of the soul . . . is the fundamental myth of the epic and heroic legends, and the blueprint allegory of religious experience, as of mental and physical collapse and renewal. (64,W,230)

Cool, analytical qualities are heavily present in everything he does, but organically subdued to a grasp that is finally visionary and redemptive. Without the genius, he might well have disintegrated as he evidently saw others disintegrate. . . . But his creative demon . . . works deeper than either of these two extremes. It is what involves him so vehemently with both. It involves him with both because this demon is ultimately the voice of his nature, which requires at all costs satisfaction in life, full inheritance of its natural joy. It is what suffers the impossible problem and dreams up the supernormal solution. It is what in most men stares dumbly through the bars. At bottom it is amoral, as interested in destruction as in creation. (65,S,8)

IV. TOWARDS *CROW*

Hughes' earliest poem to be included in one of his collections is a love address to a female of mythic dimensions. Blessed by the natural elements, she goes through a series of telluric transformations. Resembling a "shaped shell" full of Aeolian music, she is some oceanic goddess bodied forth in "marble of foam" at one moment and at the next a sky divinity of "soft fire with a cloud's grace," the stars swimming "for eyes in [her] face." In short, she embodies the White Goddess to whose youthful worshipper Graves' book of that title, given to him by his master at Mexborough Grammar School, had already turned into a kind of Bible. But the poet's relationship to this Earth Mother is as hopelessly desolate as the poem's powerful last image.

> O lady, consider when I shall have lost you
> The moon's full hands, scattering waste,
> The sea's hands, dark from the world's breast,
> The world's decay where the wind's hands have passed,
> And my head, worn out with love, at rest
> In my hands, and my hands full of dust,
>   O my lady. (H,19)

Characteristically, "Song" was written as if to dictation. Yet, just as suddenly as it had appeared, the "voice" went dumb again, leaving Hughes with the frustrating recollection of a lost line he failed to jot

71

down. According to the evidence of his published verse, it remained mute for over two decades. And but for "Crow's Undersong" or the dreams which inspired the Epilogue poems of *Gaudete* it might have remained silent for ever. In one of these poems the lady of "Song" seems to have turned into a Pietà-like Earth-Mother protectress of the middle-aged poet.

> An unearthly woman wading shorewards
> With me in your arms
>
> The grey in my hair. (G,183)

Except for "Song," the territory covered by *The Hawk in the Rain* and *Lupercal* resembles a country without women. The occasional caricature apart ("Macaw and Little Miss," "Secretary" and "Fallgrief's Girl-Friends"), woman's role is limited to that of the sufferer ("Childbirth," "A Woman Unconscious") or passive listener harangued about love, the "spoiled appetite for some delicacy" (H,24). The odd vampire or hag but no women. And where they emerge in the poetry after *Lupercal*, they mostly appear in some terrible state of desecration. Elaine in *The House of Aries*, a radio play first broadcast in November 1960, seems to intuit some of the wider historical reasons for this plight in a prophetic moment.

> I have cried out and become silent at the will of
> the Inquisitors,
> I have drowned in the blood of my family at the
> Reformation and Counter-Reformation,
> Every heresy's banner is a strip of skin off my back.[1]

Or as the poet himself was to point out ten years later,

> The subtly apotheosised misogyny of Reformed Christianity is proportionate to the fanatic rejection of Nature, and the result has been to exile man from Mother Nature—from both inner and outer nature . . . Since Christianity hardened into Protestantism, we can follow [Nature's] underground heretical life, leagued with everything occult, spiritualistic, devilish, overemotional, bestial, mystical, feminine, crazy, revolutionary, and poetic. (70,N,81-2)

Hughes' own poetry after 1960 is a powerful witness to this underground heretical life as well as to the poet's attempt to bring it out into the open.

1. Lady Lazarus.

Recent studies have revealed that modern psychiatry derives its basic "therapeutic" patterns from the *Malleus malificarum* procedures of the Inquisition. The very founder of psychiatry admitted that in "pronouncing possession by a demon to be the cause of hysterical phenomena," the former witch doctor is in basic agreement with his contemporary counterpart: "it would only have been a matter," wrote Freud, "of exchanging the religious terminology of that dark and superstitious age for the scientific language of today."[2] Thus Thomas Szasz, in *The Manufacture of Madness* (1970), subtitled *A Comparative Study of the Inquisition and the Mental Health Movement*, has demonstrated in hair-raising detail to what extent our methods of diagnosing and treating mental illness are analogous to those of witchcraft. A full account of the origins of Institutional Psychiatry would, of course, have to go back much further than that. Even the New Testament formula of the lunatic possessed with the devil who has to be driven out (Matthew, 17:15f.) can be traced to numerous older injunctions. Usually it is Yahweh himself who decrees that "Thou shalt not suffer a witch to live" (Exodus, 22:18) or that there "shall not be found among you . . . a charmer, or a consulter with familiar spirits, or a wizard, or a necromancer" (Deuteronomy, 18:10-11). No wonder that the witch of Endor was afraid that Saul, who made her conjure up the ghost of Samuel, only wanted to lay a snare for her life (1 Samuel, 28:9). And just as witches rather than wizards seem to have been the favorite victims of their persecutors throughout the ages, so women rather than men continue to be the most likely candidates for insulin or electroshock treatment. As Phyllis Chesler has shown in her recent *Women and Madness*, there is an average imbalance of roughly 60% female over 40% male hospitalized mental patients in U. S. psychiatric hospitals.[3]

Sylvia Plath had undergone a series of psychiatric treatments some three years before she met her future husband in February, 1956. Her prize-winning *Mademoiselle* guest editorship in the glossy world of New York's literary establishment had proved a stunning anticlimax. After a month of feeling "very ecstatic, horribly depressed, shocked, elated, enlightened, and enervated,"[4] she returned home to find that she had not been admitted to a prestigious creative writing course at Harvard and as a consequence became severely depressed. To the town psychiatrist who "treated her as a neurotic female rather than as a severe depressive," this proved sufficient warrant for subjecting the twenty-one year old poet to a series of out-patient electroshocks. More than anything else, the treatment gave her an extreme fear of ECT which in her mind became linked with the fate of the Rosenbergs, who had been sent to the electric chair during her *Mademoiselle* venture.[5] This was followed by her suicide attempt and more treatment of the same kind, by now administered to the hospitalized mental patient—"wak[ing] up in shuddering horror and fear of the cement tunnels leading down to the shock room."[6] Long before Thomas Szasz' *The Manufacture of Madness*, Plath's "Johnny Panic and the Bible of Dreams," a semi-surrealistic account of how a crew of "false priests" give her ECT punishment for being a "little witch" who "has been making time with Johnny Panic," reveals the Christian inquisitorial implications of electroshock therapy.

> The white cot is ready. With a terrible gentleness Miss Milleravage takes the watch from my wrist, the rings from my fingers, the hairpins from my hair. She begins to undress me. When I am bare, I am anointed on the temples and robed in sheets virginal as the first snow. Then, from the four corners of the room and from the door behind me come five false priests in white surgical gowns and masks whose one lifework is to unseat Johnny Panic from his own throne. They extend me full-length on my back on the cot. The crown of wire is placed on my head, the wafer of forgetfulness on my tongue . . . The signal is given . . . At the moment when I think I am most lost the face of Johnny Panic appears in a nimbus of arc lights on the ceiling overhead. I am shaken like a leaf in the teeth of glory. His beard is lightning. Lightning is in his eye. His Word charges and illumines the universe.[7]

No wonder that Thomas Szasz included "Johnny Panic and the Bible of Dreams" in his 1973 *The Age of Madness* which, as its subtitle indicates, documents *The History of Involuntary Mental Hospitalization* in an anthology of selected texts. The story originated in late 1958, after a typing job in the records office of a Boston mental hospital had provided Sylvia Plath with a refuge from a writing block. As Ted Hughes comments, it managed to "tap the molten source of her poetry as none of her poems up to then had" (77,P,14). A "deliberate exercise in experimental improvisation on set themes" (66,P,85) fully released that source. The first major outcome was "The Stones," the only poem from *The Colossus* (1960) which Sylvia Plath, by 1962, was prepared to exempt from the label Juvenilia. It describes "the city of spare parts" where the speaker is "mended" lying on "a great anvil," the "grafters" cheerfully

> Heating the pincers, hoisting the delicate hammers.
> A current agitates the wires
> Volt upon volt. Catgut stitches my fissures.
>
> .   .   .   .   .   .
>
> My swaddled legs and arms smell sweet as rubber.
> Here they can doctor heads, or any limb.[8]

Even lacking Hughes' testimony to this effect, the reader might have guessed that the poem is "full of specific details of her experience in a mental hospital, and is clearly enough the first eruption of the voice that produced *Ariel*" (66, P, 85). Several poems of that volume show that

"The Stones" also released Sylvia Plath's most crucial and shattering memory. They portray a soul torn loose from its body, which has turned into a patchwork of medical items placed on public exhibit.

> There is a charge
>
> For the eyeing of my scars, there is a charge
> For the hearing of my heart—
> It really goes.
>
> And there is a charge, a very large charge
> For a word or a touch
> Or a bit of blood
>
> Or a piece of my hair or my clothes.
> So, so, Herr Doktor.
> So, Herr Enemy.
>
> I am your opus.

"At twenty I tried to die," reports another poem.

> But they pulled me out of the sack,
> And they stuck me together with glue.[9]

Her final suicide on February 11, 1963 was not to give them another chance.

2. *The Wound* and "Theology."

The fact that Sylvia must have talked about these experiences to her husband needs little confirmation. Some of the results seem obvious from a letter of November 29, 1956, in which Sylvia, commenting on a student with paranoid fears of poor marks, advises her mother against some of the treatment that had been enlisted for herself:

> I think psychiatrists are often too busy to devote the right sort of care to this; they . . . blither about father and mother relationships when some common sense, stern advice about practical things and simple human intuition can accomplish much.[10]

Though such advice seems to reflect her husband's rather than Plath's basic attitudes, Hughes, in turn, was deeply affected by his wife's psychiatric history. What his conscious mind managed to transform into constructive thoughts about better therapy, his subconscious focused in a nightmare hieroglyph of female desecration—a woman with a "crudely stitched patchwork of faces" (G,104)—that has continued to haunt him ever since. The image first emerged in a dream whose immediate transcript provided the basis for his radio play *The Wound* (broadcast February 1, 1962). Here, a female chorus describes the dissection of a living woman conducted under the auspices of an international scientific assembly including a delegation of "Experimental psychologists of four countries":

THIRD: Under intense illuminations, they were not in the dark, they did not brave the interior unprepared, their eyes followed their fingers inward.

FOURTH: And what did they find did they find what they hoped for.

FIRST: Lusted for.

SECOND: Sliced me for.

THIRD: Did they find the gold teeth.

FOURTH: The plastic gums.

FIRST: The glass eyes.

SECOND: The steel skull-plates.

THIRD: The jawbone rivets.

FOURTH: The rubber arteries.   (W,121,122-3)

To its author, *The Wound* appears as a Gothic-Celtic version of the *Bardo Thödol* which in Jungian terms offers a "close parallel to the phenomenology of the European unconscious when it is undergoing an 'initiation process,' that is to say, when it is being analysed."[11] Analogously, Hughes feels that the *Tibetan Book of the Dead*—like his radio play—"is characteristically shaman," guiding the "dead soul to its place in death, or back into life—together with the principal terrific events" (64,E,677). What both works seem to demonstrate, in other words, is a regenerative death and rebirth experience rather than the soul's fateful reincarnation into a Buddhist *samsāra*. In *The Wound*, this initiation journey through the underworld takes the form of a dream dreamt by the poet's alter ego, Sergeant Ripley, a wounded soldier who is finally saved by his comrades.

In traditional Shamanism, the emissary from the spirit world who leads the neophyte into this self-destructive ritual, "with all possible variants of boiling, devouring, burning, stripping to the bones" (64,E,677), is often a beautiful woman who later marries the shaman. In Hughes' Gothic-Celtic version, this female psychopomp, or her several representatives, seems to fuse with the demons performing the quester's dismemberment. That at least is the treatment Ripley's fellow traveller Massey receives at the hands of the Bacchantes-like demon prostitutes at the Queen's chateau.

One of those women had Sergeant Massey by the hair. One had his leg
between her thighs and was trying to twist his foot off. His arms were
out of their sockets. (W,131-2)

Even the "Girl" who tries to make love to Ripley while both are watching
this spectacle, is presented as a potentially murderous ogress of the same
type. Even so, she, like Ripley, yearns to be saved from the desecration
which has demonized them all. When Ripley *"throws her away. She cries out,
hurt"* (W,133) protesting that she loves him. And although he refuses her
call to the end, he finally, after she has turned into his guide, becomes her
bridegroom. The nadir of destructiveness, from which such mutual regeneration takes its impulse, anticipates a similar dream sequence in *Gaudete.* Here the baboon woman with her "crudely stitched patchwork of
faces" (G,104) emerges from a mud crater studded with the heads of
women who are buried alive, and almost kills her rescuer before achieving
her own salvation. In *The Wound* a mud pool ("good earth at other times,
mother of mankind") turns into a slaughterhouse—"These women are
dragging them all into the ground, it's a massacre"—before Ripley and the
girl become each other's saviors.

> GIRL: Lean on me. Try to walk.
> RIPLEY: No, no . . . My feet are stuck in the mud.
> We'd better wait till the rain stops.
> GIRL: You can walk. You're walking.
> RIPLEY: What's your name? Ah, yes, you told me, didn't you.
> Did you?
> My memory's been dismantled.
> If ever I get back to streets do you know what I'll do?
> I'll marry you. (W,143-5)

Hughes' Gothic-Celtic version of the *Bardo Thödol* signals an important
turning point in the poet's career. The God, implored to visit the poet's
"sleeping body" so that he may see more than His eyes in "an animal's
dreamed head" (L,55), has begun to send the dreams. And like a semi-
autobiographical narrative of mythic dimensions, they were to turn into
the secret quarry of Hughes' poetry ever since. His poems from then on
resemble buoys above some ocean wreck and few of them, even among
those *From the Life and Songs of the Crow,* seem to reflect this narrative
directly. Yet the mythic folktale behind *Crow,* as recounted to me in 1970,
shows that some of its themes as first apparent in *The Wound,* have remained crucial concerns to the poet throughout *Crow, Orghast* and *Gaudete.*
Early on in Crow's adventures, of which a full account is given
elsewhere,[12] Crow makes contact with a woman who keeps repeatedly
appearing at the nadir of the episodes. She is always in some terrible con-

dition and undergoing some awful torment, so that in a way his whole quest becomes a quest to liberate her. But everything goes wrong until finally, at the very bottom of many different levels of adventure, he is in fact to save her, to lose her again, and to pursue her until she becomes his bride. And at the moment that she becomes his bride he becomes half a man. The Crow poems are from the first two-thirds of this story bringing it up to the moment just before he pieces her together while he himself disintegrates.

For all its forcefulness, this mythic nightmare was by no means the only or earliest source to inspire *Crow*. The first idea, as Hughes himself said in 1970, "was really an idea of a style . . . in a super-simple and a super-ugly language which would in a way shed everything except just what [the Crow] wanted to say" (71,F,20). Even "Hawk Roosting," although probably the first of its kind to be published, was not the earliest piece Hughes wrote in this vein. Already in his teens, the time of "Song," when he was not otherwise busy imitating Yeats or Eliot, Hughes would compose little interpretive fables and anecdotes in a plain, rough, almost flat mode of presentation. Abandoned for the heavily imagistic poetry of observation of *The Hawk in the Rain* and *Lupercal*, the style suddenly reemerged in 1961, shortly before dreaming *The Wound*, in a poem entitled "Theology" which at the time appeared to Hughes as only a note for a longer one.

> No, the serpent did not
> Seduce Eve to the apple.
> All that's simply
> Corruption of the facts.
>
> Adam ate the apple.
> Eve ate Adam.
> The serpent ate Eve.
> This is the dark intestine.
>
> The serpent, meanwhile,
> Sleeps his meal off in Paradise—
> Smiling to hear
> God's querulous calling.   (W,149)

Not before 1966, when Hughes began to write *Crow* in Ireland, did the poet recognize the full importance of "Theology." And the same, speaking in more strictly thematic terms, seems to be true of *The Wound*. While the radio play was not published until 1967, "Theology" remained tucked away in the anti-University curriculum entitled "Dully Gumption's College Courses" (1961),[13] a rather odd looking piece among the other poems. Only in *Wodwo* (1967) were both works granted their proper place as side by side centerpieces of the entire collection.

To be sure, Hughes may well have thought of "Theology" and *The Wound* by February 1962, when he proposed to be attentive to his "true gift" and to "do nothing but accept it" whenever it should reveal itself (62,C,45). But such readiness to receive the sudden flash vision from the innermost core of his mind was stifled by the tragic events that followed. In late February 1963, the month of Sylvia Plath's suicide, Hughes wrote "The Howling of Wolves," in March "Song of a Rat," during the following months "Cadenza" and "Kreutzer Sonata" as well as a few more pieces that have remained buried in journals or in *Recklings* (limited edition, 1966)—then no major poems before 1966. At least not poems written as poems. The new impulses were to come from elsewhere.

3. Children's Books and Educational Psychotherapy.

Hughes' first attempt to break this crippling silence was in an imagined dialogue with his children with whom, for several years after February 1963, he was to share a withdrawn existence in Devonshire. Three children's books, *How the Whale Became*, *The Earth-Owl and Other Moon People* and *Nessie the Mannerless Monster*, appeared in quick succession between November 1963 and April 1964. Their masterpiece, a fable about the birth of the bee from the tears of a demon, seems to locate part of the impulse that was to erupt in the didactic mythographies of *Crow*. A tale of spellbinding beauty, "How the Bee Became" has the characteristic ease of the poet's greatest, most spontaneous creations. And there is more to it to make us think of *Crow* than a God who is in turns ignorant, amazed or flattered. If *Crow* is a story of a nightmare monster's attempt to improve upon God's creation, then "How the Bee Became" tells us how a demon, living at the center of the earth, tries to create something that "will be far more beautiful than any of God's creatures" (Wh,67). The fable also anticipates *Crow* by reassessing the nature of the demonic. Though not as radically as "Theology" or the later children's story *The Iron Man* (1968), it rechannels the repressive dynamics of a ubiquitous Western thought pattern implicit in myths such as St. George and the Dragon, the Fall of Lucifer, the dragon Typhœus' similar casting down into Tartarus at the hands of Zeus, or the Mesopotamian Earth Mother Tiamat's massacre by her son Marduk. In "How the Bee Became," the suffering of the demon, whom God is characteristically unaware of, turns creative.

Such didacticism may have been only half intentional at the time. Yet what Hughes, in talking about *The Iron Man*, has said about his "writing stories for children with some sort of educational purpose," seems to apply to the earlier story as much as to "Crow's Account of St. George" and other myth parodies in *Crow*. In its original form the story of St. George,

Hughes pointed out to his academic audience in 1970, should be a "forbidden story" to teachers "interested in using imaginative literature for educational purposes." For it is

> the symbolic story of creating a neurosis . . . it's the key to the neurotic-making dynamics of Christianity. Christianity in suppressing the devil, in fact suppresses imagination and suppresses vital natural life. . . [But], of course, he leaks out in every direction as a very evil, wicked and uncontrolled and unsuspected presence. (70,M,55,65-6)

Such insights and the need to reverse the story are the outcome of Hughes' own imaginative experience. The speaker in "Quest," a poem published as early as February 1958, is a knight who rides out "to raise this monster's shadow from [his] people" anticipating his heroic self-sacrifice with "fragments of [his] body dangling from its hundred mouths."[14] How closely such fantasies anticipate a crucial moment in Hughes' creative life is evident from the poet's 1970 comment on "Gog." Its first part, written at the time of "Theology" and *The Wound*, began as a description of the German assault through the Ardennes but gradually turned into the dragon in *Revelations*. Terrified by such unsolicited visions, the poet at first retreated into the self-protective heroism of the Christian archetype. "It alarmed me so much I wrote a poem about the Red Cross Knight just to set against it with the idea of keeping it under control" (71,F,9). Of course, the self-defeating imagery of "The Knight" (1965)—the protagonist arising "Out of the blood-dark womb" and searching to destroy

> the enemy, the grail,
> The womb-wall of the dream that crouches there, greedier than a foetus,
> Suckling at the root-blood of the origins, the salt-milk drug of the mothers— (W,151-2)

already turns the heroic savior into a would-be murderer of his mother. But this total recasting of the legend was not achieved before "Crow's Account of St. George" (1970) in which the knight, who thinks he has killed a demon, suddenly awakens from his fury,

> Drops the sword and runs dumb-faced from the house
> Where his wife and children lie in their blood. (C,20)

The intent behind this drastic inversion is in principle equal to what inspired the happier reversals of *The Iron Man* or "How the Bee Became." And it may well have derived part of its impulse from the earlier narratives. What Hughes seems to propose in both is a semi-magical, neo-primitive art of story telling that will serve as an antidote to the "neurotic-making dynamics" of its Christian counterpart. For the right fantasy, as bards in ancient Ireland and India knew long before Freud, "can free the neurotic, temporarily at least, from his neurosis":

> Nobody has the faintest idea how it works. A mentally sick person is sick, says the theory, because there is something . . . which he represses into the cellars of his mind, down into the nervous system where it plays havoc. And this devil of suppressed life stops making trouble the moment he is acknowledged . . . The best way to welcome him and to release him, it is reckoned, is within the framework of a fantasy. Once the fantasy has made connection with the demon and given him a role, the person feels cured . . . In early times this phenomenon was understood quite well, so it became standard to include in the narrative of some stories exactly the benefits the hearers were going to get.

Besides examples from Irish folklore, Hughes quotes the *Ramayana* and another famous Indian source, *Twenty-Five Stories of the Specter and the Corpse*, which ends with the following promise from the specter:

> Neither ghosts nor demons shall have any power wherever and whenever these tales are told and whoever recites a single one of them with devotion shall be free from sin. (70, M, 58-9)

Yet it is one thing to devise anti-neurotic fables for children, and another to conjure up the fantasies that will dissolve the hardened neuroses of the adult. The latter, according to Hughes, would require the spiritual make-up of a "witch-doctor or yogi," and even the old poets, say, of pre-Christian Ireland had to go through many years of arduous training before they were able to perform this semi-religious function of a healer of souls (70,M,58). Part of their training, which the ancient shaman shares with the modern psychiatrist, is a self-destructive journey into the interior, and it is only around 1964 that Hughes seems about to embark on this quest.

4. *Eat Crow* and *Recklings*.

The dreams which inspired *The Wound* seem to prefigure the basic trajectory of this imaginary journey. Its aim was to rescue the desecrated female who in her turn restores the protagonist from the destruction he undergoes for her sake, before both are united in a mystical marriage. But any hopes to attain what *The Wound* had already put in sight were shattered by the tragic event of February 11, 1963. After that Hughes had to search out elsewhere what was lost to his own vision, and for over a year *The Chemical Wedding of Christian Rosencreutz*, by the seventeenth-century hermeticist Johann Valentin Andreae, became his prime source of inspiration. Hughes' verse drama adaptation of this novel, which in the mystical union of *sponsus* and *sponsa* typifies "processes of regeneration and change within the soul,"[15] bore the characteristic title *Difficulties of a Bridegroom*. It is equally characteristic that this work, although a quarry for poems like "Ghost Crabs," "Waking" and Part III of "Gog," remained unfinished. Yet *Eat Crow*, the only sequence from it ever to be printed,[16] shows the seminal importance of the work Hughes was pursuing under Rosicrucian guidance. Its protagonist Mr. Morgan anticipates the caricature of modern man in "A Bedtime Story" (1968), which was later incorporated into *Crow*. A person, or rather "Almost a person" (C,59), he has lost all contact with his body, emotions and memory, and in a Kafkaesque courtroom scene is subjected to a gradual dismantling of his character armor (EC,9).

Morgan's subsequent journey into self-destruction traverses the well-known scenario of Hughes' underworld. The cattle stampede with "drumming of hooves" and, more significantly, a chorus of loudly lamenting women, look forward to similar scenes in *Gaudete*, as they resume some of the basic imagery of *The Wound*. The nadir of this descent is reached in a monologue which reads like a *Bardo Thödol*-inspired inversion of Eliot's *Ash Wednesday*. Morgan's scattered bones, far from being "glad to be scattered," glory in the bloody-minded fierceness of former incarnations, and finally try to track down the quester, apparently in an effort to be readmitted into life.

> The breastbone was crying:
> 'I begot a million and murdered a million:
> I was a leopard' . . .
>
> .   .   .   .
>
> And the bones of the hand, fought: 'We were alligators,
> We dragged some beauties under, we did not let go.'
>
> .   .   .   .
>
> I got up and ran. I tried to get up and run.
> But they saw me. 'There he is,' they shouted,
> They saw me. 'It's him, it's him again, get him.'
> They came shrieking after me and I ran. (EC,18-19)

Unable to finish his story, the quester leaves off in mid-sentence, and only after a "*Long pause*" is given a new goal by the "She" who, like the "Girl" in *The Wound*, has gradually emerged from the chorus of moaning women to become his guide:

> SHE
> A crow is a sign of life. Even though it sits motionless . . .
> The crow is composed of terrible black voice . . . But voice
> that can hardly utter. He looks this way and that . . . resigned
> to the superior stamina of the empty horizon, limber and watch-
> ful.

The laws are still with the living . . . A crow has
come up from the maker of the world. (EC,19-21)

Little did Hughes know at the time that he had hit upon the creature
which was to become the most central mythograph of his entire *oeuvre* to
date. And not till after *Recklings* (1966) and *Wodwo* (1967) did he realize
how his Rosicrucian quest, as reflected in this sequence, had brought him
to the story of Crow. However, in 1971, apparently while preparing *Eat
Crow* for publication, he lifted from it the entire monologue rehearsing
Morgan's "bones all chattering together" in order to make it, little altered,
the title poem of the collection *Crow Wakes*.

Recklings are the weakest animals in the litter, those least fit for survival. Yet there was enough in the 1966 limited edition of that title that did
survive. "Logos," a key poem in Hughes' development, was reprinted in
Wodwo. "A Match," "On the Slope" and "To Be a Girl's Diary" reappeared
in its American edition as "Root, Stem, Leaf." That several others didn't
may be due to the fact that Hughes had already perfected their style in
poems that were to appear in *Crow*. Thus, much of *Recklings* appears like
the scrappy leftovers from stylistic experiments that were to bear fruit not
so much in *Wodwo* as in the 1970 collection.

Of course, several poems like the dramatic monologue "Last Lines," the
heavy-handedly satirical "Public Bar T.V." and "Tutorial," the Owen-like
"Unknown Soldier" or the magically evocative "Stealing Trout on a May
Morning" hark back to the familiar themes and stylistic modes of *Lupercal*
and *The Hawk in the Rain*. Others, like the historical fantasizings of "Poltergeist" and "Dully Gumption's Addendum" as well as the pseudo-
theological lecture "Fallen Eve" derive from the impulse that in 1961 produced "Dully Gumption's College Courses," including "Theology." Yet
much, even in the poems mentioned, is new. Hughes has shed his elaborate conceits, contorted intellectualism and argumentative rhetoric. What
has appeared instead is a dream logic of up-to-date mythic fantasies,
half-way between surrealism and allegory, replete with "folklore hieroglyphs and magical monsters" (67,P,204), and studded with symbols as
elemental as stones and water, weeping and laughter. Here for the first
time we find several of the devices characteristic of *Crow*: the repetitions
and parallelisms ("Water," "Trees"), anaphorical lists ("A Colonial") and
laconic refrains ("As Women's Weeping"), some of which may derive from
primitive poetry as well as from the neo-primitive folklore surrealism of
Vasko Popa. But the visions that claimed them as their own seem entirely
the poet's own. "Plum-Blossom" III points to their familiar source in the
apostasies of Crag Jack:

> Inside the head of a cat
> Under the bones, the brains, the blood-tissue,
> Bone of the bone and brain of the brain,
> Blood of the blood and tissue of the tissue,
> Is God's head, with eyes open. (R,21)

The poet's desire to see "more than [God's] eyes/In an animal's dreamed head" (L,55) has been fulfilled. But, as in "Hawk Roosting," the magical incantations used in its pursuit have conjured up more than God. All of nature has come to resemble a mythic stage animated by numinous forces loving and fighting each other, praying and dying. "Water is not lost, is snug, is at home—/Sometimes with its wife, stone." "The buds of the plum tree are scarred veterans/Full of last words." "The beech-bole is an angel of the earth . . ./Blind with God." The numinous has become more important than its embodiment, and we are never told who exactly in "On the Slope" is ready to die

> with the stone agony growing in her joints
> And eyes dimming with losses, widening for losses.
> (R,7,8,13,21)

The monsters of cosmic nightmare fantasy which people this mythic stage often derive from the leitmotif symbols of Hughes' earlier work. The "eye," access to the "world under the world" (L,55), has suddenly been transmogrified into "a masterful horseman" astride on the globe, surviving an apocalyptic "sky-collapse of lightning" behind the bone walls of a skull and watching a church tower crumble—

> While the ears ranged far off
> Where the laughter of great outer darkness threatened to close
>   its teeth on the skull
> And the mouth chewed lumps of sun that were melting the
>   brains. (R,18)

Similar horror visions fused with Dully Gumption's fantasies about maggot monster-like words biting "deep into the brains of the bumpkin English" (R,10) were to make their direct reappearance in *Crow:*

> Ravenous, the word tried its great lips
> On the earth's bulge, like a giant lamprey—
> There it started to suck.
>   ("A Disaster," C,21)

Next to such nightmare giants, God himself has turned into a secondary figure. He "yawns onto the black water," or, like the "Savior/Who is useful only in life," is made to remember his original function:

The Universe thickens to numbness, fumbled
By the huge lips of a phantom.

But already lambs totter out, and are apt.
And the Almighty's crept into snowdrops, where He'll be
    believed. (R,9,20,28)

The God of Logos and puritanical repression stands corrected by the nightmare of his own making. We have reached the beginning of the Crow story, whose opening scene, according to the account Hughes gave me in 1970,

> is set in heaven where God is having a repeated nightmare of a hand coming from deep space and trying to strangle him. The hand, in fact, throttles him, drags him through space, ploughs the earth with him and flings him back into heaven in a cold sweat. God cannot imagine what in his own created universe can have this power over him. And repeated attempts to make the nightmare show itself fail until God finally manages to make it speak. But its voice simply mocks God and his creation. In particular, it mocks his prime creation man as a monster and a failure. This man who has completely mismanaged his gifts and destroyed himself and the world. And God doesn't seem to be able to do anything at all about it. So he becomes more and more enraged and finally, through astute guidance by the nightmare, challenges the nightmare to prove what it is saying. In reply, the nightmare simply points to man in the gates of heaven. For it so happens that man has come up to heaven to hand his life back to God. The nightmare is jubilant and God mortified. So God challenges the nightmare to do better and this is exactly what the nightmare has been waiting for. It plunges down into matter and creates a new being. But things with this new creature go wrong because of all sorts of shortcomings and errors about the nightmare. But finally the nightmare produces Crow.

Much of this narrative derives from an earlier vision first recorded in "Logos." Characteristically, Hughes wrote this poem in Ireland during a period of spending part of every day fishing in the sea:

> But Space shudders in nightmare. Awakening
> Suddenly, she tastes the nightmare moving
> Still in her mouth
> And spits it kicking out, with a swinish cry—
>   that is God's first cry.
>
> .   .   .   .
>
>   God is a good fellow, but His mother's
>   against him. (R,39)[17]

5. *Wodwo*.

Just as *Recklings* looks forward to *Crow*, *Wodwo* (1967) charts the long initiatory ordeal that led to the 1970 volume. According to the author's widely discussed note,

> The stories and the play in this book may be read as notes, appendix and unversified episodes of the events behind the poems, or as chapters of a single adventure to which the poems are commentary and amplification. (W,9)

At least in chronological terms, it may be more appropriate to call the poems an appendix to the stories and the play. *The Wound* was written in 1961; "The Rain Horse," "Sunday," "Snow" and "The Harvesting" published or broadcast as early as 1960, the year of *Lupercal;* "The Suitor" appeared in May 1964, shortly after the last of his four early children's books. By contrast, the poems (with the single exception of "Theology") were all written after the death of Sylvia Plath, and under its impact seem to record the poet's descent into a Bardo of self-destruction. This, it seems to me, is the "single adventure" of *Wodwo*. And while prefigured in *The Wound*, it is central to the stories only as much as, say, "Meeting," a poem from *The Hawk in the Rain* about a man terrified by the "square-pupilled yellow-eyed look" (H,39) of a mountain goat, anticipates "Ghost Crabs" from *Wodwo*. In both poems man's ego is transformed by a sudden confrontation with the demonic. But in "Ghost Crabs" the transformation, as it takes place in realms of the supernatural and subconscious, is total. In "Meeting," as in the short stories collected in *Wodwo*, it is largely a matter of conscious experience and, however shattering, remains transitional.

Like the "square-pupilled yellow-eyed" goat's head in "Meeting," the transforming agent in "The Rain Horse," "The Harvesting" and "Sunday" is the mask-like or demon-eyed face of an animal. The young city gentleman, coming to revisit his native village, is attacked by a black horse resembling a "nightmarish leopard." As he jumps back he catches a "snapshot glimpse of the [animal's] red-veined eyeball." Finally the horse, after repeated attacks, "seemed to be actually inside his head" while its victim, after barely surviving his ordeal, feels "as if some important part had been cut out of his brain" (W,46,49,51,55). Similarly, Mr. Grooby, the protagonist of "The Harvesting," stops short of shooting a hare when he is struck numb by the sight of "the delicate lines" of his victim's "thin face." He finally collapses with a sunstroke listening to his own "unearthly thin scream" while an "enormous white dog's head opened beside him" (W,90,92). A perhaps semi-autobiographical and hence inverted version of the same theme is found in "Sunday." Accustomed to dreaming about "a wolf galloping through snow-filled, moonlit forest" in order to dispel his boredom in church, young Michael finds little to enjoy in his elders' after-Sunday-service entertainment of watching rats being bitten to death by old tramp Billy Red—the "rat hanging from his mouth . . . bunching and relaxing, bunching and relaxing." Yet, like the protagonists of "The Rain Horse" and "The Harvesting," he is spellbound by the animal's face. Its eyes, even in death, are "still round and bright in their alert, inquisitive expression,"—a nightmare close-up that seems to swamp his brain, until it gradually yields to a "dull, thick pain" (W,56,68,69).

As if to supplement these accounts of how the demonized forces of nature can suddenly play havoc with our sheltered self-protective egos, "Snow" and "Suitor" probe into the perversions of our solipsistic civilized consciousness. To be sure, their strategies are as diverse as two novels by Beckett and Robbe-Grillet. "Snow" reads like an absurdist caricature of Judaeo-Christian man. The protagonist, a victim of total amnesia, his hands and feet "black and shrunken on the bone," is walking through an Arctic no man's land of interminable snowstorms. While trying to reconstruct his identity from dreams, he still believes that the "facts are overwhelmingly on [his] side" and that "the chain of providential coincidences" ruling his life "is endless." Such self-delusion is not devoid of its endearing grandeur, but "Snow" is not a story about the heroic will to survive. The protagonist's desperate clinging to providence or "facts" finds a negative counterpart in his self-destructive flirtations with death. As his life and sanity depend on a chair, he often walks away from it just far enough to turn its recovery in the blinding blizzard into a chance game. The "huge futility" which such charades help dispel is as inane as the joy upon retrieving the chair, until a totally disembodied ego ends up repudiating its own melodramatic antics.

> I'm certainly not responsible for the weeping, shouting thing that falls on my chair, embracing it, kissing it, bruising his cheeks against it. (W,75-8,80)

Nouveau roman-like description with its schizophrenic self-detachment and anaesthetized geometric precision serves a particular purpose in "The Suitor." A "black column of patience," the first person narrator who watches a Peeping Tom being beaten up by the girl's chaperone, is a voyeur twice removed from his victim.

> I see the third figure rolling on the pavement, climbing to his feet, falling again, rising upright and falling again, as the tall man's arm administers over him. All this is twenty yards away, in the harsh cold wet shadows. In a few seconds, without a sound, it is over. The defeated one sits up and settles a trilby back on his head. At once I recognize the watcher from the lane-end. He slews and sits at the kerb, back bent low, as if he were spitting into the gutter. I find I have walked much closer. (W,97,98-9)

The emotions such violence has left unaffected, are suddenly unleashed by the powers of sublimation. Attracted by the softly popping flute sounds coming from the other voyeur, the suitor creeps close behind the back of his unwitting double and in "a kind of inane ecstasy" gropes with half-murderous intent for a stone in the pitch dark (W,103).

Published in 1964, "The Suitor" marks a step beyond the previous stories or "Meeting." The demonic forces of nature no longer threaten from without as in the nightmare leopard-like shape of a suddenly attacking horse. Instead, they have been interiorized, now forming a power charge of repression about to explode the deceptive façade of seeming self-control from inside. Man himself has turned into a demon, the suitor pulling a "contorting leopard-mask . . . as the flute-notes play over [his] brain":

> I writhe up my features again, stretching my mouth wide, making my eyes bulge, like a man laughing at tremendous volume or uttering a battle-cry, but in absolute and prolonged silence, while the flute notes dot and carry about the black garden and climb the wall and tap at the dark window and come circling back to the bowed attentive figure here, not three feet in front of me. (W,102-3)

With its images of cumulative destruction, trailing off in an anticlimactic gesture of futility, "Heptonstall," a poem about Sylvia Plath's burial place in North Yorkshire, reads like a motto to the remainder of *Wodwo*.

> Black village of gravestones.
> The hill's collapsed skull
> Whose dreams die back
> Where they were born.
>
> Skull of a sheep
> Whose meat melts
> Under its own rafters.
> Only the flies leave it.
>
> Skull of a bird,
> The great geographies
> Drained to sutures
> Of cracked windowsills.
>
> Life tries.
>
> Death tries.
>
> The stone tries.

Only the rain never tires. (W,165)

The lines stand in sombre contrast to those engraved on Sylvia Plath's tombstone:

> Even amidst fierce flames
> The golden lotus can be planted.

"Heptonstall" like most other poems in *Wodwo* only deals with the negative half of this promise. Images of "surrender to total Emptiness," "while zero/Itself loses consciousness" (W,39,158), vary with those of total nihilism, uttered in hasty rhythms of exhaustion ("They have melted like my childhood under earth's motherly curve/And are nowhere they are not here I know nothing," W,161) or a broken glissando of despair:

> I can understand the haggard eyes
> Of the old
>
> Dry wrecks
>
> Broken by seas of which they could drink nothing. (W,38)

The neo-metaphysical language of some earlier poems has turned into a surrealism of disintegrated conceits ("Wino," "The Green Wolf" or "New Moon in January"). A jeremiad-like prophet of doom eagerly points out the grim realities behind the fantasies of make-believe ("The Rescue"), embraces as his own the Indian belief in the ineluctable round of eternal suffering ("Karma"), or invokes a past of world wars and concentration camps whose victims "have gone down/To labour with God on the beaches" (W,161).

Dedicated to Hughes' parents, *Wodwo* abounds with memories from childhood when the boy was spellbound by his father's memories of war told "In the woe-dark under [his] mother's eye" (W,157). The parent whom Hughes had been unable to write about so far (P,102), suddenly emerges as an hieratic figure from the land of the dead:

> You dead bury your dead.
> Goodbye to the cenotaphs on my mother's breasts. (W,157)

In words even the grown-up poet dares not write down, she reveals to the young boy that the huge white angel lighting the fantasy valley of his childhood is to turn into a herald of some nameless horror:

> And through my mother's answer
> I saw all I had dreaded
> But with its meaning doubled.
> And the valley was dark.
> ("Ballad from a Fairy Tale," W,167)

Instead of celebrating their will to survive ("Thistles," "Fern"), the *Wodwo* poems more often than not extol plants and animals as the uncomplaining sufferers of creation ("Stations," "You Drive in a Circle"). But the true new champions of the unaccommodated universe are stone, water and wind. Whereas "Crow Hill" (1958) celebrated the defiant "arrogance of blood and bone" that has "thrown the hawk upon the wind,/And lit the fox in the dripping ground" (L, 14), "Pibroch" describes such survival as a desperate hanging on to life in utter dependence on the unpitying elements:

> Drinking the sea and eating the rock
> A tree struggles to make leaves—
> An old woman fallen from space
> Unprepared for these conditions.
> She hangs on, because her mind's gone completely. (W, 177)

There is prowess here just as in the fragile little harebell in which "sleeps, recovering,/The maker of the sea" ("Still Life," W, 18). But the primary emphasis is on the suffering shared by man, animals and plants alike. The crudest and at the same time most heartrending images of such unremitting agony on "Eternity's stone threshold" are found in "The Howling of Wolves" and "Song of a Rat," both written within weeks of Sylvia Plath's death. The wolves' eyes "never learn how it has come about/That they must live like this,/That they must live" while the rat attacks "heaven and earth with a mouthful of screeches" as "Iron jaws, strong as the whole earth/Are stealing its backbone" (W, 30, 162, 178).

Witness to all this despair is a poet who has himself suffered spiritual death. If *The Wound* is Hughes' Gothic-Celtic prose version of the *Bardo Thödol*, then "Stations," describing four stages after death, is its lyrical counterpart. What the 1966 poem is lacking, however, is the resurrection to life as described in the play or *The Tibetan Book of the Dead*. Its end only reinforces the beginning by rehearsing another death more absolute than the first.

> Whether you say it, think it, know it
> Or not, it happens, it happens, as
> Over rails over
> The neck the wheels leave
> The head with its vocabulary useless,
> Among the flogged plantains. (W, 39)

Images of a journey through the land of the dead abound in *Wodwo*, and "Cadenza," a poem written in the year after Sylvia's death, seems to portray an occasion for such fantasizing. A surrealist successor to Browning's "A Toccata of Galuppi's," it reveals the speaker's daydream imaginings while listening to a piece of music. In a "loaded estuary of the dead," the dreamer becomes the water bearing "the coffin that will not be silent." In this underworld we encounter a monster which recalls the mother's unrecorded prophecy in "Ballad From a Fairy Tale." The angel from the poet's childhood has been transformed into a giant "bat with a ghost in its mouth" (W,20).

The poet's guides through these nightmarish realms are animals like "The Bear" who "is the ferryman/To dead land." "Second Glance at a Jaguar" reveals the immediate ancestry for these shamanistic psychopomps. The caged Regent Park Zoo animal of the earlier poem is now "Hurrying through the underworld," "Muttering some mantrah, some drum-song of murder/To keep his rage brightening." Like other dream-animals such as the "Ghost Crabs," The Green Wolf" and "The Bear," these psychopomps are also destroyers, pressing "through our nothingness," making and unmaking, or joining

> Beginning to end
> With glue from people's bones
> In his sleep. (W,21,25-6,40-1)

According to "Theology" the myth of man's fall is "simply/Corruption of the facts," and the inhabitants of Hughes' underworld are anything but the sinners of Dante's Inferno. Rather, they are god's own followers, crucified on the "blinding pentagram of His power." "Wings" gives us a portrait gallery of these Logos worshippers whose Icarus-flight of reason has landed them in a hell of their own creation and made them vegetate under "the huge broken wing of shadow" which is both their own and the angel's whom they have disowned. Sartre, Kafka and Einstein have all incurred the sin of dissociating themselves from outer and inner nature. Sartre, with the "skull-splitting polyp of his brain," tries to regrow "the world inside his skull, like the spectre of a flower." Yet while his reason denies the supernatural ("Angels, it whispers, are metaphors, in man's image"), the world has turned into a graveyard of nightmare apparitions.

> With skull-grins, the earth's populations
> Drift off over graves, like the fumes of a rained-out campfire.

Like his god Logos, the modern rationalist is "a good fellow, but his mother's against him." She has reduced Kafka to the caricature of an "owl, 'Man' tatooed in his armpit," or answers Einstein's prayers with an image of Biblical doom.

> And he prays
>
> 'Mother! Mother!
>
> O mother

Send me love.'

But the flies

The flies rise in a cloud. (W,34,149,174-6)

Broken wings and descent, suffering and disintegration, animals transmogrified into demon psychopomps, angels turned ghost-devouring bats
presiding over a world of collective madness and mass destruction—these
and other nightmare hieroglyphs form the scenario to the "single adventure" of *Wodwo.* Yet the titular protagonist, whose soliloquy forms the
collection's epilogue, has somehow managed to survive it all. Reduced to
the bare essentials of his animal nature, the quester has turned into a "sort
of half-man half-animal spirit" which, reborn from spiritual death is "just
discovering that it is alive in the world" and stumbling around as if bedaz-
zled by its visions of past infernal horrors. Like *homo sapiens* at the dawn of
history, it tests and investigates its surroundings while reformulating
man's perennial questions about life with the ingénue precision of a radically pristine empiricism. As such, Wodwo is one more among the poet's
alter ego projections which like Crag Jack or Ripley mark major stages in
Hughes' development. The persona's language, like that of other pieces in
the same volume, recalls Hughes' earlier advocacy of a new "free poem of
sorts where grammar, sentence structure etc, are all sacrificed in an attempt to break fresh and accurate perceptions and words out of the reality
of the subject chosen" (P,23,62). But the broken accents of despair have
been retuned by a new curiosity for life which, however tentative, is
keenly alert to the slightest modulations of inner and outer experience.

> But what shall I be called am I the first
> have I an owner what shape am I what
> shape am I am I huge if I go
> to the end on this way past these trees and past these trees
> till I get tired that's touching one wall of me
> for the moment if I sit still how everything
> stops to watch me I suppose I am the exact centre
> but there's all this what is it roots
> roots roots roots and here's the water
> again very queer but I'll go on looking (W,183)

Wodwo's is a language of self-erasure which, emulating Nature's own
cycles of creation and destruction, persistently obliterates its own traces.
It comes close to the absolute naturalness which an earlier piece evokes as
the poet's ideal of a language transcending words and suggesting meanings
beyond understanding, as "the incomprehensible cry/From the boughs, in
the wind/Sets us listening for below words,/Meanings that will not part

from the rock." Characteristically, it is the poet's animal guides out of the underworld which provide him with the model for this language. The gnats, "Writing on the air, rubbing out everything they write" (W,29,179), perform the "double movement of creation and erasure" (Alain Robbe-Grillet)[18] which is adequate for that moment when, as Hughes puts it, "the iron nails remain fixed in the wounds, with an eternal iron fixity, and neither hands nor feet can move" (76,P,10). They sing

> That they are the nails
> In the dancing hands and feet of the gnat-god. (W,180)

Or the skylarks, whose song draws the quester into celestial spheres, consume themselves in an ecstasy of self-annihilation, "Battering and battering their last sparks out at the limit—"

> Like those flailing flames
> That lift from the fling of a bonfire
> Claws dangling full of what they feed on. (W,170)

The poem's onomatopoeic feats tend to obscure its deeper meaning which Hughes finally reinforced by adding two further sections to "Skylarks" in his *Selected Poems* (1972). Here, the lark who has reached the highest point in its heaven-scaling flight is compared with a mouse drowning in a well—"Lamenting, mounting a little." By now, the new symbol of affirmation—

> A towered bird, shot through the crested head
> With the command, Not die
>
> But climb
>
> Climb
>
> Sing (W,168-9)—

has turned into a cypher of pseudo-heroic pathos associated with Cuchulain's vain attempt to resist death by supernatural strength. For by the time "Skylarks" was remodelled, the poem's original, tentative message of hope had once more been stifled by the tragic events in the poet's life.

> Manacled with blood,
> Cuchulain listened bowed,
> Strapped to his pillar (not to die prone)
> Hearing the far crow
> Guiding the near lark nearer
> With its blind song

"That some sorry little wight more feeble and misguided than thyself
Take thy head
Thine ear
And thy life's career from thee." (SP,100)

Even the crow which in the years and months before 1969 had evolved into another mythograph of hope, again sings a "blind song" of death. But none of these additions were included in later editions of *Wodwo* which itself ends on a double note of survival and hope. Preceding the title poem which also closes the volume, "Full Moon and Little Frieda" reinforces the mood of pristine wonder and curiosity which the poet makes us experience through the eyes of Wodwo and his little daughter:

'Moon!' you cry suddenly, 'Moon! Moon!'
The moon has stepped back like an artist gazing amazed at a work
That points at him amazed. (W,182)

V.

Crow

The story of the mind exiled from Nature is the story of Western Man. It is the story of his progressively more desperate search for mechanical and rational and symbolic securities, which will substitute for the spirit-confidence of the Nature he has lost. The basic myth for the ideal Westerner's life is the Quest. The quest for a marriage in the soul or a physical re-conquest. The lost life must be captured somehow. It is the story of spiritual romanticism and heroic technological progress. It is a story of decline. When something abandons Nature, or is abandoned by Nature, it has lost touch with its creator, and is called an evolutionary dead-end. According to this, our Civilisation is an evolutionary error. (70,N,81)

The Existential Choice, taken to its absolute limit of wholeheartedness, becomes inevitably a religion—because man is deeper and more complicated than merely rational controls can keep hold of. Then his beliefs, disciplines, and prohibitions have to be cultivated against the odds as in a world of poisons one chooses—sensibly after all—food that nourishes. (65,S,10)

V. CROW

In his introduction to a catalogue of engravings by Leonard Baskin, published in 1962, Hughes focused on the image of a dead crow which appeared to him as the "immortal Angel of Life [in] the aspect of the Angel of Death" (62,Ba). In 1964 Hughes wrote *Eat Crow* and reviewed Eliade's *Shamanism*, a book which allowed him to locate his ongoing mythic dream in relation to both primitive mentality and its civilized manifestations in "the poetic temperament we call 'romantic'." Shamanistic rituals, Hughes concluded, must be "something closer to biological inevitability than to any merely cultural tradition" (64,E,677). And what better proof could there be of this than the Rosicrucian fantasies he was then struggling to record in his verse play *Difficulties of a Bridegroom*. Yet little as he succeeded in the dramatic medium, his studies of primitive poetry finally helped him find the strategies to embody his private myth in poetry. Thus, Baskin's suggestion that Hughes should write some poems to illustrate his crow engravings was enough to unleash a flood of totally unprecedented poems much like the spontaneous outpourings of song in which the shaman, when about to be cured, articulates his visions. As Hughes remembered early in 1970,

the story behind *Crow* brought me to the point where the poems arrived

97

naturally, precipitated themselves naturally. In a way the whole adventure was a machinery I designed gradually to produce the poems until it
produced them of its own accord. . . . There was no planning in the
poems themselves. Most of them were revealing to me as I wrote them
and they usually wrote themselves quite rapidly. With several of them
that now seem ordinary enough I had the sensation of having done something taboo and very horrible after I'd written them down.

As an example that created such a moment of complete shock, Hughes
quoted the final lines of "Criminal Ballad," which along with those of
"Crow's Account of St. George" seem to mirror one of Hughes' nightmare
obsessions:

> And he could not turn towards the house
> Because the woman of complete pain rolling in flame
> Was calling to him all the time
> From the empty goldfish pond
> And when he began to shout to defend his hearing
> And shake his vision to splinters
> His hands covered with blood suddenly
> And now he ran from the children and ran through the house
> Holding his bloody hands clear of everything
> And ran along the road and into the wood
> And under the leaves he sat weeping
>
> And under the leaves he sat weeping
>
> Till he began to laugh. (C,27-8)

1. Pseudo-Biblical and Mythical Poems.

At first sight the mythological allusiveness of *Crow* seems to belie
Hughes' claim that there was no planning in the poems themselves. Not
only does the protagonist, in a variety of apocryphal narratives, share the
stage with the Biblical Creator, the Serpent or Adam and Eve. He also
encounters Proteus, Ulysses, Hercules and Beowulf, poses as Oedipus or
parodies the latter's fortunes in "Song for a Phallus." The sequence, in
short, recalls Joyce's *Ulysses* which, in Eliot's well-known phrase, manipulates "a continuous parallel between contemporaneity and antiquity" with
the effect "of controlling, of ordering, of giving a shape and a significance
to the immense panorama of futility and anarchy which is contemporary
history."[1]

Yet a closer look at *Crow* shows that the poet's use of traditional mythology contravenes Eliot's comment in every single point. Instead of developing a parallel between present and past, the poem evokes a supratemporal world of global religious dimensions in which Western myths figure side by side with the Tibetan Buddhist Womb Door or an Eskimo Genesis. And far from giving order to the chaos of modern life, classical and Biblical myths for the most part appear as the very roots of this chaos.

Naturally for a sequence about Crow "created by God's nightmare's attempt to improve on man" (71,F,18), the poems with pseudo-Biblical content follow the pioneer example of "Theology" (1961) by inverting the orthodox Christian doctrine. "In the beginning was Scream" instead of the Word ("Lineage," C,2). The Serpent, originator of sin and death, is changed back into a phallic symbol of life ("A Childish Prank"). Resting on the seventh day, it appears as the true lord of creation which is disrupted by God, an interloper who instead of the apple uses cider to cause the fall of man in a bout of drunken debauchery ("Apple Tragedy"). Causing a similar disruption, God tries to teach Crow the meaning of "love" but "Crow's First Lesson" is at every turn refuted by the "horror of Creation" (C,9). God, as usual, "exhausted with Creation" and convulsed in nightmare, cannot answer Crow's questions, leaving the protagonist in a stupor of defiant silence—

> humped, impenetrable.
> Half-illumined. Speechless.
> ("Crow Communes," C,18)

Eventually, the quester realizes that beyond the traditional God—"the man-created, broken down, corrupt despot of a ramshackle religion" who "accompanies Crow through the world in many guises, mis-teaching, deluding, tempting, opposing and at every point trying to discourage or destroy him"[2]—there must be another God,

> bigger than the other
> Loving his enemies
> And having all the weapons.
> ("Crow's Theology," C,24)

His subsequent quest "aims to locate and release" this true creator who has become "God's nameless hidden prisoner." Crow encounters him "repeatedly but always in some unrecognisable form."[3] For Crow himself is imprisoned in an ego which declares his every act a crime ("Crow's Nerve Fails") and darkens his vision with its civilized concerns ("Crow's Vanity"). Hence he can perceive little more than the destructive aspect of this other God: in the "King of Carrion" with his palace of skulls, in the Sun which he challenges in mock heroic combat ("Crow's Fall") or in another bird whose song resounds like an oracle of Juggernaut destructiveness:

I am the maker
Of the world

That rolls to crush
And silence my knowledge.
                ("Robin Song," C,41)

Even the mythic female whom Crow at first fails ("Crow Tries the Media") but subsequently half manages to sing about, is mainly revealed in her negative elementary character ("Crow's Undersong").

However limited these insights, they give the tricksterish bird sufficient self-confidence to contravene God at every turn in "over-correct[ing]" his faulty creation.[4] Even God's ever more gruelling retaliation in trying to crush Crow, tear him to pieces or bury him, effects little more than to strengthen the protagonist in his arrogant attitude while bringing despair to the torturer ("Crow's Song of Himself"). When the Serpent, in the guise of a nuclear bomb-like ecological monstrosity, threatens to take over God's creation, Crow "Beat the hell out of it, and ate it" ("A Horrible Religious Error," C,34). Or when God's creation finally falls apart, "Crow nailed . . . heaven and earth together," causing a "horror beyond redemption . . . Crying: 'This is my Creation,'/Flying the black flag of himself" ("Crow Blacker Than Ever," C,57).

A truer counter-image to God's creation than Crow's tricksterish over-corrective is implied in "Snake Hymn," the last of the pseudo-Biblical fables. Both in content and tone the poem harks back to "Theology." Quietly yet unerringly it dismantles the Christian doctrines of the fall, the crucifixion and God's infinite love until nothing remains but a few basic facts about sex, birth, life and death:

Nothing else has happened.
The love that cannot die
Sheds the million faces
And skin of agony.

To hang, an empty husk.
Still no suffering
Darkens the garden
Or the snake's song. (C,75)

Like these pseudo-Biblical fables to which "Snake Hymn" is the appropriate summing up, the poems involving classical myths usually follow a highly dramatic "dialectics of mockery and apotheosis" reminiscent of Jerzy Grotowski's similar efforts in the theatre.[5] Unlike his Greek namesake, "Oedipus Crow" chooses to flee rather than search out his destiny and is mutilated by circumstances rather than by his own hand. The untragic protagonist remains unredeemed. "One-legged, gutless and brainless, the rag of himself—," he is tripped up by Death, who holds him up with a laugh, Crow dangling "from his one claw—corrected" for some unknown crime, a Kafkaesque "warning" to others whose mere existence is their hereditary sin (C,32). Instead of climaxing in the tragic deed of horror, his agonies follow a shamanistic pattern of repeated dismemberment, which for all its gruesomeness is "full of buffoonery, mimicry . . . and magical contortions" (64,E,677). The line about Crow who after losing a leg is "cheered by the sound of his foot and its echo," would suit a satyr play rather than the more rarified mood of classical tragedy.

Hughes' reversal of the same myth in "Song for a Phallus," originally to be part of his adaptation of Seneca's *Oedipus*, maintains this savage black humor throughout. Instead of curing the plague-ridden Thebes by answering the Sphinx's riddle, Hughes' Oedipus searches for the solution by splitting the monster from top to toe, but only releases a host of further monsters. The riddle's final answer is rendered in one of Hughes' recurrent nightmare hieroglyphs: a deliberate or unconscious destruction of the female revealing the guilt-laden interrelatedness of nature. Man in "Revenge Fable" kills his mother with the result that "His head fell off like a leaf" (C,58). Crow, repeating man's technological abuse of Mother Nature, finally

> Crashed on the moon awoke and crawled out
>
> Under his mother's buttocks.
>   ("Crow and Mama," C,5)

Similarly, Oedipus hatchets his mammy, who had emerged from the gory intestines of the Sphinx, only to find

> himself curled up inside
> As if he had never been bore
>   ("Song for a Phallus," C,65)

A similar inversion of the Proteus myth results in another parable about man's destructive search for knowledge ("Truth Kills Everybody"), while Crow's pursuit of Ulysses and Hercules turns the ancient heroes into victims to be assimilated by the protagonist's deadpan imperturbable "Crowego." Ovid's principle of metamorphosis, which some of these poems use as their structural pattern, serves to show that destiny is both elusive and ineluctable. In pursuit of Ulysses, Crow only manages to catch a worm; grappling with Hercules' two puff-adders, he strangles in error Dejanira ("Crowego"); trying to grasp Proteus, Crow finds that he has caught Achilles who in turn assumes multiple other shapes from a 2000 volts naked powerline to Christ's hot pounding heart. Yet unlike the secrets which the classical Proteus finally yields to his questioner, the truth totally eludes and even kills Crow ("Truth Kills Everybody").

2. The Influence of Primitive Poetry.

Although *Crow*, like *The Waste Land*, is bound to send critics on a wild goose chase after crows and the Holy Grail, the author's intention was "to produce something with the minimum cultural accretions of the museum sort . . . as it might be invented after the holocaust and demolition of all libraries."[6] Naturally this pursuit found its prime model in primitive song which Hughes, in his 1962 review of C.M. Bowra's study on the subject, discovered to be full of the qualities of "ideal poetry"—"full of zest, clairvoyantly sensitive, realistic, whole, natural, and passionate." More specifically, he noted a tendency toward parallelism and couplets, the "artful use of repetition and variation, and possibly rhyme" (62,B,781). An example like the following may well have helped inspire the basic structure of "A Disaster," "Truth Kills Everybody" and several other Crow poems.

> The great Koonak mountain in the south yonder,
> I see it.
> The great Koonak mountain in the south yonder,
> I behold it,
> The gleaming light in the south yonder,
> I look at it.
> Beyond the Koonak it stretches,
> The same light that wraps
> Koonak towards the sea.
> See how in the south the clouds
> Swell and change;
> See how in the south
> They make one another beautiful.[7]

Another of Bowra's examples is characteristic of a more advanced stage of primitive poetry, where, again as in several Crow poems, "repetitions are fewer and the variations more adventurous":

> Ostrich, rising and flying,
> Long-necked and big-toed,
> Belly full of rock-flint, great bird,
> Wide-mouthed male ostrich,
> Flying, running, great bird,
> Give me one of your grey feathers.

.   .   .   .
Male ostrich, looking up,
Belly that says *khari, khari,*
Ostrich, whose bowels alone are not fit to eat,
Give me one of your leg-bones, ostrich!

He who has two bones, which say *hui-hui,*
Male ostrich, who has wonderful marrow,
Who with his face says *gou-gou,*
Might I possess you, my ostrich![8]

The poem's structure vividly recalls Hughes' "Littleblood" although its content for understandable reasons does not. For ostriches and bears may have their rightful place in the neo-primitive poetry of a Snyder or Rothenberg. In the work of an English poet, who instead may invoke "the last wolf killed in Britain" (L,13), they would look out of context. No wonder that native European rather than non-Western primitive poetry came to exert the major influence on *Crow*. Hughes was fortunate to hit upon one of its rare treasures, a six volume anthology of *Carmina Gadelica* in which one can find examples of all the primitive poetic strategies analysed by Bowra. As he told me in August 1977,

> Alexander Carmichael's collection contains a lot of old Gaelic spells, chants, healing songs, invocations and so on. It's a long time since I saw it but that really is the source of it as much as anything. Some of these poems were really extraordinary and at the same time gave me a feeling that this was a source I could really lay claim to. Whereas with ordinary primitive literature you always feel like being a bit of a tourist if you use it. There is obviously a lot of ways in which you *can* use it but you can't suddenly seize that as a style.

Again recalling "Littleblood," the following poem, entitled "Little Bird," strikingly confirms what is said here:

Little Bird! O Little Bird!
  I wonder at what thou doest,
Thou singing merry far from me,
  I in sadness all alone!

Little Bird! O Little Bird!
  I wonder at how thou art,
Thou high on the tips of branching boughs,
  I on the ground a-creeping!

Little Bird! O Little Bird!
  Thou art music far away,

> Like the tender croon of the mother loved
> In the kindly sleep of death.[9]

Hughes' comparison between literary and folklore surrealism, drawn in his 1967 essay on Vasko Popa, indirectly describes the poet's own development under the influence of primitive poetry. Thus, several of the *Wodwo* poems seem to "hide behind perverse imagery" as if they had "abandoned the struggle with circumstances and consequently lost the unifying focus that comes of that"; they appear to have lost "morale and surrendered to the arbitrary imagery of the dream flow." All such surrealist vagaries disappeared from *Crow* whose "folktale surrealism"

> is always urgently connected with the business of trying to manage practical difficulties so great that they have forced the sufferer temporarily out of the dimension of coherent reality into that depth of imagination where understanding has its roots and stores its X-rays. There is no sense of surrender to the dream flow for its own sake or of relaxation from the outer battle. In the world of metamorphoses and flights the problems are dismantled and solved, and the solution is always a practical one. This type of surrealism, if it can be called surrealism at all, goes naturally with a down-to-earth, alert tone of free enquiry. (67,P,204-5)

These more recent stylistic influences reinforced two earlier ones which the poet, as late as 1970, described as the most forceful in his entire career (71,F,12,14). In Hughes' view, the techniques of parallelism, repetition and variation etc., which Bowra had located in primitive song, left a powerful legacy in Hebrew poetry and Shakespeare. It was this multiple heritage compounded of Biblical, Shakespearean, modernist and primitive elements rather than any single source which Hughes managed to reclaim in the little fables, visionary anecdotes, apocryphal lectures and totem songs of *Crow*.

3. The Story of Crow.

Hardly born from his "egg of blackness," "Trembling featherless elbows in the nest's filth" (C,1,2), Crow is subjected to a first encounter with Death in "Examination at the Womb-Door" and made to experience the basic cruelty of existence as victim ("A Kill") and destroyer ("Crow and Mama") even before he struts forth into the actual world through a black doorway described as the eye's pupil in the world's earthen wall ("The Door"). Here, his childish pranks with God or the latter's inane babblings about love are quickly muted by the horrors of nuclear devastation ("Crow Alights," "That Moment"). Where God's teachings leave Crow with nothing but a sense of guilt, his own search for instruction only results in forlorn helplessness ("Crow Hears Fate Knock on the Door"). In no time Crow has moved from childlike laughter to guilt-ridden despondency. And though he is quick to choose self-preservation as a way out of this moral dilemma, Crow eats his grub weeping ("Crow Tyrannosaurus") or experiences how his inner "prophecy" of a will to power is "Slowly rending [his] vital fibres" ("Crow Hears Fate Knock on the Door," C,11).

Crow's explorations of the world often proceed in a backward journey through history. Thus the nightmare visions of nuclear destruction are followed by "Crow's Account of [a] Battle" in traditional strategic warfare. The protagonist's growing sense of evil, destruction and guilt crystallizes in "The Black Beast," which Crow tries to track down with the ferocity of Ahab chasing the White Whale. Life in the world has already corrupted him to the point where he repeats most of man's errors, so that this hunt gradually assumes the proportions of man's recent ecological devastation of Mother Nature.

> Crow roasted the earth to a clinker, he charged into space—
> Where is the Black Beast? (C,16)

Crow is unaware that the Black Beast may after all be found in his own being.

In terms of its title, *From the Life and Songs of the Crow*, the sequence's opening poems up to "The Black Beast" primarily deal with Crow's life. "A Grin," an enigmatic folktale allegory whose meaning seems to transcend the quester's limited insights at this point, could be seen as the first of his actual songs. As against the unremitting "horror of Creation," the "cortege/Of mourning and lament," "sorrow on sorrow" (C,9,12) which we have witnessed so far, it allows the first glimmer of real hope to emerge from visions of further passion, agony and destruction. Thanatos' derisive grin fails to find a "permanent home" or "tenure/In eternal death" however hard he tries for it in the grimaces of a murderer, a woman in labor, a firing machine-gunner or lovers at the moment of death-like self-annihilation. For "none of it lasted." Even the "face/In the electric chair" finally relaxed. After Crow's schoolboy-like triumph over death in "Examination at the Womb-Door," the poem reaffirms the refusal of death's dominion in oblique yet at the same time more realistic terms.

> The grin
> Sank back, temporarily nonplussed
> Into the skull. (C,17)

Crow, in his idiosyncratic interpretation of St. George, proceeds to unmask England's patron saint as the key figure in the "neurotic-making dynamics of Christianity." As shown earlier, his account is a direct comment on why the legend of St. George, "the symbolic story of creating a neurosis," should, in Hughes' view, be a forbidden story for children

(70,M,65-6). For like Crow himself, St. George is a creature who in his craze for order, "truth" and dominion over nature, has denied the Black Beast in himself. And it is doubly ironic that one of the shapes of this Beast which, in inversion of the original legend, outwits St. George, making him murder his family instead of a monster, is that of a bird like Crow:

> A bird-head,
> Bald, lizard-eyed, the size of a football, on two staggering
>   bird-legs. (C,19)

Crow's growing experience teaches him how the world has been devastated and atrophied by the Word as by a magical monster:

> The word oozed its way, all mouth,
> Earless, eyeless.
>   . . . sucking the cities
> Like the nipples of a sow.
>   ("A Disaster," C,21; cf. "The Battle of Osfrontalis")

Yet the Word's ultimate impotence leads Crow to surmise a creator beyond Logos ("Crow's Theology"). His subsequent "fall" from the heights of all these half-assimilated insights is one of tricksterish hubris. But always quick to have recourse to his basic strengths, Crow, charred black by his attack on the sun, "spraddled head-down in the beach-garbage, guzzling a dropped ice-cream" while most birds escape from everyday reality into more rarified realms ("Crow and the Birds," C,26).

While following an implied surrealistic folktale narrative of sorts, the sequence accumulates much of its deeper meaning from an ever more densely woven texture of interrelating themes such as the basic cruelty of life, man's ineluctable guilt and the closeness between ecstasy and agony. "Criminal Ballad" picks up several of these strands. Man, the unconscious "Abattoir/Of innocents" from "Crow Tyrannosaurus" (C,12), is given a semi-biographical portrait. At every point, from birth to adulthood, his life is the death of somebody else, until suddenly, in an image recalling *Macbeth*, his hands are covered with blood, perhaps after he has unwittingly murdered his wife and children. Like Crow he starts crying, but the despair has reached a hysterical pitch where tears turn into laughter.[10] In a later poem, the same laughter in despite of life's agonies, has, like "A Grin" and "The Smile," grown into another phantom allegory in the surrealistic fantasy world of *Crow*—

> laughter scampers around on centipede boots
> Still runs all over on caterpillar tread
> And rolls back onto the mattress, legs in the air
>   ("In Laughter," C,37)

"Crow on the Beach" resumes the story of the protagonist. He has become more and more alienated from a world which turns a cold shoulder on all his crowomorphic needs and desires. But at least Crow has learnt that hearing "the sea's ogreish outcry and convulsion"

> he was the wrong listener unwanted
> To understand or help—(C,29)

Not so "The Contender" in whose self-inflicted suffering a Grin seems to have found the "permanent home" it couldn't find elsewhere.

> He lay crucified with all his strength
> On the earth
> Grinning towards the sun
>
> .   .   .   .
>
> Grinning through his atoms and decay
> Grinning into the black.

In his sacrifice for mankind the hero not only performs a "senseless trial of strength" but finds the whole of humanity and nature ranged against himself. Man's misery, which Christ's and Prometheus' suffering helped relieve, merely increases the Contender's agony:

> their tears salted his nail-holes
> Only adding their embitterment
> To his effort. (C,31,32)

In the following poem, progress and technology, as championed by the original Prometheus, have become mere chimeric projections of "Crow's Vanity"—

> Mistings of civilisations   towers   gardens
>
> .   .   .   .
>
> Mistings of skyscrapers   webs of cities—

the protagonist looking for "a glimpse of the usual grinning face" in "the evil mirror" and breathing heavily with excitement (C,33). Yet Crow continues indefatigably, playing further pranks with God's creation or trying out the media in order to sing about a nameless "her" and finding the entire world united in wanting to smother his attempt. No wonder that for a moment "Crow's Nerve Fails." Guilt-ridden since his "First Lesson" in which God tries to make him pronounce the word "love," Crow has learned that, like man who is "a walking/Abattoir/Of innocents" (C,12), he is a creature whose "every feather [is] the fossil of a murder" (C,36). And pondering this universal guilt he gains the conviction that there is neither atonement nor heaven.

The world's only response to its disasters are noises which reverberate like cosmic roars of laughter. Bemused, "Crow Frowns," wondering about the signatures of his own strength. Rather than in a Promethean striving for human progress or the Christian expectation of a better hereafter gained through grace or right moral conduct, he finds the answer in a koan-like paradox:

> We are here, we are here.
> He is the long waiting for something
> To use him for some everything
> Having so carefully made him
>
> Of nothing. (C,39)

In Crow's world every thought, no less than every act, leads to unmitigated disaster. Even the attempt to escape this vicious circle in a thought of quietude only results in further action reducing the protagonist to the inertia of self-destructive pusillanimity ("Magical Dangers").

Crow's own songs, or those he listens to, often read like cryptic answers to the protagonist's bewilderments. "Robin Song" seems to tell him that as creator and destroyer in one, the true God is the very image of life's natural cruelty. Along with "Owl's Song," "Dawn's Rose," "Notes for a Little Play," "King of Carrion," "Two Eskimo Songs" and "Littleblood," the poem is one of a series of lyrical masterpieces that focus the collection's multiple shades of meaning. As hunted victim, helpless sufferer and maker

> Of the world
> *That rolls to crush*
> *And silence* [its] *knowledge,* (C,41)

the Robin, like its creator, embodies the various facets of life in a mythograph that may be disturbing to Christians but could elicit little more than an approving nod from readers nurtured, say, on the *Bhagavad Gita* or much of primitive literature. The parallel concept of a creation emanating from a final "emptiness of inexhaustible contents" or *śūnyatā*,[11] of which "Conjuring in Heaven" gives a semi-burlesque account, causes similar consternation to Crow, although an earlier poem already spoke of how the creator had "so carefully made him/Of nothing" (C,39).

But Crow is slow to learn and often makes errors which he had earlier managed to avoid. After calmly surveying the devastations caused by words ("A Disaster") and even warding off their attempt to encroach upon his life ("The Battle of Osfrontalis"), he finally cannot resist the temptation of trying out words himself. Yet all they teach him, in a sequence of metamorphoses following the pattern of several other poems, is the ultimate elusiveness of phenomena. Crow undergoes an experience which Hughes describes as his own in *Poetry in the Making*:

> It is when we set out to find words for some seemingly quite simple
> experience that we begin to realize what a huge gap there is between our
> understanding of what happens around us and inside us, and the words
> we have at our command to say something about it. (P,119)

The hare Crow chases with a "lovely pack" of words permanently eludes
him by assuming ever new shapes even though the hunter changes his
words according to these various metamorphoses. Finally, the hare reappears leaping for the hill,

> Having eaten Crow's words.
>
> Crow gazed after the bounding hare
> Speechless with admiration.
> ("Crow Goes Hunting," C,43)

An appropriate afterword to Crow's unsuccessful experiments with
words, "Owl's Song" celebrates an art which like Hughes' own will
neither flinch from the unredeemable suffering of man nor be muted by
the ultimate silence.

> He sang
> How everything had nothing more to lose
>
> Then sat still with fear
>
> Seeing the clawtrack of star
> Hearing the wingbeat of rock
>
> And his own singing. (C,44)

And again Crow seems to learn. For his "Undersong" is an example of just
such poetry which makes "audible meanings without disturbing the silence, an art of homing in tentatively on vital scarcely perceptible signals,
making no mistakes, but with no hope for finality, continuing to explore"
(67,P,202).

"Crow's Undersong" offers an important landmark in Hughes' general
development. For here the White Goddess lost since the nineteen year old
poet's address to the Lady of "Song" (H,19) and buried under "all that
stone" of the dark churches which already "Stooped over [his] cradle"
("Crag Jack's Apostasy," L,55) makes her first reappearance in his work.
In 1970, shortly before publishing "Crow's Undersong," Hughes described the historical development of which his own is both a result and
foreshortened mirror image: "Christianity deposes Mother Nature and
begets, on her prostrate body, Science, which proceeds to destroy Nature." But since the early sixties this process has been reversed. "Nature as

the Great Goddess of mankind, and the Mother of all life" has reemerged as a dominant force in our culture (70,N,82-3). Unlike this programmatic statement, the poem explores the possibilities of this rebirth rather than stating it as a fact. Its very opening line is a negation:

> She cannot come all the way.

But from then on, the voice which went dumb after dictating "Song" not only seems to recover speech but to deliver its message of hope in direct contrast to the earlier poem. There the lady turned away from the poet; though destined to survive, she was not to come home. Now she is coming back. The precious despair of "Song" has yielded to a vitalism of hope, an elaborate, almost Petrarchan refinement replaced by "a super-simple and super-ugly language" which "shed[s] everything except what [it] wanted to say" (71,F,20):

> She has come amorous it is all she has come for
>
> If there had been no hope she would not have come
>
> And there would have been no crying in the city
>
> (There would have been no city) (C,45)

The life, of which the female in "Crow's Undersong" is the guarantor, also means suffering, an insight further developed in "Crow's Elephant Totem Song." The hyenas devour the graceful little elephant for giving them illusions about a "Land of Peaceful." In Crow's universe there is no such paradisaic beyond, and even though the elephant after his resurrection keeps on singing "About a star of deathless and painless peace/. . . no astronomer can find where it is." What the reader finds instead, is that the resurrected elephant with his

> Deadfall feet and toothproof body and bulldozing bones
> And completely altered brains
> Behind aged eyes, that were wicked and wise

has come surprisingly close to his murderers whose behavior has remained consistent even in afterlife. Their song, proclaiming that their life—

> In hourly battle with a death
> The size of the earth
> Having the strength of the earth—

is the only "Land of Peaceful" there is, is the poem's central message (C,46,47).

Along with "Crow's Undersong" and "Crow's Elephant Totem Song,"

"Dawn's Rose" seems to stem from the sequence's earlier conception in *Eat Crow*.[12] While the two songs expand upon the figure of Morgan's female guide and the choral dialogue of Morgan's bones "all chattering together," "Dawn's Rose" reads like a versified version of the earlier work's conclusion. Here again we encounter the crow which as "a sign of life," "has come up from the maker of the world" before dawn, sitting "in the early gray light," watching a "gray desert of tumbled stone[s] . . . in their usual trance, rapt to the circles of galactic dust" and singing "the song of silence," its mind "resigned to the superior stamina of the empty horizon" (EC,18-21).

"Dawn's Rose" is the collection's only poem about a crow rather than about Crow himself who reappears in "Crow's Playmates." Once more repeating a mistake which man has made before him, the protagonist, in an effort to escape loneliness, invents all kinds of gods. But such wishful imaginings backfire, disassociating Crow from direct contact with the elements and making him realize, after yet another vaudeville-like learning process, that existence essentially means loneliness.

In "Crowego" the protagonist, gazing "Like a leopard into a fat land," after he has devoured Ulysses, strangled Dejanira and drunk Beowulf's blood, seems to have turned into one of his totem animals. Like Hughes himself who considers the "comparative religion/mythology background" to be irrelevant to *Crow*,[13] its protagonist is indifferent to the heroes of our past.

> His wings are the stiff back of his only book,
> Himself the only page—of solid ink. (C,50)

Replacing the mythic figures of this erudite tradition are semi-allegorical phantasmata like "A Grin," "Laughter" or "The Smile." The last in this series of poems, which in regular intervals map the wider cosmic background to Crow's adventures, "The Smile" prepares us for the conclusion of the entire sequence. The poem, like this conclusion, is far from a happy one. It is more like the end of Shakespeare's Gloucester whose heart

> 'Twixt two extremes of passion, joy and grief,
> Burst smilingly.
> (*King Lear*, V, iii, 200-1)

"The Smile" reads as if Hughes had set out to translate these lines into cosmic terms. Searching unsuccessfully for a home in people's faces which elude it with their own deceitful smiles, the Smile, unlike its parallel allegory, the Grin, finally manages to find a tenure in death. Touching a dying man's lips, it succeeds in

> altering his eyes
> And for a moment
> Mending everything
>
> Before it swept out and away across the earth. (C,52)

As if to forestall the poem's misinterpretation in terms of our traditional tragic humanism, we are made to see a more ominous smile in the following poem. A person who in various ways tries to take destiny into his own hands is frustrated at every turn and finally, in a process of piecemeal destruction, reduced to his own ashes—

> And so the smile not even Leonardo
> Could have fathomed
> Flew off into the air, the rubbish heap of laughter
> Screams, discretions, indiscretions etcetera
>   ("Crow Improvises," C,53)

Even the smile of relaxation in death only lasts for a moment before life and suffering continue. And while Crow is alive, he is prepared to answer the guffaws of fate with his own defiant laughter to the point of emulating the cosmic phantasmata in their very antics. Just as Laughter "scampers around on centipede boots/. . . And rolls back onto the mattress, legs in the air" (C,37), Crow

> rolls on the ground helpless,
>
> And he sees his remote feet and he chokes he
> Holds his aching sides— (C,55)

"Crow's Battle Fury" or defiant laughter in the face of life's agonies suddenly turns into a shamanistic ritual of self-disintegration and renewal. This shattering of the self in laughter and the subsequent "labour of fitting it together again" (66,P,81) is described in imagery Hughes shares with Plath:

> (With his glared off face glued back into position
> A dead man's eyes plugged back into his sockets
> A dead man's heart screwed in under his ribs
> His tattered guts stitched back into position
> His shattered brains covered with a steel cowl)
>
> He comes forward a step,
>   and a step,
>   and a step— (C,56)

Donning a grin in the attempt to counter God's sham world of love with a counter-creation of agony, "Crow Blacker Than Ever" again overcorrects things in trying to change them. Even so, he acts no worse than his humanitarian fellow brethren who, like the "person" in a "Revenge Fable," commit suicide in killing off Mother Nature or, like his counterpart in "A Bedtime Story," lose all contact with body and soul.

Creation has failed again. We are back to the original Crow narrative about God's nightmare's attempt to improve upon God's creation by creating Crow, and God's own attempt to frustrate this second Genesis. As Crow's "Song of Himself" informs us, God, despite repeated attempts, has little success in destroying Crow. Yet although the protagonist's defiance has matured into genuine strength, he still reacts in panic when confronted with the ultimate mystery of his life. He has yet to learn that wherever he may turn he will always be confronted with his own self. Like Oedipus in "Song for a Phallus," he instead goes on trying to hew his way towards the "truth." The real truth is finally revealed to him when he is faced with "fear," tries to strike it down but in doing so only knocks himself down ("Crow Sickened," C,62).

Neither "Song for a Phallus" nor "Apple Tragedy" mention Crow, but they both have their place in the thematic and stylistic texture of *Crow* as a whole. By contrast, "Crow Paints Himself Into a Chinese Mural," a piece rescued from the unpublished 1964 verse play *Difficulties of a Bridegroom*, is as alien to the sequence as the melodramatically overstated "The Lovepet" seems superfluous to it. Along with "Crow Hears Fate Knock on the Door," "Crow's Fall," "The Contender," "Crow Tries the Media" and "Crow's Elephant Totem Song," both poems were added to the American edition of *Crow*, and there was good reason for eliminating "The Lovepet" from the second Faber edition which otherwise retains the American additions. It would have been equally appropriate to eliminate "Crow Paints Himself Into a Chinese Mural." With its surrealistic diffuseness this poem would fit into *Wodwo* but is at variance with the didactic, imagistic and mythopoeic precision of *Crow*. True enough, the two poems cannot be said to disrupt an Aristotelian unity with beginning, middle and end. But even within the open texture of *Crow* their inappropriateness is sufficiently felt, and particularly so at a point where they distract from an ever increasing thematic density as the sequence draws towards its conclusion.

"Crow's Last Stand" is an appropriate introduction to this last section. Whatever hope there is, is based upon survival despite utter reduction. Burnt to a charred stump by his old antagonist the sun,

> Crow's eye-pupil, in the tower of its scorched fort, (C,69)

is all that remains of the protagonist. The world is indifferent to his needs and emotions, yet holds him imprisoned in its everlasting torture chamber. There is no way of ignoring what a previous poem evokes as the "sea's ogreish outcry and convulsion" (C,29).

> He turned his back and he marched away from the sea
>
>> As a crucified man cannot move.
>>   ("Crow and the Sea," C,70)

All his attempts to come to grips with the world only lead to his utter destruction ("Truth Kills Everybody"), and whatever strength he develops in this battle is a fiendish "arrogance of blood and bone" (L,14). In no time Crow has turned into a monster, "Holding the very globe in terror" ("Crow and Stone," C,72). And little is going to change even if Crow should survive forever. For the Eternal-Feminine which gave him birth is herself an image of the destructiveness and suffering he has come to embody. Her brow, the "notable casket of gems," shows "many a painful frown"; "her perfect teeth" have a "hint of a fang at the corner"; not to mention her vagina which as "the ticking bomb of the future" is a source not only of life but of apocalyptic doom ("Fragment of an Ancient Tablet," C,73). A follow-up to "Apple Tragedy," "Notes for a Little Play" with its ironically understated title, deals with one such apocalypse, a total nuclear holocaust and its survivors, "Mutations—at home in the nuclear glare," dancing a strange nuptial dance "in the darkness of the sun,/Without guest or God" (C,74). Whether these strange items are the successors of man or even of Crow, there is one force alone which can guarantee the survival of either, the force which Plato misinterpreted as Eros and Christianity as agape.

> The blood in Adam's body
> That slid into Eve
> Was the everlasting thing
> Adam swore was love.
>   ("Snake Hymn," C,75)

Love's true image is more like that of the crawling beast with two backs reminiscent of Francis Bacon's paintings.

> His kisses sucked out her whole past and future or tried to
> He had no other appetite
> She bit him she gnawed him she sucked
> .   .   .   .
> And their deep cries crawled over the floors
> Like an animal dragging a great trap.

And yet there is more to it than the mere coupling of two animals. Sex may not be the first step in an ascent towards ideational values, but its death-like ecstacies can be a means of spiritual rebirth in which *sponsa* and *sponsus* become each other's saviors. In shamanistic terms, a mutual dismemberment is followed by mutual reintegration. After their aggressive sexual acts,

> Their heads fell apart into sleep like the two halves
> Of a lopped melon, but love is hard to stop
>
> In their entwined sleep they exchanged arms and legs
> In their dreams their brains took each other hostage
>
> In the morning they wore each other's face.
> ("Lovesong," C,76,77)

Again Crow is the last one to get the message, so once more he tries to make the world answer his need for affection. But

> The touch of a leaf's edge at his throat
> Guillotined further comment.
> ("Glimpse," C,80)

As many a previous lesson could have taught him, speechless wonder is the only appropriate response to a world of apocalyptic doom in which "King of Carrion" rules over silence.

"Fleeing From Eternity" reaffirms these experiences in an inverse sequence. The rise of man's consciousness is a process of self-reduction. Originally faceless, eyeless and mouthless, man becomes aware of things by being deprived of them. Unlike Oedipus, he learns to experience the world through suffering until finally he "gashed holes in his face" with a sharp rock and

> Through the blood and pain he looked at the earth.

The only solace afforded him in this "cemetery earth" comes from his contacts with his shamanistic Earth Mother representative or *ayami*,[14] "a woman singing out of her belly," who assumes part of the burden of his own suffering.

> He gave her eyes and a mouth, in exchange for the song.
> She wept blood, she cried pain. (C,82,83)

A song in exchange for learning to taste the bitterness of life sounds like a fitting description of Hughes' own art, and the second "Eskimo Song" as well as "Littleblood," the collection's culminating achievement, provide us with the appropriate illustrations. Like the book as a whole, "How Water Began to Play" suggests a conclusion beyond its actual end, and "Littleblood" gives us a glimpse of that beyond. Genuine playfulness or *līlā* only begins after all hope has vanished, when Water "had no weeping left" and "lay at the bottom of all things/Utterly worn out utterly clear" (C,83). Littleblood, a surrealistic fairy tale creature, has experienced this total vulnerability and absurdity of existence—

> hiding from the mountains in the mountains.
> Wounded by stars and leaking shadow
>
> .   .   .   .
>
> Reaping the wind and threshing the stones.

Like the survivors of nuclear holocaust in "Notes for a Little Play," it has begun to dance a strange dance "in the darkness of the sun,/Without guest or God" (C,74)—"drumming in a cow's skull/Dancing with a gnat's feet/With an elephant's nose with a crocodile's tail." And to this creature, as his future Muse, the poet addresses his final appeal.

> Grown so wise grown so terrible
> Sucking death's mouldy tits.
>
> Sit on my finger, sing in my ear, O Littleblood. (C,84)

4. From *Crow* to *Orghast*:

But for the event remembered in its dedication, *Crow* without doubt would be a different book. The deaths of Assia and Shura in March 1969 not only brought the actual writing of the poems to a sudden standstill; the sequence as it was put together about a year later also seems to differ markedly from the original impulse behind *Crow*. Even when Hughes, early in 1970, talked to me about the typescript he was then about to send off to Faber, his almost obsessive focus was on Crow's descent into the underworld where the quester rescues a desecrated female through his own disintegration before both become bride and bridegroom. Yet of this the published sequence reflects as little as of the actual Crow story as a whole. Poems that bear a direct relation to either were apparently excluded from both the British and American editions of *Crow* and only a few of these were allowed to surface in small editions after 1970.

One such poem, "Crow's Song About God," is about the first part of the Crow story. Man sitting under the gatepost of heaven and trying to hand his life back to God has suffered the disintegration familiar from similar descriptions in both Hughes' and Plath's poetry.

Eyesockets empty
Stomach laid open
To the inspection of the stars
The operation unfinished
(The doctors ran off, there was some other emergency). (Po,17)

Another poem deals with a female victim of similar desecration, perhaps the one destined to become Crow's bride,—

She tried to keep her breasts
They were cut from her and canned
She tried to keep her cunt
It was produced in open court she was sentenced—
                              ("Crow's Song About England,"Po,14)

A third describes God's unsuccessful attempt to provide Crow with a substitute bride made out of the burnt carcasses of hags of which cartloads are shipped into the furnaces of heaven ("Crow's Courtship," Po,15). Yet none of these poems published shortly after *Crow* covers the rescue of the desecrated female by her bridegroom, a happy end which the tragic events of March 1969 removed from the poet's reach.

If Hughes, nonetheless, persisted in his quest, it was by retracing his steps and resuming his mythopoeic journey from its beginnings. Hughes' 1973 description of the Crow story, in which the protagonist's creator, originally God's nightmare, has turned into "the mysterious, powerful, invisible prisoner of the being men called God,"[15] indicates the most general direction which this recasting of the story was to take. The result was *Orghast*[16] whose interior mythology, as the poet has commented, was "of a piece with parts of [his] earlier writing."[17] To readers of Hughes who witnessed the actual spectacle amongst the royal tombs at Persepolis, *Orghast* must have appeared like a sudden floodlit revelation of the secret quarry from which Hughes' poems had been hewn for several years. But just as the poems were half undecipherable messages from some distant mythic battlefield, so its direct dramatisation in *Orghast* remained inarticulate in a language of mere sounds.

What most clearly emerges from the various accounts of the play, is a tale of repression and rebirth which in a way parallels, continues and inverts the myth, told in Hesiod's *Theogony* and the Mesopotamian *Enuma elish*, of the victory of the male over the female principle. Krogon (the half brother of Marduk, Kronos and Zeus) imprisons his mother Moa—like Tiamat or Gaia the "womb of all"—along with his father, the sun, who between them represented the divine harmony of nature. But their repressed energy strives to resume its flow of creativity, enjoyment and death as well as to overthrow the increasingly oppressive rule of Krogon who lives in constant terror of these forces. Their release is finally achieved through

Pramanath (Prometheus), an inverted analogue of Christ, who is born into time as Krogon's child, Sogis. Himself one of Moa's children, Sogis succeeds in freeing his mother and destroying Krogon who withers to a "senile, birdlike thing, croaking empty sounds" before the universe resumes its natural course, undivided and reconciled to itself. Yet all we have of these and subsequent episodes in *Orghast* are more or less vague descriptions by spectators and an outline of the Orghast mythology in A. C. H. Smith's edition of Hughes' notes. Asked about their reliability, Hughes, in 1977, only shrugged his shoulders.

VI.

Gaudete

Religious negotiations had formerly embraced and humanized the archaic energies of instinct and feeling. . . . Without religion, those powers have become dehumanized. The whole inner world has become elemental, chaotic, continually more primitive and beyond our control. It has become a place of demons. But of course, insofar as we are disconnected anyway from that world, and lack the equipment to pick up its signals, we are not aware of it. All we register is the vast absence, the emptiness, the sterility, the meaninglessness, the loneliness. If we do manage to catch a glimpse of our inner selves, by some contraption of mirrors, we recognize it with horror—it is an animal crawling and decomposing in a hell. (76,M,90)

The story of Christ . . . can never be diminished by the seemingly infinite mass of theological agonizing and insipid homilies which have attempted to translate it into something more manageable. It remains, like any other genuine story, irreducible, a lump of the world, like the body of a new-born child. There is little doubt that if the world lasts pretty soon someone will come along . . . and see two thousand years of somnolent fumbling with the theme. Out of that, and the collision of other things, he will produce, very likely, something totally new and overwhelming, some whole new direction for human life. The same possibility holds for the ancient stories of many another deity. Why not? History is really no older than that new-born baby. And every story is still the original cauldron of wisdom, full of new visions and new life. (76,M,83)

VI. *GAUDETE*

In the terms of his essay on Shakespeare, the "skeleton-key fable" (71,S,182) of Hughes' imagination may have one of its roots in a recurrent nightmare of disaster, death and transformation which the poet, until a few years ago, dreamt at regular intervals since childhood: a plane, which he flies in or watches, crashes in flames and often, before it hits the ground, changes into a monster animal falling out of the sky. One of the Epilogue poems from *Gaudete* records a series of such transformations:

> The viper fell from the sun
> Jerked and lay in the road's dust,
> Started horribly to move, as I watched it.

> A radiant goose dropped from a fire-quake heaven,
> Slammed on to earth beside me
> So hard, it bounced me off my feet.

121

> Something dazzling crashed on the hill field,
> Elk-antlered, golden-limbed, a glowing mass
> That started to get up.

The poem also records how the speaker, with the help of a monster goddess, is salvaged from these disasters.

> I stirred, like a discarded foetus,
> Already grey-haired,
> In a blowing of bright particles.
>
> A hand out of a hot cloud
> Held me its thumb to suck.
>
> Lifted me to the dug that grew
> Out of the brow of a lioness. (G,188)

Such lines reflect a more recent evolution of what appears as the most "peculiarly black and ugly" aspect of Hughes' fable, which again can be traced to the poet's early life. Where Shakespeare, in Hughes' view, finally banished Mother Nature "as Sycorax, the blue-eyed hag" (71,S,181,198), Hughes' deliberate efforts to retrieve her desecrated remnants are a tale of frustration and disaster. "Song"(H,19), the teenaged poet's prayer to the White Goddess, ends on a note of utter despair. The glimmer of hope visible at the end of *The Wound*, where the desecrated demonic "girl" and the wounded soldier Ripley are about to save each other in mystical union, was wiped out by the death of Sylvia Plath. A similar fulfillment to the Crow story, which seemed fully in sight by 1969, was cut short by the deaths of Assia and Shura. *Gaudete* repeats the same basic fable, but now on a double level. Vicar Lumb's efforts to revitalize the cult of the Great Mother result in a total victimization of the female. All of them are deluded, drugged and betrayed, Felicity is murdered, Maud and the pregnant Janet are driven to suicide. Yet what fails in reality reaches at least partial fulfillment in the world of dream. The baboon woman with her "crudely stitched patchwork of faces" who is reborn through Lumb's dismemberment, gushing "from between his legs," has a "face undeformed and perfect"(G,104-6). In August, 1977, I asked the poet by letter whether the reader is to believe that such dream images can become reality or rather that any solution to the problem is as unattainable as a phantasmagorical mirage. Hughes replied: "You are asking me to explain my riddle, which I should refrain from doing."

A related query—whether *Gaudete* continues the main issues of *Crow* within an ongoing mythic narrative—elicited a more detailed but similarly enigmatic reply:

Gaudete obviously is connected to *Crow*. *Crow*, in full, with big developments, would be the yolk, and *Gaudete* would be the shell. I projected the life of Lumb in the underworld, and it became entangled with *Crow*, and the episodes became like the real events of which the *Gaudete* events are like the shadow on the wall in the cave.

Are Lumb's underworld experiences, unlike his Doppelgänger's adventures in real life, the true reality? Or do they reflect a hallucinatory phantasmagoria of wishful thinking deflated by the test of everyday experience? Whatever the answer, once, if ever, the whole fable is completed, there can be little doubt as to the motive power behind the gradually unfolding pattern of poems and narratives. It is a nightmare impulse searching for the pristine "bliss of the divine harmony."[1]

The actual story of the Reverend Lumb was conceived well before Hughes, around 1966, started to compose his first Crow poems. Originally written as a film scenario, it was begun in 1962, finished by 1964, and to be submitted to a Swedish film director. Nothing came of it, and to this day Hughes has never reread the manuscript which is still in his possession. But as apparent in the satyr play-like *Burning of the Brothel* (1966) about a fornicating minister in a whorehouse, the story had a powerful hold on his imagination. What finally made him start rewriting the story around 1971, was a series of actual dreams connected with the mythopoeic narrative behind *Crow*. The underworld passages in *Gaudete* are like intermittent glimpses of this continuous hallucinatory sequence. About a hundred further as yet unpublished poems written out of the same impulse, which Hughes describes as the inner yolk to the outer shell of Lumb's adventures, are completed—yet apparently without completing the Crow story which prompted them. To the poet, talking to me in August, 1977, the entire venture had turned into a *déjà vu* experience pointing backwards rather than towards a conclusion.

Gaudete is Hughes' most personal book to date, and its protagonist—sometimes the Reverend Lumb himself, at other times his double—seems to resemble the kind of self-caricature found in Dostoyevsky's anti-hero in *Notes from Underground* or Kafka's K. in *The Trial*. This is most apparent in the old "veteran of negatives" (G,176) who in the Epilogue poems pays his devotion to a nameless female deity, as well as in the Doppelgänger who in the narrative itself pursues his ill-fated messianic endeavors. Lumb with his new religion, occult practises and Earth Mother worship, makes himself the active promoter of what Hughes has called the recent "reemergence of Nature as the Great Goddess of mankind" (70,N,83) and in the process runs into difficulties. Appropriately enough, the primary source for the underworld narrative in *Gaudete* was the poet's dreams which began to proliferate as he turned them into a framework for the original story. Crucial in all this was a dream which Hughes, in conversation, interpreted as a perfect image of the divided self: a very brilliantly lit dream about fishing at a lake where he met himself and had a fight, tore his own hand off and threw it away. Lumb's adventure at the lake, after he has wounded one of the cuckolded husbands, is a direct account of that dream. His underworld double, in the shape of a naked "lean leaping figure," half human and half seal, tries to abduct Felicity, who, about to escape with Lumb, is instrumental in destroying the vicar's mission. But Lumb manages to foil his Doppelgänger's attempt. In a deadly struggle

> Lumb knocks him down and the two men wallow pummelling,
>
> .   .   .   .
> A cramp has locked their grip, hand in hand.
>
> With a sudden screech, the other rips free
> Holding aloft his stump from which the hand has vanished,
>
> .   .   .   .
> Lumb tugs to lever up the demonic fingers
> of the torn off hand, which still grips his own hand.
>
> The other is wallowing in the lake. . .
>
> .   .   .   .
> Lumb flings the freed hand out into the lake after him. (G,80, 82-3)

1. The Story of the Reverend Lumb and His Doppelgänger.

From the original Lumb's abduction until his return to the world, this motif of the two Doppelgänger with their double mission on earth and in the underworld is the backbone of the entire narrative. Here is Hughes' summing up of the story in a program leaflet for an acting version of *Gaudete* performed in August, 1977, in London:

> An Anglican clergyman, the Reverend Nicholas Lumb, is carried away into the other world by elemental spirits. Just as in the old folktale these spirits want him for some special work in their world.
>
> To fill his place in this world, for the time of his absence, the spirits make an exact duplicate of him out of an oak log, and fill it with elemental spirit life. This new Nicholas Lumb is to all appearances exactly the same as the old, has the same knowledge and mannerisms, but he is a log.
> Or rather, a log and an elemental spirit. A changeling.

This changeling proceeds to interpret the job of ministering the Gospel of love in his own log-like way. He organises the women of his parish into a coven, a love society. And the purpose of this society, evidently, is to produce the Messiah. So all the women have to be brought under Lumb's power and made pregnant by him since he is to be the father of the Messiah.

But while he applies himself to this, he runs into difficulties. The elemental oak log changeling begins to feel a longing to become human, a great nostalgia for independent ordinary life, in the world of ordinary people, free of his peculiar destiny. He plans to escape with a girl who is as yet not part of his coven.

At this point, seeing what he intends to do, the spirits who created him decide to cancel him. Or it may be that the original Lumb has done the work they wanted him to do, and so the changeling's time is up. The result is that all the husbands of the parish become aware of what is happening to their wives [and kill Lumb] . . .

At the death of the changeling the original Nicholas Lumb reappears in this world, in the West of Ireland, where he roams about half crazy, composing hymns and psalms to a nameless female deity.

The "Prologue" to *Gaudete* sets the scene in a post-holocaust North England town turned mass grave. Here the original Lumb encounters a female, half animal and half human, whose lifelessness is the appropriate emblem of the Waste Land surrounding her. But like Parzival who didn't ask the question that could have cured the king, Lumb

> stands in confusion
> And looks round at the shadowed hollow faces
> Crowding to enclose him
> Eyepits and eyeglints.
>
> He declares he can do nothing
> He protests there is nothing he can do
> For this beautiful woman who seems to be alive and dead.
> He is not a doctor. He can only pray. (G,14-15)

What the original Lumb fails to achieve in the nether regions becomes the earthly mission of his Doppelgänger created by the badger-like inhabitants of the underworld who first whip Lumb's bald skull and then tie him to a tree bole for a second beating. Lumb loses consciousness and when he wakes up again finds that the tree bole has been transformed into another man: "Lumb sees this other is himself. . . . Seeing the ridged red track of the whipstroke across that glossy skull, Lumb feels gingerly over his own skull . . . He finds only clean whole skin" (G,16-17). The new Lumb makes his entry into the world through the bloody Womb Door of a slaughterhouse as men, laughing like maniacs, try

> to drown him with blood
> And to bury him in guts and lungs. (G,19)

Gaudete, the sequel to this "Prologue," records the last day and failure of Lumb's mission on earth. As Lumb plans his escape with Felicity, the underworld powers slowly regain control over his destiny. Lumb's housekeeper, the mysterious Maud, foresees the future events by peering into her crystal ball: Felicity, during a love orgy in the cathedral will be murdered, apparently by a seal-like emissary from the nether world.

> A lumpish form is dodging behind the bride
> Who suddenly falls, face downwards, across the steps,
> And lies frozen, in the hard sunlight.
> A knife hilt is sticking from the nape of her neck. (G,63)

Several occurrences herald the fulfilment of these prophecies. After Lumb has foiled his Doppelgänger's attempt to abduct Felicity, another messenger from the beyond appears to Maud walking in the graveyard.

> A woman is walking ahead of her.
> Maud follows the woman.
> The woman walks to the far end of the path.
> Maud does not see her go but now the woman is no longer
>   there. (G,94)

Is this woman, whose tombstone carries the inscription Gaudete, associated with the female whom the original Nicholas Lumb encountered in the "domed, subterranean darkness" (G,13)? What the poem leaves unclear, Hughes clarified in conversation. The graveyard apparition is that of the dead woman Lumb was supposed to cure in the underworld. And

> Maud is her Doppelgänger and so in a way has control over Lumb to bring about this renovation of women and therefore of life in general in this world. But while she is inadequate to it he is even more so, the whole situation being impossibly crystallized in the immovable dead end forms of society and physical life.

Before these disasters take their final toll on both perpetrators and victims, Lumb manages what his double failed to accomplish in the underworld. After a car accident engineered by "Stub-fingered hairy-backed hands" which suddenly "come past his shoulders/ And wrench the steering wheel from his grip," he has to pass the outer ring of the inferno with the scenario, reminiscent of *The Wound* and *Eat Crow*, of cattle stampede and cudgel-swinging men hailing their blows on the intruder. Suddenly he discovers "the men of his parish,/Faces upward or downward" in the mud. And then

> One by one he finds them
> The women of his parish are congregated here,
> Buried alive
> Around the rim of a crater
> Under the drumming downpour. (G,98,102-3)

Lumb tries to get through to them in every imaginable way. But the women only stare past him "across the plain of mud/As if the last horror/ Were approaching beneath its surface" and continue to scream in anguish

> As if something hidden under the mud
> Were biting into [them]. (G,102-3)

In sharp contrast to their helpless agony is the "horrible reptile slowness" of an "almost human" creature who "is calling to him/Through a moving uncertain hole in the mud face." Despite his failure to save the other women, Lumb feels that "this one creature . . . he can free," and as he "draws the mud being up" from "the sink at the centre," "a human shape . . . embraces him as he embraces it." The face that gradually washes clear under the pouring rain looks like Lady Lazarus transmogrified into a nightmarish creature from the land of the dead.

> It is a woman's face,
> A face as if sewn together from several faces.
> A baboon beauty face,
> A crudely stitched patchwork of faces,
> But the eyes slide,
> Alive and electrical, like liquid liquorice behind the stitched lids.
> (G,103-5)

Momentarily paralyzed by the tight embrace of this creature who clings to him "as if she were drowning," Lumb, the dabbling would-be father of the new Messiah who has impregnated half the women of his parish, is himself made to act the part of a woman in childbirth. And, just as this pseudo-Virgin Mary is a man, so his child is a woman who becomes the new Savior simply by being saved from her own desecration. Like the soul of a man recently dead, Lumb watches his own body give birth to this primitive Mother Goddess Messiah.

> Somehow he has emerged and is standing over himself.
> He sees himself being delivered of the woman from the pit,
>
> The baboon woman,
> Flood-sudden, like the disembowelling of a cow
> She gushes from between his legs, a hot splendour
> .   .   .   .

He can hear her whole body bellowing

.   .   .   .   .   .

Men are fighting to hold her down, they cannot.

.   .   .   .

He sees her face undeformed and perfect. (G,105-6)

Upon Lumb's return to the upper world, the memory of his night-marish quest focuses on an "archaic stone carving" of a Venus-of-Willendorf-like divinity.

> The simply hacked-out face of a woman
> Gazes back at Lumb
> Between her raised, wide-splayed, artless knees
> With a stricken expression.
> The square-cut, primitive fingers, beneath her buttocks
> Are pulling herself wide open—
>
> An entrance, an exit.
> An arched target centre. (G,110)

But the vicar's ultimate response to the Earth Mother's plea is equal to the Red Cross Knight's destructiveness in "Gog," which the imagery here seems to recall.[2] The final catastrophe is foreshadowed in Lumb's sub-sequent vision: enthroned beside Maud, he looks down upon a tossing sea of lamenting women assembled in the Cathedral. The dumb housekeeper has suddenly turned beautiful but her love union with Lumb is like that of two infernal ministers presiding over an orgy culminating in a complete sacrificial holocaust. This climax to Lumb's vision is evoked in the image-ry of the "great recurrent dream" which has haunted Hughes since early childhood. While Lumb embraces Maud, the cathedral with all the women inside is exploding in a griffon-like conflagration of fire and smoke—

> As if the Cathedral
> Were being crushed in the upreaching foot
> Of an immense upside down griffon
> Which is falling
> Into a crater of black smoke
> The griffon being aflame,
> Beating deeper and deeper,
> A star of struggling rays,
> A glowing spot
> Muffled away
> By the banging—

Till only a hard banging remains.

Lumb
Lies unconscious on the carpet, face crawling with sweat
In front of the burned-out fire. (G,122-3)

From then on—Maud listening "To the banging on the door downstairs"—it is as if nightmare had turned to reality. While the murderous conspiracy of cuckolded husbands draws its ever narrowing circle around Lumb, the vicar's frantic preparations for escape are cut short by his dream bride, who drops the ignition keys of his van into a "freshly-dug not yet occupied grave" (G,136). In Lumb's "cancellation by the powers of both worlds," Maud more and more turns into a henchman of the underworld working in collusion with the destructive forces of this world. The fatal link is provided by Felicity's sudden decision to attend the meeting in the Cathedral, a moment when the "Two worlds,/Like two strange dogs" seem to be circling each other (G,125).

What follows resembles a black mass version of the ritual Lumb might have been able to perform if he had lived up to his mission. Felicity, drugged with a mushroom sandwich, her naked body dressed in a hind skin, is made to enact the sacrificial role of an "inconceivably huge and urgent love-animal" invested with all the frustrated yearnings of the other naked, dancing and screaming women in the cathedral. Even before Lumb, bobbing under antlers, a "russet bristly pelt . . . flapping at his naked back," mounts her "from behind, like a stag," Felicity is convinced that "some final crisis of earth's life is now to be enacted/Faithfully and selflessly by them all." Yet what her deliriousness anticipates as some apocalyptic moment, strikes the others with the senseless confusion caused by some unexpected, brutal crime. Whether guided by the human arms and fingers of the "giant expressionless badger," by Maud who hits "Felicity's bowed nape" (G,140-7) with her two locked fists, or by both, Lumb's dagger, previously stolen from the Vicar's "magical apparatus" (G,135), is suddenly seen sticking in Felicity's neck. The subsequent scenes seem to be spotlit with intermittent flashes recalling Lumb's previous underworld adventures. While the other women, in their chaotic despair and confusion,

are clinging to his knees, his waist, his arms, his neck
As if they too were drowning, (G,149)

Maud, as if inspired by infernal memories "of that whip across his skull" (G,16), flogs Lumb "over his bald skull with the cable-hard, twisted, horny stag's pizzle" (G,149). And after Lumb's dead body, "splayed like a stunned frog" by a bullet from Hagen's Mannlicher .318, has been pulled ashore, the scenario recalls the cudgel-swinging man hunters and stampeding cattle herds which failed to kill the protagonist in the underworld (G,168). The men hasten to eliminate all traces of the nightmare of which they have become the unwilling participants. Maud, found "Curled on the floor around Lumb's dagger," is made to join her two victims in the conflagration Lumb foresaw in his vision (G,169-170).

This narrative which, around 1971, began to connect itself with the Crow myth initially appeared to Hughes as the more interesting part of the story. But his hopes that in writing it down he might somehow manage to make it come together, remained unfulfilled. Hughes has a rough idea about the remainder of Lumb's underworld adventures but prefers to keep the story to himself. "It's very long and I've written quite a lot of it. I keep pulling bits out of it and publish them in a number of places. But I want to get it right."[3] As a result of this failure, Hughes' interest gradually turned back to the original story of Lumb's sexo-messianic exploits and his murder at the hands of the cuckolded husbands. The result appears like a series of brightly lit cinematic exposures like Janet's suicide; architect Dunworth, a loaded pistol in hand, discovering his "red-haired wife/ . . . lying naked on the couch, almost hidden/By the naked body of Lumb" (G,85); or Garten secretly taking a photograph of the priest with the blacksmith's wife. But this suspense drama of sex orgies, jealousy and revenge is best left to tell its own tale. It fully achieves what Hughes set out to do: "Something like a Kleist story that would go from beginning to end in some forceful way pushing the reader through some kind of tunnel."[4]

2. Verse Form and Narrative Technique.

Hughes' talents as lyrical poet, playwright, short story writer, children's author and mythic spellmaker are amazingly diverse. What is more, almost every one of his major volumes has managed to take readers and critics by surprise. After the primarily imagistic poetry of *The Hawk in the Rain* and *Lupercal*, the "single adventure" of *Wodwo* and the didactic mythographies of *Crow*, *Gaudete* more than ever came as such a surprise. A mixture of prose and verse narrative (apart from the epilogue cycle of poems about half the length of *Crow*), it conveys the visual effect of a cinematic experience. At the same time its poetic language has a synaesthetic impact on all the five senses as well as on the subconscious sensorium behind and beyond them. The initial attempt to write the story in prose remained unsuccessful until Hughes, while working on another film script, hit upon this new combination—a prose-verse narrative with the verse written in a way that, as Hughes puts it, "would stop you dead at every moment."[5]

More than any previous book, *Gaudete* owes much of its idiom to a lifelong apprenticeship with the poet whom Hughes has read and reread more than any other. Here, as in Shakespeare, we find what Hughes has called the playwright's "utility general-purpose style" combining "a colloquial prose readiness and variety with a poetic breadth" (62,D,1070),—a language which seems to have been

> invented in a state of crisis, for a terribly urgent job, a homely spur-of-the-moment improvisation out of whatever verbal scrap happens to be lying around . . . The meaning is not so much narrowly delineated as overwhelmingly suggested, by an inspired signalling and hinting of verbal heads and tails both above and below precision, and by this weirdly expressive underswell of a musical near-gibberish, like a jostling of spirits. (71,S,11)

A flash vision attentiveness to detail demands the reader's total concentration. What at first reading often creates a slight shock of surprise assumes, as soon as it has been absorbed, the convincingness of something we have simply overlooked. When Lumb's escaping car is hit by a bullet from Westlake's gun, for instance, "One of the van's rear windows goes black" (G,76). We expect to hear a sound but are given a visual impression. Hughes' language in *Gaudete*, to speak in the terms that Goethe applied to Shakespeare, is best appreciated if listened to with closed eyes. Only then do we experience the full sensory evocativeness of this one-time film scenario which, like Shakespeare's texts, implies a dramatic realization more powerful than one might hope to reproduce in actuality.

Part of this uniquely poetic impact derives from a lavish use of images and, in particular, of similes. As the dream narrative keeps reminding us of further dimensions behind the everyday world of the actual story, so these devices establish a further and deliberate network of correspondences between the various realms of conscious and subconscious experience. They also deepen the psychographic X-ray portraits of characters and situations otherwise revealed to us in the unmistakable gesture, facial expression or mood. Here, for instance, is Dr. Westlake listening to Jennifer talking about her affair with Lumb after her sister Janet's suicide.

> Westlake
> Keeps losing Jennifer's words
> As he gazes fascinated
> Into the turbulence of her body and features.
> He jerks back into detachment
> Noting again, between the inflamed eyelids,
> Her irises clear and nimble-delicate as a baboon's,
> And the insanity there, the steel cutting acetylene
> Of religious mania.

> And immersing himself in her voice, which flows so full of
>   thrilling touches
> And which sobs so nakedly in its narration,
> He is scorched by the hard fieriness,
> A jagged, opposite lightning
> Running along the edge of it
> Like an insane laughter—
>
> Something in his marrow shrivels with fear. (G,57)

What is imagery here partly turns into the actual events of the story. The
"steel cutting acetylene/Of religious mania" foreshadows the mass mania
of the drugged and naked women in the cathedral. Jennifer's "irises clear
and nimble-delicate as a baboon's" link her encounter with Dr. Westlake
with that between Lumb and the actual baboon woman whose eyes slide
"Alive and electrical, like liquid liquorice behind the stitched lids"
(G,104). What also seems to be intimated here is that Jennifer, like Lumb,
Maud and perhaps everyone else, has a Doppelgänger in the underworld.

A metaphor encompassing the entire narrative probably stems from the
book's original cinematic structure. If "A Bedtime Story" from *Crow* is
about modern man whose vision has been atrophied by his camera, then
the photomontage technique of *Gaudete*, with its zoom lens close-ups and
sudden changes of focus, evokes a trap that gradually closes upon the protagonist. The precision telescope guiding the bullet that will kill Lumb is
on his track from the very beginning. Major Hagen's binoculars roaming
through the countryside and suddenly settling on two figures—Lumb
making love to the Major's wife—thus set the general tone for the entire
story. The world of ossified dead end social forms that finally kill off
Lumb and his mission, is peopled with voyeurs who masochistically and
perversely glory in the self-destructive power afforded them by their
cameras and telescopes. While Janet is hanging herself, her father, Major
Estridge, stands glued to his telescope watching Mrs. Holroyd, whom he
"treasures . . . among his collection of ideals," enlarged, "within the mag-
nified circle," to a ghastly caricature of his wishful idealizations. His
"brain wrings/To a needling pang, as if a wire might snap," at what he
sees:

> Turning, she sets Lumb's hands on her breasts and bites his neck.
>
> His hands gather up her skirts. (G,47)

Inversely, Garten, after taking the picture that will lead to the Vicar's
death, is

Exultant, the fuse spluttering in him
Of what he has in the camera. (G,90)

Self-elected into a voyeuristic "focus of excitement" which gradually engulfs everybody's attention, Garten uses the photograph as his weapon in a futile attempt to dislodge Lumb from Felicity's affection. Similar impotence turned destructive is implicit in the description of Hagen aiming his deadly shot at Lumb from his long-distance rifle. Lumb's mystical bride has turned into an angel of destruction.

The Mannlicher .318
Regards Lumb's distant skull dutifully, with perfectly
    tooled and adjusted concentration.
Germanic precision, slender goddess
Of Hagen's devotions
And the unfailing bride
Of his ecstasies in the primal paradise, and the midwife of
    Eden's beasts,
Painlessly delivered, with a little blood,
And laid at his feet
As if fresh from the Creator's furnace, as if to be named.
With her, only with her
Hagen feels his life stir on its root. (G,117,137,167)

3. The Epilogue Poems.

Despite the bitter irony of this conclusion to Lumb's narrative, the actual end of *Gaudete* does not return to the desolate gloom of the young poet's "Song" about the White Goddess who will not "come home" (H,19). Hughes' alter ego champion of the Great Mother has failed in his mission, but despite Lumb's death, the bride of his and the poet's devotions survives in the poem. Her celebrations in the volume's concluding lyrics recall Eliot's "Shantih shantih shantih" echoing through the Waste Land of modern civilization. According to the epilogue story, they were written by the original Nicholas Lumb who, after the death of his Doppelgänger, reappeared "in the West of Ireland, where he roam[ed] about half crazy, composing hymns and psalms to a nameless female deity." The Jesuit priest who is handed these poems by three girls may be skeptical about the miracle performed by their author. A "solemn-looking, long-faced" man, "his bald shiny head . . . lumped with scars," he had suddenly appeared to the girls out of nowhere, whistled a weasel-like creature with strangely human eyes out of a lough before he vanished again, leaving behind him a "tattered notebook" full of verse. Yet in the very attempt to minimize these feats, the priest is about to turn into another Nicholas Lumb with excitement.

> "If that is a miracle," he said finally, "To bring an otter up out of the lough, then what must that poor man think of the great world itself, this giant, shining beauty that God whistled up out of the waters of chaos?"
> And as he spoke the priest was suddenly carried away by his words . . . and who knows what spark had jumped on to him from the flushed faces of the three girls? . . . [H]e described the first coming of Creation, as it rose from the abyss, an infinite creature of miracles, made of miracles and teeming miracles. And he went on, describing this creature, giving it more and more dazzlingly-shining eyes, and more and more glorious limbs, and heaping it with greater and more extraordinary beauties, till his heart was pounding . . . and the tears pouring from his eyes. (G,173-5)

This Creation evoked in the priest's ecstatic words is not unlike the creature addressed in most of Lumb's subsequent hymns and psalms. Just as the Jesuit's description recalls the archetypal grandeur of Vishnu with "many faces, eyes, arms, bellies, and legs" (*Bhagavad Gita*, XI, 23)[6] so Lumb's nameless female deity is an all-encompassing numen of multiple mythic dimensions.

After he has been carried in her arms, the speaker has a hard time recognizing the goddess in the skull of the "maneater" that was out to devour him. And as he questions her identity, the basic cruelty of life spells out the answers:

> Who are you?

> The spider clamps the bluefly—whose death panic
> Becomes sudden soulful absorption.

> A stoat throbs at the nape of the lumped rabbit
> Who watches the skylines fixedly. (G,177,183)

Such lines recall *Crow* although their contents mark a step beyond the earlier sequence. Unlike his trickster bird predecessor, the speaker, despite his numerous other heresies, shows little interest in inverting Biblical mythology in apocryphal lectures or fables. The following description of the deity shows how his own sporadic use of this material tends to take such inversion for granted.

> She rides the earth
> On an ass, on a lion.
> She rides the heavens
> On a great white bull.

> She is an apple
> Whoever plucks her
> Nails his heart
> To the leafless tree. (G,184)

Point by point inversion has turned into a complex *à rebours* symbology in which the fall and the crucifixion turn into icons of a commitment to and an enslavement by life and its eternal suffering. Similarly, there is the

> Agony in the garden. Annunciation
> Of clay, water and the sunlight,

or the deity's "congregations at their rapture," worshipping in animal sounds rather than in the "fistula" of human speech (G,176,199).

The true creator behind the Christian god revealed little more than his negative elementary character to Crow. By contrast, Lumb's female divinity, though clearly the creator and destroyer in one, for the most part appears as the comforter and guarantor of survival. Her kiss of life resurrects the dead. And as the power who by her kiss of death can liberate us from the "veils of wrinkle and shawls of ache," she is the eternal savior (G,192,198). In sum, she seems to fulfill the poet's own search for a new divinity which, as he put it in 1970, "won't be under the rubble when the churches collapse" (71,F,19):

> Churches topple
> Like the temples before them.
>
> The reverberations of worship
> Seem to help
> Collapse such erections.
>
> In all that time
> The river
> Has deepened its defile
> Has been its own purification
>
> Between your breasts
>
> Between your thighs. (G,190)

While such pun-riddled symbolism seems to be new in Hughes' poetry, the speaker's wish to become one of the goddess's warriors invokes his fellow champions amongst plants and animals familiar from earlier poems such as "Thistles" or "Crow Hill" (L,14;W,17):

> The grim badger with armorial mask
> Biting spade-steel, teeth and jaw-strake shattered,
> Draws that final shuddering battle cry
> Out of its backbone.
>
> Me too,
> Let me be one of your warriors. (G,189-90)

Yet though she may grant his wishes, the goddess, being everywhere and in everything, remains ultimately aloof and unfathomable. "Looking for her form," the speaker only finds "fern." "Trying to be a leaf" in her kingdom, her very fullness makes him reel back

> Like the electrocuted man
> Banged from his burst straps. (G,180,192)

In several ways these invocations of the goddess continue or at least parallel Lumb's previous adventures. As the baboon woman in the underworld embraced the vicar, "Her grip . . . cutting into his body like wires" (G,105), so the goddess when questioned about her identity, grabs the speaker,

> So the blood jumps into my teeth
>
> And 'Quick!' you whisper, 'O quick!'
> And 'Now! Now! Now!'
>
> Now what?
>
> That I hear the age of the earth?
>
> That I feel
> My mother lift me up from between her legs? (G,177)

The sequence's very opening poem seems to describe the creature Lumb has become through his failure,—a "veteran of negatives," "the survivor of cease" (G,176). And there is enough to recall the victimization of women Lumb brought about in the dabbling mismanagement of his mission. Again and again we meet the suffering, desecrated or dead representatives of the female divinity worshipped by the speaker. While the latter is taking "a few still-aimless happy steps," feeling "the sun's strength," there is "some female groaning" behind him in a cave, "In labour—/Or in hunger—/Or in fear, or sick, or forsaken—." Or suddenly he hears a screech and running to help finds "The woman who wore a split lopsided mask—" (G,178,181).

Other poems seem to transcend the story of Lumb's misfortunes. The vicar, at least in some of his traits, can be seen as the poet's ironical self-portrait. In the Epilogue lyrics this resemblance is even closer, the speaker, unlike the bald-headed Lumb, being more than once described as grey-haired. Most personal perhaps is the following poem about a dead beloved woman in the morgue.

> It was the third time. And it smashed.
>
> I turned
> I bowed
> In the morgue I kissed
> Your temple's refrigerated glazed
> As rained-on graveyard marble, my
> Lips queasy, heart non-existent
>
> And straightened
> Into sun-darkness
>
> Like a pillar over Athens
>
> Defunct
>
> In the glaring metropolis of cameras. (G,186)[7]

When I expressed surprise at the confessional nature of the *Gaudete* lyrics, Hughes referred me to their triple source. One is a collection of South Indian *vacanas* or devotional lyrics in free verse translated by A. K. Ramanujan and first published in 1973.[8] To be sure, influence here, as in the case of primitive poetry, meant recreating what was found to be congenial rather than borrowing individual lines or images. But the basic resemblances between the Dravidian *vacanas* and Hughes' *Gaudete* lyrics are obvious enough. Their common devotion as addressed to a divinity—whether Śiva or a nameless goddess—is intensely personal, willing to share its ecstasies with animals and plants rather than with confederates of an organized religion. And rather than bestowing gifts of grace, prosperity or righteousness, the deity responds by annihilating the worshipper.

> He bartered my heart,
> looted my flesh,
> claimed as tribute
> my pleasure,
> took over
> all of me.[9]

Like the author of this poem, twelfth-century poetess Mahādevī, the speaker of Hughes' lyrics feels that all he has "For an axle/Is your needle/ Through my brains"; he is reduced to an outcast in worshipping her ("Now I lie at the road's edge./People come and go./Dogs watch me.") or undergoes total self-transformation:

> Where I lay in space
> Is the print of the earth which trampled me
>
> Like a bunch of grapes.
>
> Now I am being drunk
> By a singing drunkard.   (G,179,193)

Hughes particularly admires the *vacanas* of Allama Prabhu, and, like these, his own poems combine a straightforward spontaneity of basic statement with a studied allusiveness of puns, conceits and allegories. Even in translation, the *vacanas*, like the *Gaudete* lyrics, can be seen to exploit another, linguistic contrast, resulting in a "quickening of etymologies." Played off against the Dravidian Kannada, Sanskrit words and names in the *vacanas* become "double-faced . . . by etymological recovery."[10] But long before Hughes had a chance to learn such tricks from A. K. Ramanujan's introduction in order to use them in *Gaudete* (e.g. "I hear your congregations at their rapture/Cries from birds, long ago perfect/And from the awkward gullets of beasts/That will not chill into syntax," G,176), he had analysed a similar "dialect instinct" in Shakespeare,—

> the instinct to misuse latinisms, but in an inspired way. This is really a primitive, unconscious but highly accurate punning. A familiar example would be the notorious "aggravate." In its vulgar use, this means "to goad beyond endurance," which is not merely a Joycean fusion of irritate, anger, exaggerate, but a much deeper short circuit to the concrete Anglo-Saxon "gr" core of growl, grind, eager, grief, grate etc. The word inherits a much more powerful meaning by this wrenching misuse in English than by its precise use in its Latin sense.   (71,S,11)

Another source of inspiration for the *Gaudete* lyrics is more personal. As Hughes told me in 1977, he first read Ramanujan's translations after suffering from a chronically sore throat for about a year. Suspecting that he might have cancer,

> I began to write these *vacanas* as little prayers—about a hundred of them, some of which will be published in *Orts*. And then, when I was shaping up *Gaudete*, I realised there should be something at the end and that this sort of poem would be ideal if I could write it in the right context.

This context, the third source of inspiration, which brought the other two to a focus, was provided by the poet's dreams.

The poem about the dream which Hughes dreamt about once a week during childhood and adolescence seems to best spell out the story of this amalgamation process. It is natural enough that the poet's fears of death should bring back this nightmare about a crashing plane transmogrified into a fantasy animal slamming into the earth beside the dreamer and knocking him off his feet. And how closely does its description (quoted above on pages 121-122) resemble the surrealist cryptographies in the following *vacana* by Allama Prabhu!

> When the toad
> swallowed the sky,
> look, Rāhu
> the serpent mounted
> and wonder of wonders!
> the blind man
> caught the snake.
>
> Thus, O Lord,
> I learned
> without telling the world.[11]

Even closer are the resemblances between the two poems' overall import. Like most of its genre, Allama's little *vacana* is a description of enlightenment, decipherable with reference to a system of allegorical exegesis as surrealistically elaborate as the poem's actual imagery.

> The sky is the soul, the toad is the life-breath in its highest centre (*brahmarandra*); Rāhu the cosmic serpent . . . is the serpent-path that winds through the body's centres (*cakras*) awakened by yoga.[12]

Hughes' poem cannot be explicated by relation to a similar framework of reference. And it certainly does not take the speaker all the way towards enlightenment. Despite their message of hope, its concluding lines, all of which, Hughes told me, reflects a single dream, remain within the phantasmagorical realm of the unconscious or *sambhoga-kāya*:

> I stirred, like a discarded foetus,
> Already grey-haired,
> In a blowing of bright particles.
>
> A hand out of a hot cloud
> Held me its thumb to suck.
>
> Lifted me to the dug that grew
> Out of the brow of a lioness. (G,188)

Yet what these and other images from the *Gaudete* poems share with Allama's, points to more than their common source in the collective unconscious. They may also show that Hughes, following the new lodestar of mystical visionaries, is about to extricate himself from his one-sided commitment to the primitive or what Jung described as primitive man's enslavement by the phantasmagoria of the unconscious.[13] Here is another *vacana*, recalling the above *Gaudete* lyric, about "the last stages of the process of enlightenment. The wind is the devotee's life-breath; the sky, the soul; the lullabies are the words *śivōham śivōham*, 'I am Śiva, I am Śiva.'"

> The wind sleeps
> to lullabies of sky.
>
> Space drowses,
> infinity gives it suck
> from her breast.
>
> The sky is silent.
> The lullaby is over.
>
> The Lord is
> as if He were not.[14]

Both Lumb's story and the lyrics present an unprecedented new stage in Hughes' artistic development. Yet only the poems mark a simultaneous advance in the poet's spiritual growth. To put it in other and perhaps more precise terms: if Lumb suggests certain traits of the poet himself, then the poems, as composed by his double, express the insights of a man who has suffered spiritual death. So it is possible that Hughes may arrive at an answer to the "cruel riddle" (71,S,182) which he believes—I think erroneously—Shakespeare did not solve. And the answer may well turn out to be one similar to that implied in Shakespeare's romances with their repeated celebration of a rebirth into life enjoyed in its here and now as expressed in the words Florizel addresses to his beloved:

> When you do dance, I wish you
> A wave o' th' sea, that you might ever do
> Nothing but that—move still, still so,
> And own no other function. Each your doing,
> So singular in each particular,
> Crowns what you are doing in the present deeds,
> That all your acts are queens.
>
> (*The Winter's Tale*, IV, iv, 140-6)

Since the last chapter was completed in the spring of 1978, Hughes has published several further volumes. The most important are *Cave Birds*, the reworking of a volume first published in 1975 and subtitled *An Alchemical Cave Drama* (London: Faber and Faber, 1978); *The Remains of Elmet* (London: Faber and Faber, 1979) with poems about his native Yorkshire; and *Moortown* (London: Faber and Faber, 1979) containing Hughes' verse journal of his experiences farming in Devon plus three further sequences, *Prometheus on His Crag*, *Earth-numb* (with the sub-section *Orts*), and *Adam and the Sacred Nine*. None of these books marks a radical new departure but *Cave Birds*, perhaps for that very reason, represents an unprecedented summing up of Hughes' development and achievement to date.

Much of the book sounds only too familiar. One poem, addressed to the "shyest bird among birds," sitting in its nest among the bones (CB,38), in both tone and diction, reads like a companion piece to "Littleblood" (C,84). Another parallels Wodwo's anxious questioning of the world:

> Where am I going? What will come to me here?
> Is this everlasting? Is it
> Stoppage and the start of nothing?
>
> Or am I under attention?
> Do purposeful cares incubate me? (CB,34)

More importantly, the general scenario—an apocalyptic world of evolutionary collapse in which the protagonist is put on trial by an assembly of birds—recalls the heretical inversions of Judaeo-Christian cosmology in *Crow*. Equally familiar are some of the major themes: the insufficiency of humanitarianism when faced with life's basic cruelty, silence and acceptance as the only valid stance towards the world, and the ineluctable guilt of man—

> His heart—
> The soul-stuffed despot.
>
> His stomach—
> The corpse-eating god.
>
> And his hard life-lust—the blind
> Swan of insemination.
>
> And his hard brain—the sacred assassin. (CB,24)

Also well-known from Hughes' verse, at least since *Recklings* (1966), are the main forms and poetic strategies: the surrealist fables, semi-allegorical parables and gnomic riddles; the epic similes, fairy tale-like openings and neo-primitive variations in repetition; or the pun-riddled symbols, violently metaphorical adjuncts (e.g., "The carapace/Of foreclosure./The cuticle/Of final arrest." CB,8) and semi-mythical aphorisms (as in the poem about the knight whose "spine survives its religion" while the "sun /Strengthens its revelation." CB,28).

But in its overall impact *Cave Birds* differs from the previous collections. Survival, Crow's hard won reward after bitter struggles, has turned into a certitude guaranteed by reincarnation. And its oracles are mythic creatures like the "green mother" or the protagonist's alchemical bride ("A riddle," CB,44),—the first female voices in Hughes' poetry to speak in tones other than of anguish and lamentation:

> Why are you afraid?
> In the house of the dead are many cradles.
> The earth is a busy hive of heavens.
>
> .   .   .   .
>
> I am your guide.
>
> ("A green mother," CB,40,41)

Cave Birds, in this way, fuses hitherto separate modes of creativity in Hughes' career. In his previous work, the critical writings and children's books often suggested solutions which his deepest poetic visions seemed to deny him. *The Iron Man*, for instance, inverts the "neurotic-making dynamics" (70,M,55) of its Judaeo-Christian archetype (the monster slain by the hero) with the result of integrating what is customarily repressed. "Crow's Account of St. George," by contrast, merely shows how such repression leads to self-destruction.[1] To recall another example, whereas Hughes' 1970 review of Max Nicholson's *The Environmental Revolution* draws attention to "the re-emergence of Nature as the Great Goddess of mankind" (70,N,83), Lumb's efforts to revive her worship in *Gaudete* end in total disaster.[2] *Cave Birds* for the first time seems to bridge that rift.

While clearly stemming from the same source as *Wodwo*, *Crow* and *Gaudete*, the new volume has the more optimistic bent and conclusively articulated vision of Hughes' critical prose and writings for children. In fact, no previous collection reflects the poet's central saga of the quester's descent into the underworld to save his desecrated bride more directly than *Cave Birds*. And in part, this journey amounts to a self-critical retracing of Hughes' poetic adventures and explorations since his beginnings. Whoever he is—a human being or a bird-like half-beast as in Baskin's illustrations—the speaker of the opening poem at first sounds remarkably like the roosting hawk in *Lupercal*:

And the inane weights of iron
That come suddenly crashing into people, out of nowhere,
Only made me feel brave and creaturely.

When I saw little rabbits with their heads crushed on roads
I knew I rode the wheel of the galaxy. (CB,7)

But seconds later, he chokes on his own bravado, until he learns to feel guilt and to keep silence (CB,10). Unlike Crow, he quickly finds comfort in his desolation with a nameless "she" who "seemed so considerate" (CB,14). But the worst is still to come. "Something was happening" (CB,31), like several previous poems in Hughes' *oeuvre*, describes the death of a beloved woman. But before long, her mythic counterpart, who subsequently becomes the quester's bride, is reborn. As in "Crow's Undersong," the eternal Feminine, lost since the teenaged poet's address to the Lady of "Song" (H,19), has come back.

> After there was nothing there was a woman
>
> .   .   .   .
>
> Whose breasts had come about
> By long toil of earthworms
> After many failures, but they were here now
> And she protected them with silk
>
> .   .   .   .
>
> She had made it but only just, just—(CB,48)

Readers familiar with "Lovesong" will not be surprised to find that this is followed by a sexual scene closely resembling the earlier poem in its violence and intensity (CB,52 cf. C,76-7). But *Cave Birds* takes the decisive step beyond this point reached in *Crow* and makes real what in the baboon woman episode of *Gaudete* remains an event in the world of dream. The new volume carries its subtitle for a good reason. For its central piece, "Bride and groom lie hidden for three days,"[3] is the fulfilment of a quest which started with Hughes' attempt, shortly after Sylvia Plath's death, to write a verse drama adaptation of *The Chemical Wedding of Christian Rosencreutz*, Andreae's seventeenth century Hermetic narrative about how *sponsus* and *sponsa* become each other's saviors through their union:

> She gives him his eyes, she found them
> Among some rubble, among some beetles
>
> He gives her her skin
> He just seemed to pull it down out of the air and lay
>   it over her
> She weeps with fearfulness and astonishment

. . . .

So, gasping with joy, with cries of wonderment
Like two gods of mud
Sprawling in the dirt, but with infinite care

They bring each other to perfection. (CB,56)

Hughes explains how the poem relates to "Lovesong."[4] Coming to a river, Crow encounters a monstrous Ogress who gets him to carry her through the water. But as they cross, her weight increases driving Crow deeper and deeper into the riverbed until he is near drowning. Then she asks him seven questions which he must answer correctly if her weight is to decrease again. While Crow's answers move from one pole of total disaster in the relationship with the female to the opposite pole of successful, blissful union, the Ogress on his back turns into a beauty before suddenly escaping into the oak forest on the other side of the river, a happy land, in which she eventually becomes his bride.[5] "Lovesong" is one of Crow's earlier answers to the question: "Who paid most, him or her?" "Bride and groom lie hidden for three days" answers a later question: "Who gives most, him or her?" But whatever its function in the original story, the poem, in the way it is placed in *Cave Birds,* clearly anticipates the positive conclusion of the entire quest and perhaps the direction of Hughes' work in future years.

Abbreviated References
for Writings by Ted Hughes

ABBREVIATED REFERENCES FOR WRITINGS

BY TED HUGHES

I. BOOKS (in alphabetical order)

C	*Crow.* New York: Harper & Row, 1971.
CB	*Cave Birds. An Alchemical Cave Drama.* London: Faber and Faber, 1978
EC	*Eat Crow.* London: Rainbow Press, 1971.
G	*Gaudete.* London: Faber and Faber, 1977.
H	*The Hawk in the Rain.* London: Faber and Faber, 1957.
L	*Lupercal.* London: Faber and Faber, 1960.
O	*Seneca's Oedipus.* Adapted by Ted Hughes. Garden City, N.Y.: Doubleday, 1972.
P	*Poetry in the Making.* London: Faber and Faber, 1967.
Po	*Poems — Ruth Fainlight, Ted Hughes, Alan Sillitoe.* London: Rainbow Press, 1971.
Pr	*Prometheus on His Crag.* London: Rainbow Press, 1973.
R	*Recklings.* London: Turret Books, 1966.
SP	*Selected Poems 1957-1962.* London: Faber and Faber, 1972.
W	*Wodwo.* London: Faber and Faber, 1967.
Wh	*How the Whale Became.* London: Faber and Faber, 1963.

II. CRITICAL ESSAYS, INTERVIEWS, REVIEWS etc.
(in chronological order)

57,H*	"Ted Hughes Writes." *Poetry Book Society Bulletin,* 15 (September 1957).
61,A	Review of Joy Adamson. *Living Free,* etc., *New Statesman,* 62 (10 November 1961), p. 712.

147

62,B*   Review of C. M. Bowra. *Primitive Song. Listener*, 67 (3 May 1962), p. 781.

62,Ba*   Introduction. *Leonard Baskin Catalogue.* 1962.

62,C*   "Context." *London Magazine*, 1, 11 (February 1962), pp. 44-45.

62,D*   "The Poetry of Keith Douglas." *Listener*, 67 (21 June 1962), pp. 1069-71.

62,J   Review of S. P. Johnson. *Everyman's Ark. New Statesman*, 64 (9 November 1962), p. 666.

63,D*   "The Poetry of Keith Douglas." *Critical Quarterly*, 5 (1963), pp. 43-48.

63,Di*   Review of C. R. Anderson. *Emily Dickinson's Poetry. Listener* 70 (12 September 1963), p. 394.

63,H   Introduction. *Here Today.* London: Hutchinson, 1963.

63,O   Review of Philip O'Connor. *Vagrancy. New Statesman*, 66 (9 August 1963), pp. 293-294.

63,S   Review of Keigo Seki, ed. *Folktales of Japan*, etc., *Listener*, 70 (12 December 1963), p. 999.

64,D   Introduction & Biographical Note. Keith Douglas. *Selected Poems.* London: Faber and Faber, 1964.

64,E*   Review of Mircea Eliade. *Shamanism. Listener*, 72 (29 October 1964), pp. 677-678.

64,M*   Review of Louis MacNeice. *Astrology.* etc., *New Statesman*, 68 (2 October 1964), p. 500.

64,S   Review of Snorri Sturluson. *The Prose Edda.* Translated by Lee M. Hollander, etc., *New York Review of Books*, 3, 10 (31 December 1964), pp. 6-7.

64,T*   Review of F. D. G. Turville-Petre. *Myth and Religion of the North. Listener*, 71 (19 March 1964), pp. 484-485.

64,W*   Review of Patrick White. *Voss. Listener*, 71 (6 February 1964), pp. 229-230.

65,G*   Review of John Greenway. *Literature Among the Primitives*, etc., *New York Review of Books*, 5, 9 (9 December 1965), pp. 33-35.

65,H   Interview with John Horder. *Guardian* (23 March 1965).

65,P*   "Sylvia Plath," *Poetry Book Society Bulletin,* 44 (February 1965).

65,Pa   Review of I.M. Parsons, ed. *Men Who March Away. Poems of the First World War. Listener,* 74 (5 August 1965), p. 200.

65,S*   "The Genius of Isaac Bashevis Singer." *New York Review of Books,* 4, 6 (22 April 1965), pp. 8-10.

66,P*   "Notes on the Chronological Order of Sylvia Plath's Poems." *Tri-Quarterly,* 7 (Fall 1966), pp. 81-88.

66,T*   Review of C. Fitzgibbon, ed., *The Selected Letters of Dylan Thomas, New Statesman,* 72 (25 November 1966), p. 783.

67,P*   "Vasko Popa." *Tri-Quarterly,* 9 (Spring 1967), pp. 201-205.

68,L   "Lore Abiding." *New Statesman,* 75 (24 May 1968), pp. 699-700.

68,D*   Introduction. *A Choice of Emily Dickinson's Verse.* London: Faber and Faber, 1968.

70,M   "Myth and Education." *Children's Literature in Education* 1 (1970), pp. 55-70.

70,N*   Review of Max Nicholson. *The Environmental Revolution. Your Environment* 1, 3 (Summer 1970), pp. 81-83.

71,F*   "Ted Hughes and Crow. An Interview with Ekbert Faas." *London Magazine* 10, 10 (January 1971), pp. 5-20.

71,O*   "Orghast: Talking Without Words." *Vogue* (December 1971).

71,P   "Sylvia Plath's *Crossing the Water*: Some Reflections." *Critical Quarterly* 13, 2 (Summer 1971), pp. 165-172.

71,S   Introduction & Note. *A Choice of Shakespeare's Verse.* London: Faber and Faber, 1971.

76,M*   "Myth and Education." *Writers, Critics, and Children,* ed. Geoff Fox etc., New York: Agathon Press, 1976, pp. 77-94.

76,P*   Introduction. János Pilinszky. *Selected Poems*. Translated by
            Ted Hughes & János Csokits. Manchester: Carcanet
            New Press, 1977.

77,P   Introduction. Sylvia Plath. *Johnny Panic and the Bible of
            Dreams and other prose writings*. London: Faber and
            Faber, 1977.

---

*Item reprinted in whole or in part in Appendix I or II below.

Notes

NOTES

A Personal Pre-Preface

1 *London Magazine*, 10, 10 (January 1971), pp. 5-20.

2 *Towards a New American Poetics: Essays & Interviews, Charles Olson, Robert Duncan, Gary Snyder, Robert Creeley, Robert Bly and Allen Ginsberg* (Santa Barbara: Black Sparrow Press, 1978), p. 32.

PREFACE

1 See Shakespeare, *King Lear. A Casebook*, ed. F. Kermode (London: Macmillan, 1969), pp. 36, 44.

2 See Hegel, *On Tragedy*, ed. A. and H. Paolucci (New York: Harper & Row, 1975), p. 135.

3 See *Shakespeare Our Contemporary* (London: Methuen, 1965), p. 116.

4 A full account of their relationship has yet to be given. Margaret Dickie Uroff, in a somewhat disappointing study *Sylvia Plath and Ted Hughes* (Urbana, Ill.; University of Illinois Press, 1979), gives us little more than parallels between the poets' works. While claiming that the "direction of [her] study is provided by Hughes' comment that influences open new prospects," Uroff curiously ignores the poet's warning that "the influences that really count are most likely not literary at all." (Quoted approvingly on p. 8.)

5 *The Spirit in Man, Art, and Literature*. Bollingen Series XX (Princeton, N.J.: Princeton University Press, 1972), p. 73.

I. ORIGINS

1 From an unpublished essay on Laura Riding of 1970; see below, pp. 188-9.

2 *On Poetry and Poets* (London: Faber and Faber, 1969), p. 211.

3 "The H.D. Book," II, 2. *Caterpillar*, 6 (January 1969), pp. 16-38, 17.

4 See *America a Prophecy. A New Reading of American Poetry from Pre-Columbian Times to the Present*, ed. J. Rothenberg and G. Quasha (New York: Random House, 1974), p. xxx.

5 *Modern Poetry in Translation*, ed. Ted Hughes and Daniel Weissbort, No. 1 (November 1965).

6 See A. C. H. Smith, *Orghast at Persepolis* (New York: The Viking Press, 1973), p. 108.

7 See *The Special View of History*, ed. Ann Charters (Berkeley: Oyez, 1970), pp. 33, 39.

8 See Faas, *New American Poetics*, pp. 91, 118.

9 *On Aggression* (London: Methuen, 1970), p. x.

10 See *New Statesman*, 63 (23 March 1962), 420-421

11 "Interview," *Road Apple Review*, I, 4 and II, 1 (Winter 1969– Spring 1970), pp. 59-68, 59.

12 "Interview," pp. 64, 67-8.

13 See Heinrich Zimmer, *Philosophies of India*, ed. J. Campbell, Bollingen Series XXVI (Princeton, N.J.: Princeton University Press, 1971), p. 598 and passim.

14 D. T. Suzuki's paraphrase of *śūnyatā* in *Mysticism: Christian and Buddhist*. World Perspectives. Volume Twelve. Planned and edited by R. N. Anshen (Westport, Conn.: Greenwood Press, 1975), p. 28.

15 *Le théâtre et son double* (Paris: Gallimard, 1964), p. 155.

16 See Smith, *Orghast*, pp. 93, 94, 95.

17 From an unpublished review of *The God Beneath the Sea* by Leon Garfield and Edward Blishen.

18 See Smith, *Orghast*, p. 96, 97.

19 *Orpheus, Listening and Writing* (Spring 1971), pp. 1-23, 20, 21, 23.

II. POETICS

1 From a letter to the author received on August 23, 1977.

2 See 71,F,14.

3 *Observer*, March 27, 1960.

4 See J. J. Y. Liu, *Chinese Theories of Literature* (Chicago: University of Chicago Press, 1975), p. 73. For the following see also Faas, *New American Poetics*, pp. 9ff.

5 *Complete Works: Selected Letters (English and French)*, ed. W. Fowlie (Chicago: University of Chicago Press, 1966), pp. 303-309.

6 See S. Bush, *The Chinese Literati on Painting. Su Shih (1037-1101) to Tung Ch'i-Ch'ang (1555-1636)*: Harvard-Yenching Institute Studies XXVII (Cambridge, Mass.: Harvard University Press, 1971), p. 56.

7   *The Letters*, ed. M. B. Forman (London: Oxford University Press, 1952), p. 107.

8   See Makoto Ueda, *Zeami, Basho, Yeats, Pound. A Study in Japanese and English Poetics.* Studies in General and Comparative Literature, vol. I (The Hague: Mouton, 1965), pp. 39, 52-53.

9   See O. Sirén, *The Chinese on the Art of Painting* (New York: Schocken Books, 1971), pp. 21-22.

10   *Selected Literary Criticism*, ed. A. Beal (New York: Viking Press, 1956), p. 87.

11   Ueda, *Zeami, Bashō, Yeats, Pound*, p. 38.

12   See *Selected Writings*, ed. R. Creeley (New York: New Directions, 1966), p. 25.

13   See Sylvia Plath, *Letters Home. Correspondence 1950-63*, ed. Aurelia Schober Plath (New York: Bantam Books, 1977), pp. 302, 303, 352, 394.

14   *A Course of Instruction of Magic Theory and Practise* (Wuppertal: Dieter Ruggeberg, 1971), pp. 76, 77, 291.

15   *Laṅkāvatāra-sūtra*, A Buddhist Bible, ed. D. Goddard (Boston: Beacon Press, 1970), p. 300.

16   See *The Tibetan Book of the Dead*, ed. W. Y. Evans-Wentz. With Psychological Commentary by C. G. Jung (London: Oxford University Press, 1960), p. xlix.

17   *The Tibetan Book of the Great Liberation*, ed. W. Y. Evans-Wentz. With Psychological Commentary by Dr. C. G. Jung (London: Oxford University Press, 1972), p. 1.

18   See, for instance, Ueda, *Zeami, Basho, Yeats, Pound*, p. 25, or Chang Chung-yuan, *Creativity and Taoism. A Study of Chinese Philosophy, Art, and Poetry* (New York: Harper & Row, 1970), p. 16.

19   See Liu, *Chinese Theories of Literature*, pp. 69, 114.

20   Chang Chung-yuan, *Creativity and Taoism*, p. 87.

21   See *Anthology of Chinese Literature*, ed. C. Birch (New York: Grove Press, 1967), pp. 205-6

22   Olson, *Selected Writings*, p. 28.

23   *Philosophical Investigations* (New York: Macmillan, 1968), p. 47e.

24   See Chang Chung-yuan, *Creativity and Taoism*, pp. 43-4.

25   *Prosa*, 4 vols. (Frankfurt am Main: S. Fischer, 1952-9), II, 12.

26   "Laura Riding," see above, chapter I, note 1.

27   Ibid.

28   See, for instance, Keith Sagar, *The Art of Ted Hughes* (Cambridge: Cambridge University Press, 1975), pp. 123ff.

29   *Language, Thought, and Reality. Selected Writings*, ed. J. B. Carrol (Cambridge, Mass.: Massachusetts Institute of Technology Press, 1964), passim.

30   *The Chinese Written Character as a Medium for Poetry*, ed. E. Pound (San Francisco: City Lights Books, 1968), p. 21.

31   *Apocalypse* (London: Heinemann, 1972), p. 45.

32   *Human Universe and Other Essays*, ed. D. Allen (New York: Grove Press, 1967), p. 18.

33   See Smith, *Orghast*, p. 51.

34   *Selected Writings*, p. 18; also see Fenollosa, *Chinese Written Character*, p. 15.

35   See Geoffrey Reeves, "The Persepolis Follies of 1971," *Performance* I (December 1971), pp. 47-71, 64.

36   *Le théâtre*, pp. 181-2.

37   See Smith, *Orghast*, pp. 42, 180.

38   See Reeves, "The Persepolis Follies," p. 66.

39   See Smith, *Orghast*, p. 43.

40   "Interview," *Spectrum*, 21, 34 (20 November 1970), p. 12.

41   See Smith, *Orghast*, p. 210.

42   See Frances A. Yates, *Giordano Bruno and the Hermetic Tradition* (New York: Random House, 1969), pp. 28, 266.

43   See H. C. Berendt, *Parapsychologie* (Stuttgart: W. Kohlhammer, 1972), pp. 77ff.

44   See Fritjof Capra, *The Tao of Physics* (Bungay, Suffolk: Fontana, 1976), p. 16.

III. BEGINNINGS

1   From an unpublished BBC interview with Peter Orr, "The Poet Speaks," XVI, Tape No. 527, British Council, 1963.

2   *Complete Writings*, ed. Geoffrey Keynes (London: Oxford University Press, 1969), pp. 155, 156.

3   "To J. H. Reynolds, Esq.," *Poetical Works*, ed. H. W. Garrod (London: Oxford University Press, 1959), p. 383.

4   *Pour un nouveau roman* (Paris: Gallimard, 1963), p. 21.

5 See *The Art of Sylvia Plath*, ed. Charles Newman (Bloomington, Ind.: Indiana University Press, 1970), pp. 183-184.

6 Sagar, *Ted Hughes*, p. 22.

7 *Selected Essays* (London: Faber and Faber, 1966), p. 286.

8 *Spectator*, October 11, 1957.

9 *London Magazine* 8, 3 (March 1961), p. 21.

10 In conversation with the author.

11 From unpublished BBC interviews of 1963; see above, note 1.

12 See above, page 40.

13 *The Spirit in Man*, p. 90.

14 *The Spirit in Man*, p. 82.

IV. TOWARDS CROW

1 *Audience* 8, 2 (Spring 1961), pp. 77-105, 99.

2 See Thomas S. Szasz, *The Manufacture of Madness. A Comparative Study of the Inquisition and the Mental Health Movement* (New York: Dell, 1970), p. 73.

3 *Women and Madness* (Garden City, N.Y.: Doubleday, 1972), pp. 114-132.

4 *Letters Home*, p. 129.

5 See E. Butscher, *Sylvia Plath: Method and Madness* (New York: Simon and Schuster, 1977), pp. 112, 122.

6 *Letters Home*, p. 143.

7 Thomas S. Szasz, ed., *The Age of Madness. The History of Involuntary Mental Hospitalization Presented in Selected Texts* (Garden City, N.Y.: Doubleday, 1973), pp. 316-317.

8 *The Colossus* (London: Faber and Faber, 1968), pp. 87-88.

9 *Ariel* (London: Faber and Faber, 1968), pp. 18, 55-56; see also pp. 14-15, 70.

10 *Letters Home*, p. 145.

11 *Tibetan Book of the Dead*, p. XLIX.

12 See below, p. 85.

13 *London Magazine* 8, 3 (March 1961), pp. 20-21.

14 See Sagar, *Ted Hughes*, p. 161.

15 Frances A. Yates, *The Rosicrucian Enlightenment* (Frogmore, St. Albans, Herts.: Granada Publishing, 1975), p. 97.

16   Parts of it in July 1965, in *Encounter*, the entire sequence in 1971, in a Rainbow Press limited edition.

17   The poem underwent slight changes before it was republished in *Wodwo*. See above, p. 46.

18   *Pour un nouveau roman*, p. 160.

V. CROW

1   *The Dial* 75 (July-December 1923), p. 483.

2   See liner notes for *Crow*, Dublin: Claddagh Records CCT 9-10, 1973.

3   See *Crow*, Claddagh Records.

4   See "Ted Hughes's Crow," *Listener*, 84 (30 July 1970), p. 149.

5   *Towards a Poor Theatre* (New York: Simon and Schuster, 1968), p. 22.

6   See Sagar, *Ted Hughes*, p. 107.

7   *Primitive Song* (New York: The World Publishing Company, 1962), p. 80.

8   *Primitive Song*, pp. 79-80.

9   Alexander Carmichael, ed. *Carmina Gadelica. Hymns and Incantations*, 6 vols. (Edinburgh: Oliver and Boyd, 1941), IV, 365.

10   See above, p. 98.

11   See Suzuki, *Mysticism*, p. 28.

12   See above, p. 82f.

13   See Sagar, *Ted Hughes*, p. 107.

14   See M. Eliade, *Shamanism. Archaic Techniques of Ecstasy*, Bollingen Series LXXVI. (Princeton, N.J.: Princeton University Press, 1972), pp. 71ff., 80f.

15   See *Crow*, Claddagh Records.

16   See above, pp. 18, 46-7.

17   For this and the following see Smith, *Orghast*, pp. 93ff., 97.

VI. GAUDETE

1   See Smith, *Orghast*, p. 94.

2   See W,151: "Out through the dark archway of earth, under the ancient lintel overwritten with roots/Out between the granite jambs, gallops the hooded horseman of iron."

3 In conversation, September 1, 1977.

4 In conversation, August 1977, see below, p. 214.

5 In conversation, August 1977.

6 Ed. A. C. Bhaktivedanta Swami Prabhupãda (New York: Macmillan, 1972), p. 558.

7 Compare A. Alvarez' description of Sylvia Plath in *The Savage God. A Study of Suicide* (Harmondsworth: Penguin Books, 1975), p. 56.

8 *Speaking of Śiva*, (Harmondsworth: Penguin Books, 1973).

9 *Speaking of Śiva*, p. 125.

10 *Speaking of Śiva*, p. 47.

11 *Speaking of Śiva*, p. 154.

12 *Speaking of Śiva*, p. 197.

13 See "Archaic Man," *Collected Works*, 19 vols., ed. H. Read, M. Fordham, G. Adler (New York: Pantheon Books, 1953), IX, 50-73.

14 *Speaking of Śiva*, pp. 164, 199.

Postscript

1 See above, pp. 79-80, 105-106.

2 See above, p. 18.

3 First published in Sagar, *Ted Hughes*, pp. 167-168.

4 In conversation, September 1, 1977.

5 See below, p. 213.

Appendix I.
Excerpts from Ted Hughes' Critical Writings

APPENDIX I:
EXCERPTS FROM TED HUGHES' CRITICAL WRITINGS

Ted Hughes Writes . . . (1957)

. . . In each poem, besides the principal subject—and in my poems this is usually pretty easy to see, as, for instance, the jaguar in the poem called "The Jaguar"—there is what is not so easy to talk about, even generally, but which is the living and individual element in every poet's work. What I mean is the way he brings to peace all the feelings and energies which, from all over the body, heart, and brain, send up their champions onto the battleground of that first subject. The way I do this, as I believe, is by using something like the method of a musical composer. I might say that I turn every combatant into a bit of music, then resolve the whole uproar into as formal and balanced a figure of melody and rhythm as I can. When all the words are hearing each other clearly, and every stress is feeling every other stress, and all are contented—the poem is finished . . .

. . . .

There is a great mass of English poetry in which the musical element—the inner figure of stresses—is not so important as other elements. To me—no matter what metaphysical persuasion or definable philosophy a poem may seem to subscribe to—what is unique and precious in it is its heart, that inner figure of stresses . . . (57,H)

Context (1962)

The poet's only hope is to be infinitely sensitive to what his gift is, and this in itself seems to be another gift that few poets possess. According to this sensitivity, and to his faith in it, he will go on developing as a poet, as Yeats did, pursuing those adventures, mental, spiritual and physical, whatever they may be, that his gift wants, or he will lose its guidance, lose the feel of its touch in the workings of his mind, and soon be absorbed by the impersonal dead lumber of matters in which his gift has no interest, which is a form of suicide, metaphorical in the case of Wordsworth and Coleridge, actual in the case of Mayakovsky.

Many considerations assault his faith in the finality, wisdom and sufficiency of his gift. Its operation is not only shadowy and indefinable, it is intermittent, it has none of the obvious attachment to publicly exciting and seemingly important affairs that his other mental activities have and in which all his intelligent contemporaries have such confidence, and so it receives no immediate encouragement—or encouragement only of the most dubious kind, as a flagellant, questioning his illuminations, might be encouraged by a bunch of mad old women and some other half-dead gory flagellant; it visits him when he is only half suspecting it, and he is not sure it has visited him until some days or months afterwards and perhaps he never can be sure, being a sensible man aware of the examples of earlier poets and of the devils of self-delusion and of the delusions of whole generations.

Wordsworth himself is an example of both the true poet and the false, the man trusting his gift and producing the real thing, and the man searching for his satisfaction among more popular and public causes. And his living poetry is a good example of how the greatness and even the timely significance of poetry depends on qualities of depth, breadth, intensity and accent in the spirit of it, rather than in reference to many matters.

The important issues of the two decades following the French Revolution were, in England, overwhelmingly social and political, one would say. Wordsworth and Coleridge and Blake were the great poets of that time, in English, and were as involved, intellectually, in those issues as anybody well could be, but that seems to have had very little to do, directly, with their poetry. From their surviving poetry alone one might suspect Wordsworth would have done better to leave his mountains and broaden his mind somewhat on life, that Coleridge ought to have wakened up to his time and come out of the dark ages and away from those fogs of the South Pole of all places, that Blake needed friends of a more worldly and liberal conversation. This flower, this little girl, this bird, this old man paddling in a pool, this boat-stealing and woodcock-snaring, these soul-notes of a mountain-watcher, and these magical damsels in a magical forest and this dream flight with a dead bird, and these angels and black boys and roses and briars, all this infatuation with infancy and innocence, what did these have to do with the great issues of the time? Nothing whatsoever, till the spirit that worked through Wordsworth and Coleridge and Blake chose them for its parables. And looking back now, if we wish to see the important issues of those two decades, we see nothing so convincing and enlightening to so many of us, as the spirit which seems to touch us openly and speak to us directly through these poems.

Damon, quoted by Plato, says that the modes of music are nowhere altered without changes in the most important laws of the state. Is a musician to listen to his gift then, or study legislation? The poet who feels he needs to mix his poetry up with significant matters, or to throw his verse into the popular excitement of the time, ought to remember this strange fact. . . . (62,C)

Keith Douglas (1962)

. . . Most English poets, if they start writing in their teens, spend their first five or ten years unrecognizable under their bowing and scraping respect for the English poets of the past. It is part of our patrician and conservative culture that we should be almost paralysed by the lofty examples of our seniors, out of sheer dutiful good manners. Our beginners in poetry, like our lower ranks in war, seem to have lacked initiative somewhat, in this century. Keith Douglas was not cursed with this fear of being insubordinate in vital matters.

. . . .

The excellences of Douglas are already there:* the marriage of verbal brilliance with verbal rightness, technical accuracy and brio with the absolutely natural living sound of his voice. It is a voice unique in modern English poetry for the endless variety of its intonations while still working at high artistic pressure and with the presence of a whole human being—not just a lyrical or metaphysical or formal fragment of one. Most important of all is this last: his special brand of honesty, which is also courage and also an obsession to get the facts down clear and straight, with no concessions to so-called poetry.

. . . .

His poetic gift did not go underground in the face of his war experience, as for instance Edward Thomas's did, but it came forward and developed in the conflict. This seems in character with his aggressive nimbleness of mind, his impatience to counter-attack on an impression, and it may also be related to certain limitations that his imagination had not time to outgrow.

. . . .

Little about his work is dated, though the mass of it is exercise and unsuccessful attempt. And in this poetry there is the beginning of a style, a tempered wholeness of mind, that could deal in poetry with whatever it came up against, a versatile, ruthless, direct style not limited to certain subjects in certain moods. It is a utility general-purpose style, as for instance Shakespeare's was; a style that combines a colloquial prose readiness and variety with a poetic breadth; a ritual intensity and music of an exceedingly high order with a clear wholehearted passion.

. . . .

There is nothing studied about Douglas's poems. They have the freshness and trenchancy of a jotting, yet the good ones leave no doubt about the completeness and subtlety of his impression or the thoroughness of his artistic conscience . . . (62,D)

---

*I.e., in the early poem "Encounter with a God" of 1936.

Leonard Baskin (1962)

. . . Technique is not a machine to do work, like a car engine that runs best of all with little or no load, but the act of work being done. So-called "technique without substance" is our polite word for fakery, or the appearance of something happening that is not happening, and attracts our attention at all only because we will look for some minutes at absolutely anything that seems to say "look at me," so humble and great is our hope. In Baskin's work one can no longer easily talk about "technique" after the engraving called "The Hanged Man." This figure was the earliest emergence of the second of the two phases, represented here, through which his art has so far passed, and the point at which an outstanding talent, of unmanageable density and potential, suffered the inner explosion that transformed it into genius and one of the deepest and most intense imaginations of our time.

From that point the "technique" seems no longer an aptitude of the artist, but a possession of the vision, the physical, prehensile grasp of an unusual spirit. This spirit is of such intensity that wherever it appears it permits nothing but itself to remain. It is not interested in the furniture or incidental lighting of existence, or any view from the window. It has identified itself with the naked form of the Angel of Life. So these engravings, in their endless variety, are the self-portraits of the Angel of Life in its wholeness: men, beasts, birds, insects, plants and supernatural beings, each in the terrible immobility of being forced and fated to move at once in two opposite directions, for the Angel of Life is also, in spite of itself, to its own horror, the Angel of Death.

How could such images be other than single, like suns, the dead epidermis burned away, without panorama? If they are multiple, they revolve around each other, like suns, in a single image, over nothingness, like God, or a last breath, or a birth-cry, a dead body, a small face singled for confrontation by the nothingness and the calamity of existence.

. . . .

"The Hanged Man" is not dead: it is the Angel, shattered by death, dispersed to the Universe, re-assembled by joy, that here takes up a position in which it is equal to the whole of its past and the whole of its future. So the dead crow, just the size of crow, as he is just the size of a man, is The Hanged Man's equal. Every feather of the crow is there and perfect, and the crow is dead, yet this bird again is the immortal Angel of Life. In the aspect of the Angel of Death. And the dog of joy, which we are to love, opens its mouth to exult and, appalled, hears the roar of the beast of death. These are emissaries from the sole source. The small, grubby, haughty, reasonable devils of lies and compromise, the frivolous and complacent devils, the optimistic joyless devils, the whole black gibbering cloud of our unreality, leave us in terror or faint with humiliation when we look rightly into these engravings.

In our time, the heroic struggle is not to become a hero but to remain a living creature simply. The Scientific Spirit has bitten so many of us in the nape, and pumped us full of its eggs, the ferocious virus of abstraction. We yield to the larvae, warmly numbed, and we all speak well of them and their parent. The Scientific Spirit, as we say, is hard-headed, it fears nothing, it faces the facts, and how it has improved our comforts! And yet what is this master of ours? The Scientific Spirit was born of the common hunt for the nourishing morsel, nursed by the benign search for objective truth, schooled in the pedagogic idolatry of the objective fact, graduated through old-maid specialised research, losing eyes, ears, smell, taste, touch, nerves and blood, adapting to the sensibility of electronic gadgets and the argument of numbers, to become a machine of senility, a pseudo-automaton in the House of the Mathematical Absolute. So it ousts humanity from man and he dedicates his life to the laws of the electron in vacuo, a literal self-sacrifice, and soon, by bigotry and the especially rabid evangelism of the inhuman, a literal world-sacrifice, as we all too truly now fear. Any artist who resists the suction into this galactic firestorm and holds to bodily wholeness and the condition of the creature, finds ranged against him the worldly powers of our age and everything that is not the suffering vitality of nature. The victims of radio-activity and of the death-camps, the corpse of a bird, an agony too private to name, become the only unequivocal portraits of life, of the Angel a hundred faces behind the human face. In this way, the particular misery and disaster of our time are, uniquely, the perfect conditions for the purest and most intense manifestation of the spirit, the Angel, the ghost of ashes, the survivor of the Creation, which has chosen to reveal itself in the works of Leonard Baskin. (62,Ba)

Primitive Song (1962)

. . . We imagine primitives to possess some of the qualities of ideal poetry—full of zest, clairvoyantly sensitive, realistic, whole, natural, and passionate; and so we might well look at their songs hopefully. And since only a captious anthropologist could doubt that in broad human essentials the songs reproduce the features of our own literature's embryonic stage, we wonder if these earliest stirrings of the poetic impulse might show something analogous to the gills in the human embryo, something as revealing of the inmost buried nature of the thing.

. . . .

Most of these songs are composed, as far as their subject-matter and motivations are concerned, of cryptics and particularities which open not into a world of common general ideas and familiar forms of life, as our poetry does, but into a world of rituals and objects unique to each tribe or group. Any analysis of this poetry that fails in its grasp of this substantive detail is going to be weaving about in a partial vacuum, just as would any analysis of a modern poem that failed to show a convincing grasp of the intellectual and spiritual inheritance which all such poems must inevitably use.

.   .   .   .

Poetry at its most primitive seems first to occur as a one-line chant of nonsense syllables in accompaniment to the rhythm of a stamping dance. Chimpanzees have got this far, and with them there is evidently not much before it. From that point, its development is moot, but among its early achievements are hints of the parallelism that becomes so powerful in Hebrew poetry and Shakespeare, a tendency to couplets, artful use of repetition and variations, and possibly rhyme. Its ultimate development, in this phase, is in the elaborately symbolic Australian song-cycles of the adventures of gods, which must be reckoned the stage before epic, and in the ritual dialogues of the Congo pygmies, which are a long step toward drama. Within that span, lyrics and laments attain great refinement. The bulk of the songs are power-charms, tools and practical agents in the business of gaining desired ends, or deflecting the spirits of misfortune from planting their larvae in the psyche . . . (62,B)

Emily Dickinson (1963)

. . . Like Whitman and Emerson, her contemporaries, she has been enlightened by an ecstatic vision, a basic poetic experience that recurs almost like a physical state, and, with her, at an abnormal intensity. In this mystical moment she encounters either her own soul, or the soul within the Creation and within its creatures. But she is more interesting than Whitman or Emerson, and more up-to-date, in that she is not sure she likes the looks of this soul-thing. Her ecstasy—"ecstasy" is one of her favoured words—is also terror, convincingly. She wants to believe that the great Creation-sustainer is God's love but it affects her often enough as if it were the final revelation of horrible Nothingness:

> Most, like Chaos—Stopless—cool,
> Without a Chance, or Spar,
> Or even a Report of Land
> To justify—Despair.

This fundamental ambiguity proliferates through her work, informing her imagery, her sense of words, her verse technique, her poetic personality, in all kinds of ways. Her relationship to this soul is as to a lover, or betrothed. She dotes on everything he touches, but doubts the way he will treat her. Those curious marriage poems instate her as a nun, as priestess of the Beautiful, of the Absolute, or as a corpse, for they are usually also funeral poems.

As a rule, she is happier meeting Him clothed in visible Nature than naked in solitude. Her wonderful imagery of scenes, weather, and creatures belongs mainly to her ecstatic, confident phase. When she tries to describe her mystical experience direct, as it occurs to her in meditation, it is generally too terrifying for words. Some of her best pieces are those in which she projects the inner visitation into an outer event; then terror and ecstasy become oddly mingled, as in those metaphorical accounts of electrical storms, ominous, exalted glimpses of objects, eerie openings of the Cosmos—

> A wind that rose, though not a leaf
> In any forest stirred—

The solidest, and perhaps the most characteristic, pieces belong to the after-phase of doubt and ironic query. ". . . we both believe, and disbelieve, a hundred times in an Hour, which keeps believing nimble," she wrote in a letter. But the more she needed to believe, in immortality, in the eternal orders of bliss, and the longer she lived with only hints and no evidence but frequent intimations to the contrary, the more agonisingly she doubted. Accordingly, the image of the final investigator, the same throughout her work, becomes more and more obsessive: and it is a person piercing the façade with the act of death. This is also a plain, self-descriptive image, of herself at the greatest moment of her life, during the poetic vision, where the whole problem keeps on renewing itself: her frozen, deep-sleep posture of communion with the mystery.

. . . .

Emily Dickinson lived with her "lexicon." A great number of her poems are simply an imaginative reconnaissance through the hinterland of a word—

> Exultation is going
> Of an inland soul to sea—

and there seems to lie a similar labour of exploration and restoration, of spacious inner drama and inner geography, behind all her words. She has little interest in rhythm: it is not the impetus of a feeling that matters, so much as its temperature, its luminosity; not the striking but the undermining power. She enters her idea slowly, relentlessly, blazing her trail almost unconsciously with those mesmerized dashes. Her slow, small metre is, among other things, a device for bringing each syllable into close up and liberating its resonances:

> Could mortal lip divine
> The undeveloped freight
> Of a delivered syllable
> Twould crumble with the weight.

The focus is so deep and steady that she manages to hold words in precise, yet at the same time somehow free, relationships: the individual words seem trembling on the point of slipping into utterly new meanings that are pressing to be uncovered. In this, she invites comparison with Shakespeare. Like his, her language is solid with metaphor, saturated with the homeliest imagery and subtlest applications. And since her prevailing cast of mind, during composition, is playful and paradoxical, bold and shy at the same time, this is the perfect occasion for riddles. Her poems are, in fact, games. Before they are records of her soul, or her world, or her experience, they are word-games, endlessly complicated and symmetrical . . . (63,Di)

Keith Douglas (1963)

. . . He is a renovater of language. It is not that he uses words in jolting combinations, or with titanic extravagance, or curious precision. His triumph lies in the way he renews the simplicity of ordinary talk, and he does this by infusing every word with a burning exploratory freshness of mind—partly impatience, partly exhilaration at speaking the forbidden thing, partly sheer casual ease of penetration. The music that goes along with this, the unresting variety of intonation and movement within his patterns, is the natural path of such confident, candid thinking.

There is nothing studied about this language. Its air of improvisation is a vital part of its purity. It has the trenchancy of an inspired jotting, yet leaves no doubt about the completeness and subtlety of his impressions, or the thoroughness of his artistic conscience.

. . . .

The war brought his gift to maturity, or to a first maturity. In a sense, war was his ideal subject: the burning away of all human pretensions in the ray cast by death. This was the vision, the unifying generalisation that shed the meaning and urgency into all his observations and particulars: not truth is beauty only, but truth kills everybody. The truth of a man is the doomed man in him or his dead body. Poem after poem circles this idea, as if his mind were tethered. At the bottom of it, perhaps, is his private muse, not a romantic symbol of danger and temptation, but the plain foreknowledge of his own rapidly-approaching end—a foreknowledge he becomes fully conscious of in two of his finest poems. This sets his writing apart from that of Hemingway, with which it shares certain features. Hemingway tried to imagine the death that Douglas had foresuffered. Douglas had no time, and perhaps no disposition to cultivate the fruity deciduous tree of How to Live. He showed in his poetry no concern for man in society. The murderous skeleton in the body of a girl, the dead man being eaten by dogs on the moonlit desert, the dead man behind the mirror, these items of circumstantial evidence are steadily out-arguing all his high spirits and hopefulness.

Technically, each of the poems of this second phase rests on some single objective core, a scene or event or thing. But one or two of the latest poems, and one in particular, start something different: the poems are "On a Return from Egypt" and "Simplify Me When I'm Dead." Their inner form is characterised not by a single object of attraction, but a constellation of statements . . . (63,D)

Myth and Religion of the North (1964)

. . . This particular mythology is much deeper in us, and truer to us, than the Greek-Roman pantheons that came in with Christianity, and again with the Renaissance, severing us with the completeness of a political interdict from these other deities of our instinct and ancestral memory. It is as if we were to lose Macbeth and King Lear, and have to live on Timon and Coriolanus; or as if a vocabulary drawn wholly from the Greek-Roman branch were to take over absolutely from our Anglo-Saxon-Norse-Celtic: there's no doubt which of these two belongs to our blood. The combination of the two is our wealth, but in the realm of mythologies, the realm of management between our ordinary minds and our deepest life, we've had no chance to make a similar combination. Even after Shakespeare, it's interesting to see what an infusion the few artificial revivals of that lost inheritance have proved: William Morris's Icelandic stories, the most genuine productions of the pre-Raphaelite period, led directly to Yeats's whole-hearted attempt to recover the pre-Christian imagination of Ireland, and the results were a powerful source of the energy of the whole Irish nationalist movement. But, as I say, one has only to look at our vocabulary to see where our real mental life has its roots, where the paths to and from our genuine imaginations run, clearly enough. It's false to say these gods and heroes are obsolete: they are the better part of our patrimony still locked up . . . (64,T)

Superstitions (1964)

. . . The word "rationality" is having a bad time. The laws of the Creation are the only literally rational things, and we don't yet know what they are. The nearest we can come to rational thinking is to stand respectfully, hat in hand, before this Creation, exceedingly alert for a new word. We no longer so readily make the grinding, funicular flight of cerebrations from supposed first principles. On all points of uncertainty, we give the Universe the benefit of the doubt. We'll stand to some claims: the moon is not green cheese, and birds lay eggs, and if we cross the room we reach the other side. But whether Gandhi's prayers affected European politics, whether Jehovah was or was not a highly irascible poltergeist laboriously constructed by the psychokinetic efforts of Moses and Aaron, and whoever else they could get to pray with them, we leave open. Whether or not an ill-wish gets up and walks the streets, or enemies' dreams meet, fight and mutilate each other, with consequences, or unhuman electrical powers occasionally play a kind of witty or witless chess with men, are fantastic ideas no means can possible disprove, but which could conceivably at any moment come within the detection of new instruments. We reject them, if we do, because they inhabit a gulf where our careful civilization would disintegrate. Yet they are ancient ideas which from time to time men all over the world have found taking on power in their minds, just as they found the wild Heraclitean/Buddhist notion that the entire Universe is basically made of fire.

Modern physicists have reasserted this last one in civilised terms. Their "rationality" has evaporated in an astonished watchfulness and the struggle to keep a grasp on the human dimension of things—evidently not easy, as we see in such men as Teller. They've landed themselves, and us, in a delicately balanced, purely electrical Creation, at the backdoor of the house of activities formerly called "supernatural." For a purely electrical Creation is one without walls, where everything, being an electrical power, can have an electrical effect on every other thing, and where electrical effects are vital effects.

. . . .

The *couvade*, where the husband suffers the wife's childbirth pains . . . is only one of the whole range of sympathetic illnesses, physical and mental, and . . . may be related to faith-healing, where as in some primitive medicine the healer takes over the illness of his patient or passes over some health. The key to this theory is the commonplace law that electrical potential flows from high tension to low. The person with the lower potential absorbs current from the one with higher, along with highly charged thought-forms, moods, colourings and so on as modifying waves. Certain conditions—high emotion in particular—seem to raise a person's potential, while depression, tiredness and fear seem to lower it. It's known, in support of Mr. Lethbridge's suggestion, that during a healing seance a faith-healer's static potential drops measurably. Another condition of the exchange is that the people involved share some sort of "sympathy"—though a very little thing will suffice to establish this. Telepathy certainly works best between friends, and can be hair-raisingly intrusive between people who are really close. And the more practical operations of witchcraft, as well as long-distance magical healing (which works too well to be easily repudiated), require some scrap of the victim's or patient's body—hair, or a blood drop.

All this opens onto a gulf—as Freud, for one, saw and feared. What are the limits of this involuntary transmission? What about the gift, recorded in several individuals (Jung cites an occasion where the gift visited him), of being able to read off, at first meeting, large stretches of the stranger's past life, seeing it unrolled like a cinema, and effortlessly, as Mozart heard his music. If that sort of reception occurs, it's quite as likely to be a common property of life's electrical constitution as a freakish personal talent. The possibilities of what a child might absorb from its lineage in this way are awful, which is what alarmed Freud.

Other inhabitants of the gulf are ghosts. Many ghosts fall to psychological or medical explanations. But the ghosts or "presences" which haunt one spot, where different people, and animals, react to them, are evidently part of the logic of the earth—which is not yet ours. Mr. Lethbridge's theory explains such a ghost as an impression—of terror, misery, hatred, or, it may be, happiness—projected into an electrical field by some individual in a state of intense emotion, and stored there as in a capacitor, or as our experience is stored in our own electrical field. When some person in a low state of potential, i.e. depressed or frightened or enfeebled in the early hours or ill, enters the same field, the impression is leaked back into his consciousness: he becomes "aware" of it. In other words, all these electrical fields within the Ge-field of the earth store up experience, though perhaps fadingly, and the question of just what forms that experience may take confronts once more the swarming worlds of the religions.

These are only the shallows of Mr. Lethbridge's intriguing venture into the gulf. And if, by some spectacular development of sensitive recording equipment, all these refreshed but really very ancient and widely shared suppositions were proved, to the crassest incredulity to be fact, what an entertaining place the world would become again! What a chaos! The only respectable sanities to survive undiscredited in all that would be physics and art. (64,M)

Shamanism (1964)

Traces and variations of Shamanism are found all over the world, but it has developed its purest or most characteristic procedures in northeastern and central Asia. The word "shaman" comes from the Tungus. Shamanism is not a religion, but a technique for moving in a state of ecstasy among the various spiritual realms, and for generally dealing with souls and spirits, in a practical way, in some practical crisis. It flourishes alongside and within the prevailing religion. For instance, some Tibetan Lamas occasionally shamanize. And whereas religions may differ fundamentally, the inner experiences and techniques and application of shamanism spring into shape everywhere similar, as if the whole activity were something closer to biological inevitability than to any merely cultural tradition—though obviously cultural traditions influence it a good deal too, in detail. The Buddhist influence on Asiatic shamanism is strong.

The vital function shamanizing can take on, even in a colossally formed religion like Buddhism, may be seen in the *Bardo Thödol*, the Tibetan "Book of the Dead." In the *Bardo Thödol* the geography and furnishings of the afterworld are Buddhist, but the main business of the work as a whole, which is to guide a dead soul to its place in death, or back into life—together with the principal terrific events, and the flying accompaniment of descriptive songs, exhortation to the soul, threats, and the rest—are all characteristically shaman. This huge, formal work has long ago lost contact with any shaman, but its origins seem clear.

The shaman is "chosen" in a number of ways. In some regions, commonly among the North American Indians, the aspirant inflicts on himself extraordinary solitary ordeals of fasting and self-mutilation, until a spirit, usually some animal, arrives, and becomes henceforth his liaison with the spirit world. In other regions, the tribe chooses the man—who may or may not, under the initiation ordeals, become a shaman. But the most common form of election comes from the spirits themselves: they approach the man in a dream. At the simplest, these dreams are no more than a vision of an eagle, as among the Buryats, or a beautiful woman (who marries him), as among the Goldi. But at the other extreme, the dreams are long and complicated, and dramatize in full the whole psychological transformation that any shaman, no matter how he has been initially chosen, must undergo. The central episode in this full-scale dream, just like the central episode in the rites where the transformation is effected forcibly by the tribe, is a magical death, then dismemberment, by a demon or equivalent powers, with all possible variants of boiling, devouring, burning, stripping to the bones. From this nadir, the shaman is resurrected, with new insides, a new body created for him by the spirits. When he recovers from this—the dream may hold him in a dead trance for several days—he begins to study under some shaman, learning the great corpus of mythological, medical and technical lore of the particular cultural line of shamanism he is in: this stage takes several years.

Some shamans shamanize to amuse themselves, but usually the performance is public and to some public purpose. The preparations are elaborate, the shamanizing prolonged and spectacular, as the shaman dances, drums, leaps—in regalia hung with mirrors and iron emblems often weighing more than fifty pounds—and sings himself into ecstasy, entering the spirit realm. In this condition he can handle fire, be stabbed and not bleed, and do incredible feats of strength and agility. His business is usually to guide some soul to the underworld, or bring back a sick man's lost soul, or deliver sacrifices to the dead, or ask the spirits the reason for an epidemic, or the whereabouts of game or a man lost. The structure of these spirit realms is universally fairly consistent, and familiar figures recur as consistently: the freezing river, the clashing rocks, the dog in the cave-entrance, the queen of animals, the holy mountain, and so on. The results, when the shaman returns to the living, are some display of healing power, or a clairvoyant piece of information. The cathartic effect on the audience, and the refreshing of their religious feeling, must be profound. These shamanizings are also entertainments, full of buffoonery, mimicry, dialogue, and magical contortions. The effect on the shaman himself is something to wonder about. One main circumstance in becoming a shaman, in the first place, is that once you've been chosen by the spirits, and dreamed the dreams, there is no other life for you, you must shamanize or die: this belief seems almost universal . . . (64,E)

Patrick White (1964)

. . . One of the remarkable things about this book [i.e., *Voss*], to my mind, is the way it is written. The still, tense, pervading watchfulness of the prose seems to me something extraordinary. Nothing throw-away or racily colloquial: something delicate, and piercing, yet a massive steady grasp. Patrick White has devised a narrative style of writing which is partly passionate incantation, partly immensely precise, scientific formality, partly wild, impressionistic poetry, with just an overtone of humorous Australian twang—and a complicated effect it makes, altogether: it engages a reader in an unusual state of attention.

The style is, in fact, a form of hypnosis, just as rhythmical verse can be, but without any of the monotony of verse. It is this deliberately shaped prose which above anything else enables him to set even the trivial events of his story into a super-real, semi-mythological dimension. In this prose, Patrick White is the most exciting poet Australia has yet produced . . . (64,W)

Literature among the Primitives (1965)

. . . Primitive literature has been terribly unlucky in the past. The recording of it began in earnest in the nineteenth century, but by just those individuals who had come to destroy—deliberately or otherwise—the unique conditions of its flourishing. Missionaries who emasculated all they heard, even when they were eager to hear, or who inspired automatic censorship in the narrators; lawmakers who had the same effect, and amateurs who were recording simply the outlines of something curious. When the anthropologists arrived, with few exceptions they were not much better, to begin with, since by cultural tradition and scientific bent they tended to despise these tales as infantile fantasies or—at best— fairytales fit (or unfit) for children. Poetasters and writers for the nursery fell on whatever material got through, and saturated it with nineteenth-century literary manners, in which guise it was introduced to the civilized West, adjusted to the circle of ministers' daughters that corrupted Tennyson. Mr. Greenway's account of what happened to some of the North American Indian material illustrates what depths this meant. Even the popular presentations of the mythologies fared no better. Primitive literature hasn't yet recovered, among the non-specialist public, from this wretched debut. That publishers still subscribe to the emasculations and prettifications and denaturings can be seen from the popular selections that still come out plentifully.

As a result of all that, the mass of the literature has been lost. By the time the modern recorders got down to it, with no squeamish reservations and with germanic faith, happily, in the great mystery of accurate detail, the primitives, with few exceptions, had been either wiped out or mentally reconstituted, their literatures dissolved with the natural circumstances and self-confidence that fostered them, and nothing remained but the fragments. Still, these fragments amount to an immense and ever-increasing hoard—lying inert in the Departments of Anthropology and the Folklore Libraries. They are lying inert because the anthropologists do not know what to do with them. Nobody knows what to do with them.

. . . .

Somewhere in *Literature Among the Primitives* he [i.e., J. Greenway] makes a disparaging remark about Kafka, so perhaps it's natural that he excludes from his selection any of those tales which are, in my opinion, the most inspired and astonishing, and in a way the most concentratedly characteristic, in the entire literature, and which resemble nothing in Western Literature except Kafka. Paul Radin's collection *African Folk Tales and Sculpture* contains quite a few of the sort of thing I mean; so does his Winebago Trickster Cycle, and B. H. Chamberlain's collection of Ainu tales. It is in the elemental autonomy of these pieces that we can detect the seminal thing that in primitive sculpture and primitive music has already operated on us.

Primitive music has altered our world, maybe radically. Primitive sculpture has been one of the chief sources of modern sculpture; it certainly led the way out of the impasse. But somehow or other, primitive literature, of one spirit with the music and the sculpture, has not arrived, not fruitfully. The only instance I know, was in the explosive transformation Radin's African collection worked on the poetry of Sylvia Plath . . . (65,G)

Isaac Bashevis Singer (1965)

. . . Looking over his novels in their chronological order (the stories are written in and among, but they belong with the novels) the first apparent thing is the enormous and one might say successful development of his vision. Vision seems to be the right word for what Singer is conveying. The most important fact about him, that determines the basic strategy by which he deals with his subject, is that his imagination is poetic, and tends toward symbolic situations. Cool, analytical qualities are heavily present in everything he does, but organically subdued to a grasp that is finally visionary and redemptive. Without the genius, he might well have disintegrated as he evidently saw others disintegrate—between a nostalgic dream of ritual Hasidic piety on the one hand and cosmic dead-end despair on the other. But his creative demon (again, demon seems to be the right word) works deeper than either of these two extremes. It is what involves him so vehemently with both. It involves him with both because this demon is ultimately the voice of his nature, which requires at all costs satisfaction in life, full inheritance of its natural joy. It is what suffers the impossible problem and dreams up the supernormal solution. It is what in most men stares dumbly through the bars. At bottom it is amoral, as interested in destruction as in creation, but being in Singer's case an intelligent spirit, it has gradually determined a calibration of degrees between good and evil, in discovering which activities embroil it in misery, pain, and emptiness, and conjure into itself cruel powers, and which ones concentrate it towards bliss, the fullest possession of its happiest energy. Singer's writings are the account of this demon's re-education through decades that have been—particularly for the Jews—a terrible school. They put the question: "How shall man live most truly as a human being?" from the center of gravity of human nature, not from any temporary civic center or speculative metaphysic or far-out neurotic bewilderment. And out of the pain and wisdom of Jewish history and tradition they answer it. His work is not discursive, or even primarily documentary, but revelation—and we are forced to respect his findings because it so happens that he has the authority and power to force us to do so.

. . . .

The key to Singer's works seems to be an experience of the collapse of the Hasidic way of life under the pressure of all that it had been developed to keep out. Something like this is a usual moral position among poets who come at some revolutionary moment, but who need to respect order. Singer comes at the moment when the profound, rich, intense Hasidic tradition, with the whole Jewish tradition behind it, debouches into the ideological chaos of the mid-twentieth century. Visited with all that the old Law excluded, such poets are burdened with the job of finding new Law. But when the hosts of liberated instinct and passion and intellectual adventure and powers of the air and revelations of physical truth are symbolized by Satan, as they must be for a Hasidic Jew, and the old, obsolete order is symbolized by the devotion and ritual that are a people's unique spiritual strength and sole means of survival, the position must be a perilous one to manage.

. . . .

Singer's vision arrived there, in despair in the absurd Universe, at a point where most comparable modern writers have remained, emotionally, despite their notable attempts to get beyond it. The Existential Choice, taken to its absolute limit of wholeheartedness, becomes inevitably a religion—because man is deeper and more complicated than merely rational controls can keep hold of. Then his beliefs, disciplines, and prohibitions have to be cultivated against the odds as in a world of poisons one chooses—sensibly after all—food that nourishes. Singer is at a point there, that is to say, where he has every sane and human reason to rebuild an appreciation of the Faith it was death for him to lose. So here again the Jewish Hasidic tradition takes on a Universal significance, as a paradigm of the truly effective Existential discipline, which perhaps it always has been. The core of the Jewish faith, unlike most larger persuasions, is one long perpetually-renewed back-to-the-wall Choice, one might say in this context, to affirm a mode of survival against tremendous odds. It has kept the Jewish heart in one piece through three thousand years of such oppressions and temptations as dissolved other peoples in a few decades. (65,S)

Sylvia Plath (1965)

In her earlier poems, Sylvia Plath composed very slowly, consulting her Thesaurus and Dictionary for almost every word, putting a slow, strong ring of ink around each word that attracted her. Her obsession with intricate rhyming and metrical schemes was part of the same process. Some of those early inventions of hers were almost perverse, with their bristling hurdles. But this is what she enjoyed. One of her most instinctive compulsions was to make patterns—vivid, bold, symmetrical patterns. She was fond of drawing—anything, a blade of grass, a tree, a stone, but preferably something complicated and chaotic, like a high heap of junk. On her paper this became inexorably ordered and powerful, like a marvelous piece of sculpture, and took on the look of her poems, everything clinging together like a family of living cells, where nothing can be alien or dead or arbitrary. The poems in *Ariel* are the fruits of that early labour. In them, she controls one of the widest and most subtly discriminating vocabularies in the modern poetry of our language, and these are poems written for the most part at great speed, as she might take dictation, where she ignores metre and rhyme for rhythm and momentum, the flight of her ideas and music. The words in these odd-looking verses are not only charged with terrific heat, pressure and clairvoyant precision, they are all deeply related within any poem, acknowledging each other and calling to each other in deep harmonic designs. It is this musical, almost mathematical hidden law, which gives these explosions their immovable finality.

Behind these poems there is a fierce and uncompromising nature. There is also a child desperately infatuated with the world. And there is a strange muse, bald, white and wild, in her "hood of bone," floating over a landscape like that of the Primitive Painters, a burningly luminous vision of a Paradise. A Paradise which is at the same time eerily frightening, an unalterably spot-lit vision of death.

And behind them, too, is a long arduous preparation. She grew up in an atmosphere of tense intellectual competition and Germanic rigour. Her mother, first-generation American of Austrian stock, and her father, who was German-Polish, were both University teachers. Her father, whom she worshipped, died when she was nine, and thereafter her mother raised Sylvia and her brother single-handed. Whatever teaching methods were used, Sylvia was the perfect pupil: she did every lesson double. Her whole tremendous will was bent on excelling. Finally, she emerged like the survivor of an evolutionary ordeal: at no point could she let herself be negligent or inadequate. What she was most afraid of was that she might come to live outside her genius for love, which she also equated with courage, or "guts," to use her word. This genius for love she certainly had, and not in the abstract. She didn't quite know how to manage it: it possessed her. It fastened her to cups, plants, creatures, vistas, people, in a steady ecstasy. As much of all that as she could, she hoarded into her poems, into those incredibly beautiful lines and hallucinatory evocations.

But the truly miraculous thing about her will remain the fact that in two years, while she was almost fully occupied with children and housekeeping, she underwent a poetic development that has hardly any equal on record, for suddenness and completeness. The birth of her first child seemed to start the process. All at once she could compose at top speed, and with her full weight. Her second child brought things a giant step forward. All the various voices of her gift came together, and for about six months, up to a day or two before her death, she wrote with the full power and music of her extraordinary nature.

Ariel is not easy poetry to criticise. It is not much like any other poetry. It is her. Everything she did was just like this, and this is just like her— but permanent. (65,P)

Sylvia Plath (1966)

In a poet whose development was as phenomenal as hers, the chronological order of the poems is an important help to understanding them. Most readers will perceive pretty readily the single centre of power and light which her poems all share, but I think it will be a service if I point out just how little of her poetry is "occasional," and how faithfully her separate poems build up into one long poem. She faced a task in herself, and her poetry is the record of her progress in the task. The poems are chapters in a mythology where the plot, seen as a whole and in retrospect, is strong and clear—even if the origins of it and the dramatis personae, are at bottom enigmatic. Her poetry has been called "confessional and personal," and connected with the school of Robert Lowell and Anne Sexton. She admired both these poets, and knew them personally, and they both had an effect on her. And she shares with them the central experience of a shattering of the self, and the labour of fitting it together again or finding a new one. She also shared with them the East Massachusetts homeland. But the connection goes no further. Her poetic strategies, the poetic events she draws out of her experience of disintegration and renewal, the radiant, visionary light in which she encounters her family and the realities of her daily life, are quite different in kind from anything one finds in Robert Lowell's poetry, or Anne Sexton's. Their work is truly autobiographical and personal, and their final world is a torture cell walled with family portraits, with the daily newspaper coming under the door. The autobiographical details in Sylvia Plath's poetry work differently. She sets them out like masks, which are then lifted up by dramatis personae of nearly supernatural qualities. The world of her poetry is one of emblematic visionary events, mathematical symmetries, clairvoyance, metamorphoses, and something resembling total biological and racial recall. And the whole scene lies under the transfiguring eye of the great white timeless light. Her poetry escapes ordinary analysis in the way clairvoyance and mediumship do: her psychic gifts, at almost any time, were strong enough to make her frequently wish to be rid of them. In her poetry, in other words, she had free and controlled access to depths formerly reserved to the primitive ecstatic priests, shamans and Holy men, and more recently flung open to tourists with the passport of such hallucinogens as LSD.

As will be shown by the sequence of her poems, and of her preoccupations right from the start, her initiation into this spiritual world was inevitable, and nothing very sudden. In her, as with perhaps few poets ever, the nature, the poetic genius and the active self, were the same. Maybe we don't need psychological explanations to understand what a difficult and peculiar destiny that means. She had none of the usual guards and remote controls to protect herself from her own reality. She lived right in it, especially during the last two years of her life. Perhaps that is one of the privileges, or prices, of being a woman and at the same time an initiate into the poetic order of events. Though the brains, the strength, the abundance and vivacity of spirits, the artistic virtuosity, the thousand incidental gifts that can turn it into such poetry as hers are another matter.

Before her first book, *The Colossus*, she had written great quantities of verse, all of it characteristic and unique, with a dense crop of inspired phrases that a poet of any age would have been glad to have secured. But she never saved lines or phrases. She wrote her early poems very slowly, Thesaurus open on her knee, in her large, strange handwriting, like a mosaic, where every letter stands separate within the work, a hieroglyph to itself. If she didn't like a poem, she scrapped it entire. She rescued nothing of it. Every poem grew complete from its own root, in that laborious inching way, as if she were working out a mathematical problem, chewing her lips, putting a thick dark ring of ink around each word that stirred for her on the page of the Thesaurus.

. . . .

Surveyed as a whole, with attention to the order of composition, I think the unity of her opus is clear. Once the unity shows itself, the logic and inevitability of the language, which controls and contains such conflagrations and collisions within itself, becomes more obviously what it is— direct, and even plain, speech. This language, this unique and radiant substance, is the product of an alchemy on the noblest scale. Her elements were extreme: a violent, almost demonic spirit in her, opposed a tenderness and capacity to suffer and love things infinitely, which was just as great and far more in evidence. Her stormy, luminous senses assaulted a downright, practical intelligence that could probably have dealt with anything. Her vision of death, her muse of death in life and life in death, with its oppressive evidence, fought in her against a joy in life, and in every smallest pleasure, for which her favourite word "ecstasy" was simply accurate, as her poems prove. She saw her world in the flame of the ultimate substance and the ultimate depth. And this is the distinction of her language, that every word is "Baraka": the flame and the rose folded together. Poets have often spoken about this ideal possibility but, where else, outside these poems, has it actually occurred? If we have the discrimination to answer this question, we can set her in her rightful company. (66,P)

Dylan Thomas (1966)

. . . Everything we associate with a poem is its shadowy tenant and part of its meaning, no matter how New Critical purist we try to be. Yeats's life is not the less interesting half of his general effort, and one wonders what his poetry would amount to if it could be lifted clear of the biographical matrix. Quite a lot, no doubt. But how much less than at present! With poets who set their poetic selves further into the third person, maybe the life is less relevant. But Thomas's life, letters and legends belong to his poetry, in that they make it mean more.

His poetic vision undid him. Or the sensitivity and psychic openness that showed him the vision also betrayed him in life. It was a vision of the total Creation, where everything, man and atom, life and death, was equal, and nothing could be ugly or bad, where everything was a vital member of a single infinite being, which he sometimes called God. It was sustained by the circulation of divine energy which he sometimes called love, sometimes joy. It was a morally undetermined, infinitely mothering creation. He had no comments or interpretations or philosophisings to add to it. His poetry was exclusively an attempt to present it. Every poem is an attempt to sign up the whole heavenly vision, from one point of vantage or other, in a static constellation of verbal prisms. It is this fixed intent, and not a rhetorical inflation of ordinary ideas, that gives his language its exaltation and reach.

In his life, the reflex of this vision was a complete openness toward both inner and outer worlds denying nothing, refusing nothing, suppressing nothing. But the vision included the hells as well as "the faces of a noiseless million in the busyhood of heaven." The hells indeed were a favoured part of the task. Poetry, he said, was to drag into "the clean nakedness of the light more even of the hidden causes than Freud could realize." He made a half-conscious attempt to take on all the underground life that the uppercrustish, militant, colonial-suppressive cast of the English intelligence excludes. It is apt that he seemed physically such a representative of the old Moorish strain of blood in South Wales. Much of his writing and general thinking was a perpetual invocation of the most hellish elementals. And as he said himself, when devils are called, they come. Maybe Yeats could have advised him how to confine their capers to his imaginative works, but it wasn't in Thomas to negotiate or protect himself on this or any other front. All life was one, and he was open to it all, and "he'd be a damn fool" if he weren't . . . (66,T)

Vasko Popa (1967)

. . . Circumstantial proof that man is a political animal, a state numeral, as if it needed to be proved, has been weighed out in dead bodies by the million. The attempt these poets are making to put on record that man is also, at the same time and in the same circumstances, an acutely conscious human creature of suffering and hope, has brought their poetry down to such precisions, discriminations and humilities that it is a new thing. It seems closer to the common reality, in which we have to live if we are to survive, than do those other realities in which we can holiday, or into which we decay when our bodily survival is comfortably taken care of, and which art, particularly contemporary art, is forever trying to impose on us as some sort of superior dimension. I think it was Milosz, the Polish poet, who when he lay in a doorway and watched the bullets lifting the cobbles out of the street beside him realized that most poetry is not equipped for life in a world where people actually do die. But some is. And the poets of whom Popa is one seem to have put their poetry to a similar test.

We can guess at the forces which shaped their outlook and style. They have had to live out, in actuality, a vision which for artists elsewhere is a prevailing shape of things but only brokenly glimpsed, through the clutter of our civilised liberal confusion. They must be reckoned among the purest and most wide awake of living poets.

In a way, their world reminds one of Beckett's world. Only theirs seems braver, more human, and so more real. It is as horrible as his but they do not despair of it to the point of surrendering consciousness and responsibility to their animal cells. Their poetic themes revolve around the living suffering spirit, capable of happiness, much deluded, too frail, with doubtful and provisional senses, so undefinable as to be almost silly, but palpably existing, and wanting to go on existing—and this is not, as in Beckett's world, absurd. It is the only precious thing, and designed in accord with the whole Universe. Designed, indeed, by the whole Universe. They are not the spoiled brats of civilisation disappointed of impossible and unreal expectations and deprived of the revelations of necessity. In this they are prophets speaking somewhat against their times, though in an undertone, and not looking for listeners. They have managed to grow up to a view of the unaccommodated Universe, but it has not made them cynical, they still like it and keep all their sympathies intact. They have gone back to the simple animal courage of accepting the odds and have rediscovered the frontier.

.   .   .   .

This helplessness in the circumstances has purged them of rhetoric. They cannot falsify their experience by any hopeful effort to change it. Their poetry is a strategy of making audible meanings without disturbing the silence, an art of homing in tentatively on vital scarcely perceptible signals, making no mistakes, but with no hope of finality, continuing to explore. Finally, with delicate manoeuvering, they precipitate out of a world of malicious negatives a happy positive. And they have created a small ironic space, a work of lyrical art, in which their humanity can respect itself.

. . . .

It is all there, the surprising fusion of unlikely elements. The sophisticated philosopher is also a primitive, gnomic spellmaker. The desolate view of the Universe opens through eyes of childlike simplicity and moody oddness. The wide perspective of general elemental and biological law is spelled out with folklore hieroglyphs and magical monsters. The whole style is a marvellously effective artistic invention. It enables Popa to be as abstract as man can be, yet remain as intelligible and entertaining and as fully human as if he were telling a comic story. It is in this favourite device of his, the little fable or visionary anecdote, that we see most clearly his shift from literary surrealism to the far older and deeper thing, the surrealism of folklore. The distinction between the two seems to lie in the fact that literary surrealism is always connected with an extreme remove from the business of living under practical difficulties and successfully managing them. The mind, having abandoned the struggle with circumstances and consequently lost the unifying focus that comes of that, has lost morale and surrendered to the arbitrary imagery of the dream flow. Folktale surrealism, on the other hand, is always urgently connected with the business of trying to manage practical difficulties so great that they have forced the sufferer temporarily out of the dimension of coherent reality into that depth of imagination where understanding has its roots and stores its X-rays. There is no sense of surrender to the dream flow for its own sake or of relaxation from the outer battle. In the world of metamorphoses and flights the problems are dismantled and solved, and the solution is always a practical one. This type of surrealism, if it can be called surrealism at all, goes naturally with a down-to-earth, alert tone of free enquiry, and in Popa's poetry the two appear everywhere together.

. . . .

The air of trial and error exploration, of an improvised language, the attempt to get near something for which he is almost having to invent the words in a total disregard for poetry or the normal conventions of discourse, goes with his habit of working in cycles of poems. He will trust no phrase with his meaning for more than six or seven words at a time before he corrects his track with another phrase from a different direction. In the same way, he will trust no poem with his meaning for more than fifteen or so lines, before he tries again from a totally different direction with another poem . . . (67,P)

Emily Dickinson (1968)

. . . The forces which now came together in the crucible of her imagination decided her greatness. One of the most weighty circumstances, and the most interesting, was that just as the Universe in its Divine aspect became the mirror-image of her "husband," so the whole religious dilemma of New England, at that most critical moment in its history, became the mirror-image of her relationship to him—of her "marriage," in fact. And so her spiritualised love and its difficulties became also a topical religious disputation on the grandest scale.

At that time, the old Calvinism of the New England States was in open battle against the leading spirits of the new age—the Higher Criticism that was dissolving the Bible, the broadening, liberalising influence of the Transcendentalists, the general scientific scepticism which, in America, was doubly rabid under the backlash of the ruthless, selective pragmatism of the frontier and the international-scale hatreds smuggled in by the freedom-grabbers. On the one hand, radical Puritan revivals were sweeping Emily Dickinson's friends and relatives away from the flesh and the world, like epidemics which she was almost alone among her friends in resisting, and on the other hand the words of Jonathan Edwards were still proclaiming that the visible Universe was "an emanation of God for the pure joy of Creation in which the creatures find their justification by yielding assent to the beauty of the whole, even though it slay them." Beyond this, the Civil War was melting down the whole nation in an ideological gamble of total suicide or renewal in unity. The Indian tribes and the great sea of buffalo waited on the virgin plains, while Darwin wrote his chapters. The powers that struggled for reconciliation in Emily Dickinson were no less than those which were unmaking and remaking America.

. . . .

In a way, it was the precision of her feeling for language, which is one department of honesty, that kept her to the painful shortcoming of her suspended judgement, and saved her from the easy further step of abstraction into philosophy and shared religion. And it is in her verbal genius that all her gifts and sufferings came to focus. She was able to manage such a vast subject matter, and make it so important to us, purely because of the strengths and ingenuities of her poetic style.

There is the slow, small metre, a device for bringing each syllable into close-up, as under a microscope; there is the deep, steady focus, where all the words lie in precise and yet somehow free relationships, so that the individual syllables are on the point of slipping into utterly new meanings, all pressing to be uncovered; there is the mosaic, pictogram concentration of ideas; there is the tranced suspense and deliberation in her punctuation of dashes, and the riddling, oblique artistic strategies, the Shakespearean texture of the language, solid with metaphor, saturated with the homeliest imagery and experience; the freakish blood-and-nerve paradoxical vitality of her latinisms; the musical games—of opposites, parallels, mirrors, chinese puzzles, harmonising and counterpointing whole worlds of reference; and everywhere there is the teeming carnival of world-life. It is difficult to exhaust the unique art and pleasures of her poetic talent. With the hymn and the riddle, those two small domestic implements, she grasped the "centre" and the "circumference" of things—to use two of her favourite expressions—as surely as human imagination ever has . . . (68,D)

The Environmental Revolution (1970)

. . . The fundamental guiding ideas of our Western Civilisation are against Conservation. They derive from Reformed Christianity and from Old Testament Puritanism. This is generally accepted. They are based on the assumption that the earth is a heap of raw materials given to man by God for his exclusive profit and use. The creepy crawlies which infest it are devils of dirt and without a soul, also put there for his exclusive profit and use. By the skin of her teeth, woman escaped the same role. The subtly apotheosised misogyny of Reformed Christianity is proportionate to the fanatic rejection of Nature, and the result has been to exile man from Mother Nature—from both inner and outer nature. The story of the mind exiled from Nature is the story of Western Man. It is the story of his progressively more desperate search for mechanical and rational and symbolic securities, which will substitute for the spirit-confidence of the Nature he has lost. The basic myth for the ideal Westerner's life is the Quest. The quest for a marriage in the soul or a physical re-conquest. The lost life must be captured somehow. It is the story of spiritual romanticism and heroic technological progress. It is a story of decline. When something abandons Nature, or is abandoned by Nature, it has lost touch with its creator, and is called an evolutionary dead-end. According to this, our Civilisation is an evolutionary error. Sure enough, when the modern mediumistic artist looks into his crystal, he sees always the same thing. He sees the last nightmare of mental disintegration and spiritual emptiness, under the super-ego of Moses, in its original or in some Totalitarian form, and the self-anaesthetising schizophrenia of St. Paul. This is the soul-state of our civilisation. But he may see something else. He may see a vision of the real Eden, "excellent as at the first day," the draughty radiant Paradise of the animals, which is the actual earth, in the actual Universe: he may see Pan, whom Nietzsche mistook for Dionysus, the vital, somewhat terrible spirit of natural life, which is new in every second. Even when it is poisoned to the point of death, its efforts to be itself are new in every second. This is what will survive, if anything can. And this is the soul-state of the new world. But while the mice in the field are listening to the Universe, and moving in the body of nature, where every living cell is sacred to every other, and all are interdependent, the housing speculator is peering at the field through a visor, and behind him stands the whole army of madmen's ideas.

. . . .

The time for Conservation has certainly come. But Conservation, our sudden alertness to the wholeness of nature, and the lateness of the hour, is only the crest of a deeper excitement and readiness. The idea of nature as a single organism is not new. It was man's first great thought, the basic intuition of most primitive theologies. Since Christianity hardened into Protestantism, we can follow its underground heretical life, leagued with everything occult, spiritualistic, devilish, over-emotional, bestial, mystical, feminine, crazy, revolutionary, and poetic. Now it has suddenly re-emerged, within the last few years, presenting respectable scientific credentials through the voice of the Computer. Science, it has often been said, which began by deposing every primitive idea, will end by reinstating them as the essential conditions for life and as true descriptions of the Universe. It is like the old-fashioned dynasties of the gods. Christianity deposes Mother Nature and begets, on her prostrate body, Science, which proceeds to destroy Nature, but which in turn, on its half-destroyed mother's body, begets the Computer, a god more powerful than its Father or its Grandfather, who reinstates Nature, its Mother and Grandmother and Great-Grandmother, as the Holy of Holies, mother of all the gods. Because this is what we are seeing: something that was unthinkable only ten years ago, except as a poetic dream: the re-emergence of Nature as the Great Goddess of mankind, and the Mother of all life. And her oracle, speaking the language to which everybody, even Technology itself, is forced to listen, is the Computer.

. . . .

Looking at this image of global unity, so prehistoric and yet so actually present, we see how far ahead of its time Conservation has been. While Politicians, Sociologists, Economists, Theologians, Philosophers and the rest pick over the stucco rubble of a collapsed civilisation, the Conservationists are nursing a new global era. It seems right that Max Nicholson should sub-title his book "A Guide for the New Masters of the Earth." And in contrast to the hopeless gloom of all comment on our civilisation, it is right that his tone should be so hopeful, and his will so purposeful. He makes it very clear that we may well be too late, that our civilisation may be too strong for us for too long. In spite of that, he leaves the reader feeling that the wonderful thing might be possible, that the earth can be salvaged, that we are not hopelessly in the grip of our abstractions, our stupidity and greed, and our shiftless, imbecile governments. He makes it seem possible that we can come to our senses in time. . . .(70,N)

Laura Riding (1970)

. . . The problem of any poet writing at present is how not to be over-whelmed by the influences of the great period now just over. The bequest of that generation is too rich. At the same time, as far as its usefulness to a living poet goes, it is obsolete. The huge poetic account they amassed is somehow—without ever having been really spent—bankrupt. Perhaps the world has changed too quickly. Now among the greater number who go on presenting dud cheques, one sees poets preferring to accept total poverty—as a more honest alternative.

But the real alternative, which Laura Riding's poetry exemplifies like nobody else's, is for the poet to do what is perhaps easier at the beginning of a good period than at the end, to ignore all influences and mine his way back to the source of poetry inside his own head. This, which one imagines ought to be the distinctive labour that makes a poet a poet, is what poets almost never manage to keep up: given our social natures, and our instinctive economies, it is almost impossible, after the first innocent inspiration. It is because her poems embody both a search and a discovery of how precisely the job can be done, that Laura Riding's poetry has operated on other poets—as she very justifiably points out—as "a new primer of poetic linguistics."

 .   .   .   .

Her pursuit is religious only in the sense that Wittgenstein's demands on and final despair with language can be called religious. She is not so alone as she claims in forcing poetry to "the breaking point," but since her *Collected Poems*—which evidently convinced her that in poetry she had failed her notion of the truth—she has published no new verse. She now claims purer poetic conscience for her silence than for her poetry.

However she may feel she failed her notion of the truth, we can say she did not fail poetry till she stopped writing. One senses a deep mistake in her sort of absolutism, an angelic sort of miserliness. Some abstract, suicidally-high demand for an ideal has got the upper hand of the creature sunk in the chattering fever of approximations and compromise which is the life of expressive speech. Nevertheless, it is the steady pressure of this demand through the poems which gives them their marvellously purposeful tension and inner moral coherence.

Perhaps her secret lies in this combination of a concentrated, ruthless drive towards things beyond language with a new-molten supple wild and free language. She has a "religious" respect for the thing to be said, but no respect at all for the available means of saying it. "The poetry does not matter." But only a poet with an immense natural verbal gift can get away with that. The naively mathematical computerised ideal of language which one associates with the linguistic philosophy closest to her main theme is the opposite of her type of precision. Her language is truly primitive speech, a medicine bag of provisional magic and rough improvisation—childlike, playful, bizarre in a perpetual restless state of dissolution and re-invention. It is a selfless language, created on the spur of the moment by her fierce, close, lucid, entranced, sensitive and wary pursuit of the actualities beyond them. Her nearly incredible precision is the precision not so much of the cold meaning of words as of expressiveness—in which many things beside a clear eye relentlessly on the object combine. Her weird music and patterning, her unfailing surprise—the greater poetic field that words begin to wield when they come fully alive—all that seems to have been incidental to her special state of attention, which was essentially contemptuous of words. Her priorities were right. To respect words more than the truths which are perpetually trying to find and correct words is the death of poetry. The reverse, of course, is also the death of poetry—but not before it has produced poetry.

As a "new primer of poetic linguistics" her poems are as fresh and exemplary as ever they were. No doubt poets will go on being as grateful for them in the future as they have been in the past.

(Previously unpublished)

Orghast (1971)

. . . For a man even to know what he really wants, is beyond him. He tries to be sincere, and he sounds phonier than ever. He swears he will dig out his real true feeling, and he flounders from shape to shape in a fog. He gets hold of what seems like the real thing, and he vows "this *is* it"—and he might even start building a life round it, to fortify it, to make sure of it. But then another contrary feeling snakes up and says "what about me?" and another, "what about me?" and another "and me?" and "we're all you, too." In the end maybe he sits despairing under a dogfight of voices—all falsehoods, but all ringingly sincere, and all dead serious, they can be alarmingly serious, one of them might even control a pistol. Yet none of these is "it." None of them is the "real" him. Then some stranger comes along and hears his voice in the next room, or sees him coming in through the door, or getting up smiling to shake somebody's hand—and in a flash they know him absolutely, as if they knew what to expect of him in every situation. It often happens like that. And almost inevitably closer acquaintance proves sooner or later that first flash vision was dead accurate. The real self, the one the man himself couldn't find, spoke loud and clear through his whole being. Or maybe just through a flicker in his voice.

. . . .

Yet this creature of truths, which provides most of the excitement in our lives, is only halfway to the truth we really need. There is another person, another being, much more important, of much greater truth, beyond this one. If this one finds it so difficult to speak his truth, what about the further, deeper one? And if this one is so hard to get to grips with, how far away from us is that other, hidden beyond and beneath?

And in fact this other rarely speaks or stirs at all, in the sort of lives we now lead. We have so totally lost touch, that we hardly realise he is absent. All we know is that somehow or other the great, precious thing is missing. And the real distress of our world begins there. The luminous spirit (maybe he is a crowd of sprits), that takes account of everything and gives everything its meaning, is missing. Not missing, just incommunicado. But here and there, it may be, we hear it.

It is human, of course, but it is also everything else that lives. When we hear it, we understand what a strange thing is living in this Universe, and somewhere at the core of us—strange, beautiful, pathetic, terrible. Some animals and birds express this being pure and without effort, and then you hear the whole desolate, final actuality of existence in a voice, a tone. There we really recognize a spirit, a truth under all the truths. Far beyond human words. And the startling quality of this "truth" is that it is terrible. It is for some reason harrowing, as well as being the utterly beautiful thing. Once when his spirits were dictating poetic material to Yeats, an owl cried outside the house, and the spirits paused. After a while one said: "We like that sort of sound." And that is it: "that sort of sound" makes the spirits listen. It opens our deepest and innermost ghost to sudden attention. It is a spirit, and it speaks to spirit.

Sometimes singers have this elemental, bottomless, impersonal, perfect quality, which seems open to the whole Creation, but they are usually old men, singing very ancient songs, or women who sing like mediums, possessed. Children acting sometimes have it, and it is the distinctive thing in the recorded chanting of religious texts, where they are distinctive at all, or in the recorded singing of primitive holy men. In all these, that lost spirit-being opens a door to a world of spirit—nothing else, it simply opens a door, and that other world is present. And it is as if the whole Creation were suddenly present.

And sometimes actors have it. It not only speaks, it moves—a particular quality of movement, or of action, can announce its presence as distinctly as a sound. The sole original purpose of the sound and action of poetic drama was to engage that world, open it, and act out its pressures and puzzle over its laws. In a play of that sort, properly performed, the poetry of the words is unimportant. What is important about them is that they should speak with everything else, where everything is speaking together, every muscle, every inflection, every position. The incidental verbal poetry of true poetic drama is the least poetic thing about it.

At least, that is the sort of drama I have always imagined as an ideal. I never thought I would see it in English, because it would need such ideal, unlikely actors, and above all a director who not only wanted what I wanted, but knew how to get it. And I could never imagine what language would carry it.

In this kind of special drama, the real poetic potential would lie in the physical events, which would be of a special sort, and in the pattern of their sequence, but above all in the actor. That actor is the problem. It has never been my illusion that the theatre should belong to the writer. The theatre belongs to the actor . . .(71,O)

Myth and Education (1976)

. . . Objective imagination, then, important as it is, is not enough. What about a "subjective" imagination? It is only logical to suppose that a faculty developed specially for peering into the inner world might end up as specialized and destructive as the faculty for peering into the outer one. Besides, the real problem comes from the fact that outer world and inner world are interdependent at every moment. We are simply the locus of their collision. Two worlds, with mutually contradictory laws, or laws that seem to us to be so, colliding afresh every second, struggling for peaceful coexistence. And whether we like it or not our life is what we are able to make of that collision and struggle.

So what we need, evidently, is a faculty that embraces both worlds simultaneously. A large, flexible grasp, an inner vision which holds wide open, like a great theatre, the arena of contention, and which pays equal respects to both sides. Which keeps faith, as Goethe says, with the world of things and the world of spirits equally.

This really is imagination. This is the faculty we mean when we talk about the imagination of the great artists. The character of great works is exactly this: that in them the full presence of the inner world combines with and is reconciled to the full presence of the outer world. And in them we see that the laws of these two worlds are not contradictory at all; they are one all-inclusive system; they are laws that somehow we find it all but impossible to keep, laws that only the greatest artists are able to restate. They are the laws, simply, of human nature. And men have recognized all through history that the restating of these laws, in one medium or another, in great works of art, are the greatest human acts. They are the greatest acts and they are the most human. We recognize these works because we are all struggling to find those laws, as a man on a tightrope struggles for balance, because they are the formula that reconciles everything, and balances every imbalance.

. . . .

So it comes about that once we recognize their terms, these works seem to heal us. More important, it is in these works that humanity is truly formed. And it has to be done again and again, as circumstances change, and the balance of power between outer and inner world shifts, showing everybody the gulf. The inner world, separated from the outer world, is a place of demons. The outer world, separated from the inner world, is a place of meaningless objects and machines. The faculty that makes the human being out of these two worlds is called divine. That is only a way of saying that it is the faculty without which humanity cannot really exist. It can be called religious or visionary. More essentially, it is imagination which embraces both outer and inner worlds in a creative spirit.

Laying down blueprints for imagination of that sort is a matter of education, as Plato divined.

The myths and legends, which Plato proposed as the ideal educational material for his young citizens, can be seen as large-scale accounts of negotiations between the powers of the inner world and the stubborn conditions of the outer world, under which ordinary men and women have to live. They are immense and at the same time highly detailed sketches for the possibilities of understanding and reconciling the two. They are, in other words, an archive of draft plans for the kind of imagination we have been discussing.

Their accuracy and usefulness, in this sense, depend on the fact that they were originally the genuine projections of genuine understanding. They were tribal dreams of the highest order of inspiration and truth, at their best. They gave a true account of what really happens in that inner region where the two worlds collide. This has been attested over and over again by the way in which the imaginative men of every subsequent age have had recourse to their basic patterns and images.

But the Greek myths were not the only true myths. The unspoken definition of myth is that it carries truth of this sort. These big dreams only become the treasured property of a people when they express the real state of affairs. Priests continually elaborate the myths, but what is not true is forgotten again. So every real people has its true myths. One of the first surprises of mythographers was to find how uncannily similar these myths are all over the world. They are as alike as the lines on the palm of the human hand . . .(76,M)

János Pilinszky (1976)

. . ."I would like to write," Pilinszky has said, "as if I had remained silent." He is not alone among modern poets, particularly those of his generation and experience, in his obsession with personal silence. As it is used by those Indian saints who refuse to speak at all until the ultimate truth speaks through them, or as Socrates used it before his judges, or as Christ used it before his accusers, silence can be a resonant form of speech. Pilinszky, who is rarely ironic and never Messianic, makes us aware of another silence.

It is impossible not to feel that the spirit of his poetry aspires to the most naked and helpless of all confrontations: a Christ-like posture of crucifixion. His silence is the silence of that moment on the cross, after the cry.

In all that he writes, we hear a question: what speech is adequate for this moment, when the iron nails remain fixed in the wounds, with an eternal iron fixity, and neither hands nor feet can move?

The silence of artistic integrity "after Auschwitz" is a real thing. The mass of the human evidence of the camps, and of similar situations since, has screwed up the price of "truth" and "reality" and "understanding" beyond what common words seem able to pay. The European poets who have been formed by this circumstance are well known. They have only continued to write, when at all, with a seasoned despair, a minimal, much-examined hope, a special irony. But because he is as he is, above all a passionately religious being, Pilinszky has shifted the problem into other dimensions—which are more traditional but also, perhaps, broader and older, more intimately relevant, more piercing.

This is not to suggest that his poetry is in its inmost spirit necessarily Christian. The poems are nothing if not part of an appeal to God, but it is a God who seems not to exist. Or who exists, if at all, only as he exists for the stones. Not Godlessness, but the imminence of a God altogether different from what dogmatic Christianity has ever imagined. A God of absences and negative attributes, quite comfortless. A God in whose Creation the camps and modern physics are equally at home. But this God has the one Almightiness that matters: He is the Truth.

. . . .

And how is it, we might well ask, that this vision of what is, after all, a

Universe of Death, an immovable, unalterable horror, where trembling creatures still go uselessly through their motions, how is it that it issues in poems so beautiful and satisfying? How do his few poor objects, his gigantic empty vistas, come to be so unforgettably alive and lit? The convict's scraped skull, the chickens in their wooden cages, the disaster-blanched wall, which recur like features of a prison yard—all have an eerie, glowing depth of perspective, like objects in an early religious painting.

Though the Christian culture has been stripped off so brutally, and the true condition of the animal exposed in its ugliness, and words have lost their meaning—yet out of that rise the poems, whose words are manifestly crammed with meaning. Something has been said which belies neither the reality nor the silence. More than that, the reality has been redeemed. The very symbols of the horror are the very things he has redeemed.

They are not redeemed in any religious sense. They are redeemed, precariously, in some all-too-human sense, somewhere in the pulsing mammalian nervous-system, by a feat of human consecration: a provisional, last-ditch "miracle" which we recognise, here, as poetic.

. . . .

If the right hand of his poetic power is his hard grasp of a revealed truth of our final condition, then his left hand, so much more human and hurt, is his mystically intense feeling for the pathos of the sensual world. "Mystical" is an unsatisfactory word, but one feels the nearness of something like ecstasy, a fever of negated love, a vast inner exposure. The intensity is not forceful or strenuous, in any way. It is rather a stillness of affliction, a passivity of transfiguration. At this point, when all the powers of the soul are focused on what is final, and cannot be altered, even though it is horrible, the anguish is indistinguishable from joy. The moment closest to extinction turns out to be *the* creative moment. Final reality, a source of extraordinary energy, has been located and embraced. It is like an eclipse of the sun: each image of living death, in all its solid, earthen confinement, has a halo of solar flames.

So we feel, finally, no revulsion. The result is not comforting. But it is healing. Ghastliness and bliss are strangely married. The imagery of the central mysteries of Catholicism and the imagery of the camps have become strangely interdependent . . . (76,P)

Appendix II.
Two Interviews Conducted by the Author

APPENDIX II:
TWO INTERVIEWS CONDUCTED BY THE AUTHOR

Ted Hughes and *Crow* (1970)

Faas: Critics have often described your poetry as the "poetry of violence." Obviously such a label overlooks the wide philosophical implications of your early work, which in your own words is inspired by the "war between vitality and death . . . and celebrates the exploits of the warriors on either side." How does such poetry relate to our customary social and humanitarian values and to what degree can it be considered a criticism of these values? Probably this is two questions in one.

HUGHES: The role of this word "violence" in modern criticism is very tricky and not always easy to follow. I wonder if it's used in other countries. Do American critics use it? It's hard to imagine how the distinction can be made, outside recent English poetry.

One common use of it I fancy occurs where the reviewer type of critic is thinking of his audience . . . his English audience. When my Aunt calls my verse "horrible and violent" I know what she means. Because I know what style of life and outlook she is defending. And I know she is representative of huge numbers of people in England. What she has is an idea of what poetry ought to be . . . a very vague idea, since it's based on an almost total ignorance of what poetry has been written. She has an instinct for a kind of poetry that will confirm the values of her way of life. She finds it in the milder parts of Wordsworth if she needs supporting evidence. In a sense, critics who find my poetry violent are in her world, and they are safeguarding her way of life. So to define their use of the word violence any further, you have to work out just why her way of life should find the behaviour of a hawk "horrible" or any reference to violent death "disgusting," just as she finds any reference to extreme vehemence of life "frightening somehow." It's a futile quarrel really. It's the same one that Shakespeare found the fable for in his "Venus and Adonis." Shakespeare spent his life trying to prove that Adonis was right, the rational sceptic, the man of puritan good order. It put him through the tragedies before he decided that the quarrel could not be kept up honestly. Since then the difficult task of any poet in English has been to locate the force which Shakespeare called Venus in his first poems and Sycorax in his last.

Poetry only records these movements in the general life . . . it doesn't investigate them. The presence of the great goddess of the primaeval

world, which Catholic countries have managed to retain in the figure of
Mary, is precisely what England seems to have lacked, since the Civil War
. . . where negotiations were finally broken off. Is Mary violent? Yet
Venus in Shakespeare's poem if one reads between the lines eventually
murdered Adonis . . . she murdered him because he rejected her. He was
so desensitized, stupefied and brutalized by his rational scepticism, he
didn't know what to make of her. He thought she was an ethical peril. He
was a sort of modern critic in the larval phase . . . a modern English critic.
A typical modern Englishman. What he calls violence is a very particular
thing. In ordinary criticism it seems to be confused a lot with another type
of violence which is the ordinary violence of our psychotic democracy . . .
our materialist, non-organic democracy which is trying to stand up with a
bookish theory instead of a skeleton. Every society has its dream that has
to be dreamed, and if we go by what appears on TV the perpetual tortures
and executions there, and the spectacle of the whole population, not just a
few neurotic intellectuals but the whole mass of the people, slumped every
night in front of their sets . . . in attitudes of total disengagement, a sort of
anaesthetized unconcern . . . watching their dream reeled off in front of
them, if that's the dream of our society, then we haven't created a society
but a hell. The stuff of pulp fiction supports the idea. We are dreaming a
perpetual massacre. And when that leaks up with its characteristic whiff
of emptiness and meaninglessness, that smell of psychosis which is very
easy to detect, when it leaks up into what ought to be morally responsible
art . . . then the critics pounce, and convert it to evidence in a sociological
study. And of course it does belong to a sociological study.

On the other hand it's very hard to see where that type of violence
becomes something else . . . a greater kind of violence, the violence of the
great works. If one were to answer that exam question: Who are the poets
of violence? you wouldn't get far if you began with Thom Gunn . . . and
not merely because his subject is far more surely gentleness. No, you'd
have to begin with Homer, Aeschylus, Sophocles, Euripides, etc., author
of Job, the various epics, the Tains, the Beowulfs, Dante, Shakespeare,
Blake. When is violence "violence" and when is it great poetry? Can the
critic distinguish? I would say that most critics cannot distinguish. The
critic whose outlook is based on a rational scepticism is simply incapable of
seeing Venus from any point of view but that of Adonis. He cannot distinguish between fears for his own mental security and the actions of the
Universe redressing a disturbed balance. Or trying to. In other words, he
is incapable of judging poetry . . . because poetry is nothing if not that,
the record of just how the forces of the Universe try to redress some balance disturbed by human error. What he can do is judge works and deeds
of rational scepticism within a closed society that agrees on the terms used.
He can tell you why a poem is bad as a work of rational scepticism, but he

cannot tell why it is good as a poem. A poem might be good as both, but it need not be. Violence that begins in an unhappy home can go one way to produce a meaningless little nightmare of murder etc. for TV or it can go the other way and produce those moments in Beethoven.

Faas: You probably know about the controversy between Rawson and Hainsworth as to whether or not you celebrate violence for its own sake.

HUGHES: I think I've probably already answered that. The poem of mine usually cited for violence is the one about the Hawk Roosting, this drowsy hawk sitting in a wood and talking to itself. That bird is accused of being a fascist . . . the symbol of some horrible totalitarian genocidal dictator. Actually what I had in mind was that in this hawk Nature is thinking. Simply Nature. It's not so simple maybe because Nature is no longer so simple. I intended some Creator like the Jehovah in Job but more feminine. When Christianity kicked the devil out of Job what they actually kicked out was Nature . . . and Nature became the devil. He doesn't sound like Isis, mother of the gods, which he is. He sounds like Hitler's familiar spirit. There is a line in the poem almost verbatim from Job.

Faas: Like "Hawk Roosting," your two Jaguar poems are often interpreted as celebrations of violence.

HUGHES: I prefer to think of them as first, descriptions of a jaguar, second . . . invocations of the Goddess, third . . . invocations of a jaguar-like body of elemental force, demonic force.

It is my belief that symbols of this sort work. And the more concrete and electrically charged and fully operational the symbol, the more powerfully it works on any mind that meets it. The way it works depends on that mind . . . on the nature of that mind. I'm not at all sure how much direction, how much of a desirable aim and moral trajectory you can fix onto a symbol by associated paraphernalia. A jaguar after all can be received in several different aspects . . . he is a beautiful, powerful nature spirit, he is a homicidal maniac, he is a supercharged piece of cosmic machinery, he is a symbol of man's baser nature shoved down into the id and growing cannibal murderous with deprivation, he is an ancient symbol of Dionysus since he is a leopard raised to the ninth power, he is a precise historical symbol to the bloody-minded Aztecs and so on. Or he is simply a demon . . . a lump of ectoplasm. A lump of astral energy.

The symbol opens all these things . . . it is the reader's own nature that selects. The tradition is, that energy of this sort once invoked will destroy an impure nature and serve a pure one. In a perfectly cultured society one imagines that jaguar-like elementals would be invoked only by self-disciplinarians of a very advanced grade. I am not one and I'm sure few readers are, so maybe in our corrupt condition we have to regard poems about jaguars as ethically dangerous. Poems about jaguars, that is, which do have real summoning force. Lots of people might consider I'm overrating the powers of those two poems, but I'm speaking from my own evidence. I wrote another jaguarish poem called "Gog." That actually started as a description of the German assault through the Ardennes and it turned into the dragon in Revelations. It alarmed me so much I wrote a poem about the Red Cross Knight just to set against it with the idea of keeping it under control . . . keeping its effects under control.

Faas: What you say about "Gog" and "The Knight" reminds me of what Blake may have gone through with "Tyger! Tyger! burning bright."

HUGHES: Blake's great poem "Tyger! Tyger!" is an example, I think, of a symbol of this potentially dangerous type which arrives with its own control—it is yoked with the Lamb, and both draw the Creator. Yeats' poem about the Second Coming is very close—and the control there is in the direction given to the symbol in the last line—"towards Bethlehem." Not so much a control as a warning, an ironic pointer—but fixing the symbol in context.

Behind Blake's poem is the upsurge that produced the French Revolution, the explosion against the oppressive crust of the monarchies. Behind Yeats' poem is the upsurge that is still producing our modern chaos—the explosion against civilization itself, the oppressive deadness of civilization, the spiritless materialism of it, the stupidity of it. Both poets reach the same way for control—but the symbol itself is unqualified, it is an irruption, from the deeper resources, of enraged energy—energy that for some reason or other has become enraged.

Faas: The solution to this whole problem of violence, as you see it, seems to lie in some form of new mythology.

HUGHES: Any form of violence—any form of vehement activity—invokes the bigger energy, the elemental power circuit of the Universe. Once the contact has been made—it becomes difficult to control. Something from beyond ordinary human activity enters. When the wise men know how to create rituals and dogma, the energy can be contained. When the old rituals and dogma have lost credit and disintegrated, and no new ones have been formed, the energy cannot be contained, and so its effect is destructive—and that is the position with us. And that is why force of any kind frightens our rationalist, humanist style of outlook. In the old world God and divine power were invoked at any cost—life seemed worthless without them. In the present world we dare not invoke them—we wouldn't know how to use them or stop them destroying us. We have settled for the minimum practical energy and illumination—anything bigger introduces problems, the demons get hold of it. That is the psychological stupidity, the ineptitude, of the rigidly rationalist outlook—it's a form of hubris, and we're paying the traditional price. If you refuse the energy, you are living a kind of death. If you accept the energy, it destroys you. What is the alternative? To accept the energy, and find methods of turning it to good, of keeping it under control—rituals, the machinery of religion. The old method is the only one.

Faas: You find yourself in opposition not only to some of your critics but also to most of the *New Lines* poets who for the most part write about life in our civilization. Robert Conquest, though he included four of your poems in *New Lines* II, did so only after rejecting the poetry of violence in his introduction.

HUGHES: I haven't read that introduction so I'm not sure what he'd mean by the poetry of violence. One of the things those poets had in common I think was the post-war mood of having had enough . . . enough rhetoric, enough overweening push of any kind, enough of the dark gods, enough of the id, enough of the Angelic powers and the heroic efforts to make new worlds. They'd seen it all turn into death camps and atomic bombs. All they wanted was to get back into civvies and get home to the wife and kids and for the rest of their lives not a thing was going to interfere with a nice cigarette and a nice view of the park. The second war after all was a colossal negative revelation. In a sense it meant they recoiled to some essential English strengths. But it set them dead against negotiation with anything outside the cosiest arrangement of society. They wanted it cosy. It was an heroic position. They were like eskimos in their igloo, with a difference. They'd had enough sleeping out. Now I came a bit later. I hadn't had enough. I was all for opening negotiations with whatever happened to be out there. It's just as with the hawk. Where I conjured up a jaguar, they smelt a stormtrooper. Where I saw elementals and forces of Nature they saw motorcyclists with machine guns on the handlebars. At least that was a tendency.

Faas: From the beginning of your career you have been considered an outsider. This has somewhat changed in recent years—mainly through your already far-ranging influence on other poets—but you still don't fall into what Robert Conquest would consider the mainstream English poetic tradition. You once referred to that tradition as a "terrible, suffocating, maternal octopus."

HUGHES: I imagine I wouldn't have said that if I hadn't burdened myself with a good deal of it. I should think my idea of the mainstream is pretty close to Robert Conquest's. What I meant by the octopus was the terrific magnetic power of the tradition to grip poets and hold them. Helped by our infatuation with our English past in general. The archetypes are always there waiting . . . swashbuckling Elizabethan, earthy bawdy Merrie Englander, devastatingly witty Restoration blade and so on. And some of the great poets are such powerful magnetic fields they remake us in their own image before we're aware. Shakespeare in particular of course.

Faas: You told me a few months ago that you tried to escape this influence by drawing on your native dialect and its medieval literature. For instance, you took the title and motto of *Wodwo* from *Sir Gawain and the Green Knight*.

HUGHES: I grew up in West Yorkshire. They have a very distinctive dialect there. Whatever other speech you grow into, presumably your dialect stays alive in a sort of inner freedom, a separate little self. It makes some things more difficult . . . since it's your childhood self there inside the dialect and that is possibly your real self or the core of it. Some things it makes easier. Without it, I doubt if I would ever have written verse. And in the case of the West Yorkshire dialect, of course, it connects you directly and in your most intimate self to middle English poetry.

Faas: The main poets that are cited as influences on your work are Hopkins, Donne, Dylan Thomas and D. H. Lawrence. In addition to that, what is your relation to Blake and Yeats? It seems that your more recent development from a poet of nature to a "sophisticated philosopher" and "primitive, gnomic spellmaker" shows an increasing resemblance to theirs.

HUGHES: Well, in the way of influences I imagine everything goes into the stew. But to be specific about those names. Donne . . . I once learned as many of his poems as I could and I greatly admired his satires and epistles. More than his lyrics even. As for Thomas, *Deaths and Entrances* was a holy book with me for quite a time when it first came out. Lawrence I read entire in my teens . . . except for all but a few of the poems. His writings coloured a whole period of my life. Blake I connect inwardly to Beethoven, and if I could dig to the bottom of my strata maybe their names and works would be the deepest traces. Yeats spellbound me for about six years. I got to him not so much through his verse as through his other interests, folklore, and magic in particular. Then that strange atmosphere laid hold of me. I fancy if there is a jury of critics sitting over what I write, and I imagine every writer has something of the sort, then Yeats is the judge. There are all sorts of things I could well do but because of him and principles I absorbed from him I cannot. They are principles that I've found confirmed in other sources . . . but he stamped them into me. But these are just the names you mentioned. There are others. One poet I have read more than any of these is Chaucer. And the poet I read more than all other literature put together is Shakespeare. More than all other fiction or drama or poetry that is.

Faas: In one of your essays you speak of Shakespeare's "utility general purpose style."

HUGHES: Maybe that's an ideal notion, and yet maybe not. It's connected to the dream of an ideal vernacular. I suppose Shakespeare does have it. I remember the point in *Lear* where I suddenly recognized this. It was very early in my reading, we were going through *Lear* in school and *Lear* as you know is the most extraordinary jumble of styles. I can't remember what I thought of Shakespeare before that but at one particular mutilated and mistaken looking phrase I suddenly recognized what Shakespearean language was . . . it was not super-difficult language at all . . . it was super-easy. It wasn't a super-processed super-removed super-arcane language like Milton . . . it was super-crude. It was backyard improvisation. It was dialect taken to the limit. That was it . . . it was inspired dialect. The whole crush and cramming throwaway expressiveness of it was right at the heart of it dialect. So immediately I felt he was much closer to me than to all those scholars and commentators at the bottom of the page who I assumed hadn't grown up in some dialect. It enabled me to see all sorts of virtues in him. I saw all his knotted up complexities and piled up obscurities suddenly as nothing of the sort . . . they were just the result of his taking short cuts through walls and ceilings and floors. He goes direct from centre to centre but you never see him on the stairs or the corridors. It's a sort of inspired idleness. Wherever he turns his attention, his whole body rematerializes at that point. It's as if he were too idle to be anything but utterly direct, and utterly simple. And too idle to stop everything happening at the speed of light. So those knots of complexity are traffic jams of what are really utterly simple confrontations. His poetic virtue is hitting the nail on the head and he eventually became so expert that by hitting one nail he made fifty others jump in of their own accord. Wherever a nail exists he can hit it on the head.

Faas: When did you first get interested in poetry?

HUGHES: When I was about fifteen. My first subjects were Zulus and the Wild West. I had sagas of involved warfare among African tribes, for some reason. All in imitation of Kipling.

Faas: From what you were saying, the influence of Hopkins, Thomas and Lawrence was not really as great as often claimed.

HUGHES: I read Lawrence and Thomas at an impressionable age. I also read Hopkins very closely. But there are superficial influences that show and deep influences that maybe are not so visible. It's a mystery how a writer's imagination is influenced and altered. Up to the age of twenty-five I read no contemporary poetry whatsoever except Eliot, Thomas and some Auden. Then I read a Penguin of American poets that came out in about 1955 and that started me writing. After writing nothing for about six years. The poems that set me off were odd pieces by Shapiro, Lowell, Merwin, Wilbur and Crowe Ransom. Crowe Ransom was the one who gave me a model I felt I could use. He helped me get my words into focus. That put me into production. But this whole business of influences is mysterious. Sometimes it's just a few words that open up a whole prospect. They may occur anywhere. Then again the influences that really count are most likely not literary at all. Maybe it would be best of all to have no influences. Impossible of course. But what good are they as a rule? You spend a lifetime learning how to write verse when it's been clear

from your earliest days that the greatest poetry in English is in the prose of
the Bible. And after all the campaigns to make it new you're stuck with the
fact that some of the Scots ballads still cut a deeper groove than anything
written in the last forty years. Influences just seem to make it more and
more unlikely that a poet will write what he alone could write.

Faas: Since *Wodwo* there has been an increasing use of mythological and
Biblical material in your poetry. Do you use this material as a means (as
Eliot said of Joyce's *Ulysses*) of "manipulating a continuous parallel between contemporaneity and antiquity . . . [and as] a way of controlling, or
ordering, or giving a shape and a significance to the immense panorama of
futility and arnarchy which is contemporary history?"

HUGHES: He speaks specifically of contemporary history which was his
own red herring I imagine. Somewhere else he speaks of *The Waste Land* as
the chart of his own condition, and of history, if at all, just by extension
and parallel.

Faas: But you too speak about the disintegration of Western civilization.
Might not Eliot have done something similar?

HUGHES: I can't believe that he took the disintegration of Western civilization as a theme which he then found imagery and a general plan for. His
sickness told him the cause. Surely that was it. He cleaned his wounds and
found all the shrapnel. Every writer if he develops at all develops either
outwards into society and history, using wider and more material of that
sort, or he develops inwards into imagination and beyond that into spirit,
using perhaps no more external material than before and maybe even less,
but deepening it and making it operate in the many different inner dimensions until it opens up perhaps the religious or holy basis of the whole
thing. Or he can develop both ways simultaneously. Developing inwardly, of course, means organizing the inner world or at least searching
out the patterns there and that is a mythology. It may be an original
mythology. Or you may uncover the Cross—as Eliot did. The ideal aspect
of Yeats' development is that he managed to develop his poetry both out-
wardly into history and the common imagery of everyday life at the same
time as he developed it inwardly in a sort of close parallel . . . so that he
could speak of both simultaneously. His mythology is history, pretty
well, and his history is as he said "the story of a soul."

Faas: So you do not use Biblical and mythological material so as to give
order and meaning to something else.

HUGHES: You choose a subject because it serves, because you need it. We
go on writing poems because one poem never gets the whole account right.
There is always something missed. At the end of the ritual up comes a
goblin. Anyway within a week the whole thing has changed, one needs a
fresh bulletin. And works go dead, fishing has to be abandoned, the shoal
has moved on. While we struggle with a fragmentary Orestes some com-

plete Bacchae moves past too deep down to hear. We get news of it later . . . too late. In the end, one's poems are ragged dirty undated letters from remote battles and weddings and one thing and another.

Faas: You told me that the main theme of *Wodwo* was a "descent into destruction of some sort." Yet even here you seem to go beyond an Eliot-like portrayal of the Waste Land of modern civilization.

HUGHES: What Eliot and Joyce and I suppose Beckett are portraying is the state of belonging spiritually to the last phase of Christian civilization, they suffer its disintegration. But there are now quite a few writers about who do not seem to belong spiritually to the Christian civilization at all. In their world Christianity is just another provisional myth of man's relationship with the creator and the world of spirit. Their world is a continuation or a re-emergence of the pre-Christian world . . . it is the world of the little pagan religions and cults, the primitive religions from which of course Christianity itself grew.

Faas: In many ways, Schopenhauer's and Nietzsche's thought bears a striking resemblance to yours.

HUGHES: The only philosophy I have ever really read was Schopenhauer. He impressed me all right. You see very well where Nietzsche got his Dionysus. It was a genuine vision of something on its way back to the surface. The rough beast in Yeats' poems. Each nation sees it through different spectacles.

Faas: Like Schopenhauer you looked towards the East in quest of a new philosophy. When did you first read the *Tibetan Book of the Dead*?

HUGHES: I can't say I ever quested deliberately for a philosophy. Whatever scrappy knowledge of Indian and Chinese philosophy and religious writings I have picked up on the way . . . tied up with the mythology and the folklore which was what I was mainly interested in. And it's the sort of thing you absorb out of pure curiosity. The *Bardo Thödol*, that's the *Tibetan Book of the Dead*, was a special case. In 1960 I had met the Chinese composer Chou Wen-chung in the States, and he invited me to do a libretto of this thing. He had the most wonderful plans for the musical results. Gigantic orchestra, massed choirs, projected illuminated mandalas, soul-dancers and the rest.

Faas: Did you ever write this libretto?

HUGHES: Yes, I rewrote it a good deal. I don't think I ever came near what was needed. I got to know the *Bardo Thödol* pretty well. Unfortunately the hoped-for cash evaporated, we lost contact for about nine years, and now of course we've lost the whole idea to the psychedelics. We had no idea we were riding the zeitgeist so closely. We had one or two other schemes . . . and maybe we'll do them some day.

Faas: The idea for "Examination at the Womb Door" in *Crow* seems to be lifted straight out of the *Bardo Thödol*, and besides such direct parallels there seem to be several more general resemblances between the two books.

HUGHES: From one point of view, the *Bardo Thödol* is basically a shamanistic flight and return. Tibetan Buddhism was enormously influenced by Tibetan primitive shamanism. And in fact the special weirdness and power of all things Tibetan in occult and magical circles springs direct from the shamanism, not the Buddhism.

Faas: What exactly do you mean by shamanism in this context?

HUGHES: Basically, it's the whole procedure and practice of becoming and performing as a witch-doctor, a medicine man, among primitive peoples. The individual is summoned by certain dreams. The same dreams all over the world. A spirit summons him . . . usually an animal or a woman. If he refuses, he dies . . . or somebody near him dies. If he accepts, he then prepares himself for the job . . . it may take years. Usually he apprentices himself to some other shaman, but the spirit may well teach him direct. Once fully-fledged he can enter trance at will and go to the spirit world . . . he goes to get something badly needed, a cure, an answer, some sort of divine intervention in the community's affairs. Now this flight to the spirit world he experiences as a dream . . . and that dream is the basis of the hero story. It is the same basic outline pretty well all over the world, same events, same figures, same situations. It is the skeleton of thousands of folktales and myths. And of many narrative poems. The Odyssey, the Divine Comedy, Faust etc. Most narrative poems recount only those other dreams . . . the dream of the call. Poets usually refuse the call. How are they to accept it? How can a poet become a medicine man and fly to the source and come back and heal or pronounce oracles? Everything among us is against it. The American healer and prophet Edgar Cayce is an example of one man who dreamed the dreams and accepted the task, who was not a poet. He described the dreams and the flight. And of course he returned with the goods.

Faas: In comparison with *Wodwo* which, appropriate to its theme, has a kind of open form, your new volume has a much denser and more coherent structure. Mainly, the poems seem to interconnect on the basis of a fairly coherent "apocryphal" narrative, as you call it, in which you turn the Biblical account of the creation, the fall of man and the crucifixion etc. upside down. But last time you told me a long story mainly concerning Crow himself which is only partly reflected in the sequence.

HUGHES: The story is not really relevant to the poems as they stand. Maybe I'll finish the story some day and publish it separately. I think the poems have a life a little aside from it. The story brought me to the poems, and it was of course the story of Crow, created by God's nightmare's attempt to improve on man.

Faas: Parts of this story already appear in "Logos." You told me that the imagery in *Crow* forced itself upon you and that writing the poems had been like putting yourself through a process. Do you feel that this process has reached its completion or that you will further enlarge upon your new mythological system?

HUGHES: In a way I think I projected too far into the future. I'd like to get the rest of it. But maybe it will all take a different form.

Faas: One of the unifying devices in *Crow*, it seems to me, is the recurrence of particular themes. Especially complex is your symbolic use of the notions of Laughter, Smiling and Grinning. To each of these notions you devoted an entire poem in which Laughter, Smile and Grin are vividly realized personifications. Would you agree that they stand for an acceptance of suffering and evil, for your attitude towards the absurd?

HUGHES: I'm not quite sure what they signify.

Faas: Another recurrent motif is Crow eating in the face of adversity, in the face of suffering, violence, etc. Or I remember the protagonist sitting under the leaves "weeping till he began to laugh."

HUGHES: Most of them appeared as I wrote them. They were usually something of a shock to write. Mostly they wrote themselves quite rapidly, the story was a sort of machine that assembled them, and several of them that seem ordinary enough now arrived with a sense of having done something . . . tabu. It's easy enough to give interpretations I think and draw possibilities out of them but whether they'd be the real explanations I don't know.

Faas: So in your poem about Laughter you weren't thinking of, say, Beckett and his notion of the absurd?

HUGHES: No.

Faas: In your essay on Vasko Popa you write that Popa in contrast to Beckett has the "simple animal courage of accepting the odds."

HUGHES: Popa, and several other writers one can think of, have in a way cut their losses and cut the whole hopelessness of that civilization off, have somehow managed to invest their hopes in something deeper than what you lose if civilization disappears completely and in a way it's obviously a pervasive and deep feeling that civilization has now disappeared completely. If it's still here it's still here by grace of pure inertia and chance and if the whole thing has essentially vanished one had better have one's spirit invested in something that will not vanish. And this is a shifting of your foundation to completely new Holy Ground, a new divinity, one that won't be under the rubble when the churches collapse.

Faas: In *Crow* the first and second creation seem to be separated by nuclear war which you hint at in poems such as "Crow Alights" and "Notes for a Little Play."

HUGHES: Yes, a complete abolition of everything that's been up to this point and Crow is what manages to drag himself out of it in fairly good morale.

Faas: Does what you say about Vasko Popa apply to painter Francis Bacon as well?

HUGHES: Yes, and I like Francis Bacon very much. He's very much in both worlds. A complicated case. Because in a way like Eliot and Beckett he's suffering the disintegration, isn't he? Yet one doesn't at all have a feeling of desolation, emptiness, or hopelessness.

Faas: You seem to have mostly abandoned such formal devices as rhyme, metre and stanza which do to some extent occur in your earlier poetry. Do you feel that these devices are generally inadequate in modern poetry or that they just don't suit what you personally want to say?

HUGHES: I use them here and there. I think it's true that formal patterning of the actual movement of verse somehow includes a mathematical and a musically deeper world than free verse can easily hope to enter. It's a mystery why it should do so. But it only works of course if the language is totally alive and pure and if the writer has a perfectly pure grasp of his real feeling . . . and the very sound of metre calls up the ghosts of the past and it is difficult to sing one's own tune against that choir. It is easier to speak a language that raises no ghosts.

Faas: Which poems in *Crow* do you like best?

HUGHES: The first idea of *Crow* was really an idea of a style. In folktales the prince going on the adventure comes to the stable full of beautiful horses and he needs a horse for the next stage and the king's daughter advises him to take none of the beautiful horses that he'll be offered but to choose the dirty, scabby little foal. You see, I throw out the eagles and choose the Crow. The idea was originally just to write his songs, the songs that a Crow would sing. In other words, songs with no music whatsoever, in a super-simple and a super-ugly language which would in a way shed everything except just what he wanted to say without any other consideration and that's the basis of the style of the whole thing. I get near it in a few poems. There I really begin to get what I was after.

Ted Hughes and *Gaudete* (1977)

Faas: I'd like to start by resuming some of the issues we touched upon in our 1970 interview. You told me that "View of a Pig" was written in a deliberate effort to create an absolutely still language.

HUGHES: "View of a Pig" was a piece really written as a note. I was writing "To Paint a Water Lily" and felt very constricted fiddling around with it. It was somehow like writing through a long winding tube, like squeezing language out at the end of this long, remote process. And "View of a Pig" was just an impatient effort to break that and to write in absolutely the opposite way. So it was written in a moment of impatience. Maybe I wrote it out twice, but just more or less as it is. And that immediately struck me as a whole way of writing that was obviously much more natural for me than that water-lily-style.

Faas: Although "To Paint a Water Lily" is one of the most beautiful poems in *Lupercal*.

HUGHES: Maybe, but it isn't as interesting to me. And my follow-up to "View of a Pig" was "Pike." But that poem immediately became much more charged with particular memories and a specific obsession. And my sense of "Hawk Roosting" was that somehow or other it had picked up the prototype style behind "View of a Pig" and "Pike" without that overlay of a heavier, thicker, figurative language. Anyway, they were written in that succession, so that I got to "Hawk Roosting" through those other two poems. All three were written in a mood of impatience, deliberately trying to destroy the ways in which I had written before, trying to write in a way that had nothing to do with the way in which I thought I ought to be writing. But then, that too became deliberate and a dead end.

Almost all the poems in *Lupercal* were written as invocations to writing. My main consciousness in those days was that it was impossible to write. So these invocations were just attempts to crack the apparent impossibility of producing anything.

Faas: So, *Lupercal*, I guess, was a kind of dead end in your development?

HUGHES: But only in that it culminated a deliberate effort to find a simple concrete language with no words in it over which I didn't have complete ownership: a limited language, but authentic to me. So in my ordinary exercise of writing I felt that the *Lupercal* style simply excluded too much of what I wanted to say. But the "Hawk Roosting" style offered infinite expansion and flexibility. It was just too difficult a road, in my circumstances. It needed a state of concentration which I was evidently unable to sustain. So I preferred to look for a different way in. *Wodwo* was one way of looking for the new ground with the old equipment. While *Crow* was the discovery of a style as close and natural to me as the *Lupercal* style, but then again I set off with an attempt to simplify it . . . with the idea of reintroducing, once I'd got control of it, all the perceptions and material I'd been able to use in the *Lupercal* style. I never got that far.

Faas: I think you met the Chinese composer Chou Wen-chung in late 1959 in Yaddo rather than in 1960 as you said in our 1970 interview.

HUGHES: Yes, you are right. My memory probably played me a trick here because it was only as late as 1960 that I began to work on the *Bardo Thödol*.

Faas: Did you write the *Bardo Thödol* along the lines of your Seneca-adaptation for Peter Brook?

HUGHES: No, not at all. I just versified the whole thing, only omitting what was unnecessarily repetitive.

Faas: Do you still have the manuscript?

HUGHES: In fact, I was digging up parts of it the other day. But it's just too much like a versified version of the *Bardo Thödol* itself.

Faas: You once mentioned to me that *The Wound* was based on an actual dream.

HUGHES: Yes, I dreamt the whole thing twice, waking up in between. And when I woke the second time I wrote down as much as I could remember, managing to get the main thread and most of the episodes.

Faas: That would have been *after* you had worked on the *Bardo Thödol*.

HUGHES: Yes, I had just finished writing right through it.

Faas: Were there any images from the *Bardo Thödol* in the dream?

HUGHES: No. But my immediate interpretation of it when I woke— although I don't find it too easily interpretable like that right now—was that the dream was my Gothic-Celtic version or transposition of the *Tibetan Book of the Dead*.

Faas: What were the sources for the exercises in meditation and invocation you and Sylvia devised in 1959?

HUGHES: The whole body of magical literature which anybody can look up. I'd prefer not to talk about it.

Faas: Around 1958 Sylvia began to write a story entitled "The Hypnotizing Husband." And there are several instances in *Letters Home* where she discusses things she learnt from you like getting over writing blocks, dispensing with symbolism, or simple concentration.

HUGHES: I often used to hypnotize her to sleep and that also seems to have made her focus and concentrate on work in certain ways.

Faas: One would have thought that *she* would have introduced you to American poetry . . .

HUGHES: Well, her knowledge of American poetry was pretty extensive. But she didn't have strong preferences except maybe for Wallace Stevens.

Faas: How strange! And she hardly mentions him at all. According to *Letters Home*, Lowell and Roethke were the only poets of their generation you both really admired.

HUGHES: Well, she came to Roethke rather late.

Faas: After you had given her his *Words for the Wind* in 1959.

HUGHES: Reading Lowell in 1958 had really set her off to break through whatever blocks there were. And then suddenly at Yaddo she was isolated, reading Roethke. At first she plundered him directly but then developed her own style out of it. But all along, though with a growing scepticism, she preserved her admiration for Wallace Stevens. He was a kind of god to her, while I could never see anything at all in him except magniloquence. Her early poetry is Wallace Stevens almost every other line. By contrast, I was infatuated with John Crowe Ransom when I first met her, and I brought her into that infatuation as well. And that had an immediate impact on the style of her writing at the time.

Faas: I still don't quite understand your admiration for Crowe Ransom.

HUGHES: Yes. His is not a world you can explore for ever and ever. But his best poems are very final objects.

Faas: Yet his vision seems so limited.

HUGHES: And yet his poems are not. In the way that a melody is not limited. You may know a melody inside out and completely by heart and still not find it limited. I think his best poems have an extreme density where every movement and every word in the line is physically connected to the way it's being spoken. There is a solid total range of sensation within the pitch of every word. There are moments in Ransom's work which have a Shakespearean density of that sort—and that's quite unique in American poetry and, I think, modern poetry generally.

Faas: Personally, I just find Ransom difficult to read.

HUGHES: Well, it's all a matter of the ear. I guess the poems have very limited content. "Tawny are the leaves turned but they still hold." I mean, how does that strike you? It had my hair stand on end when I first read it. It was the first line I ever read of Crowe Ransom's where I felt that there was something extraordinary there. It seems to be completely commonplace and yet it's very weirdly planned. "Tawny are the leaves turned but they still hold." It's still a mystery to me how that line should have stirred me so much after I'd read acres and acres of Wallace Stevens and William Carlos Williams who never had any of the like effect on me.

Faas: It has been claimed that "Theology," which was published in 1961, was inspired by Popa's "The Heart of the Quartz Pebble." Did you know Popa in 1961?

HUGHES: No, I didn't know Popa until around 1964. I first read Herbert and Holub in 1963 and then Popa in '64, '65.

Faas: "Theology" seems to be some kind of blind hit of the vein you were to strike in the Crow poems. It was published in 1961 as part of "Dully Gumption's College Courses." Do you remember the circumstances of writing that poem?

HUGHES: "Theology" was a note for a poem, and turned out itself to be a better poem than I could have written at that time. And the idea of "Dully Gumption's College Courses" was to write a kind of pocket college education for each discipline. I only wrote four or five of them. But the interesting thing to me about "Theology" was that when I looked at it again maybe a month later, I realized that it was a much more concentrated and natural kind of poem than I was capable of writing with my ordinary machinery at that time.

Faas: The next one of that kind is "Reveille" from about five years later.

HUGHES: That's an imitation in a way, an attempt to get back to that kind of writing. So it was written very deliberately and with great revisions. It was part of a sequence which I began to develop around the theme of Adam and Eve. There were one or two others which I didn't keep. "Reveille" seems to me laborious and contrived now.

Faas: A long passage in *Eat Crow* was reprinted almost verbatim as the title poem of *Crow Wakes* (1971). That passage along with the rest of *Eat Crow*, I gather, was written in 1964.

HUGHES: Yes, that was part of a long waddling verse drama, I was writing then, partly based on Andreae's *The Chemical Wedding of Christian Rosencreutz*. It was entitled *Difficulties of a Bridegroom*. I got a few other pieces out of it such as "Ghost Crabs," "Waking" and "Gog," Part III. What became the title poem of *Crow Wakes*, originally was a speech made by the bride's father who at the end of the day was petrified in a glass case. It's his account of how he got into that condition.

Faas: What attracted you to *The Chemical Wedding of Christian Rosencreutz*?

HUGHES: It is a crucial seminal work—like *Parzival* or *The Tempest*—a tribal dream.

Faas: Did the writing of *Oedipus* have an influence on your poetry?

HUGHES: Yes, that had. I did that in the middle of writing those Crow pieces. And that turned out to be useful. Because it was a simple story, so that at every moment the actual writing of it was under a specific type and weight of feeling. It gave me a very sharp sense of how the language had to be hardened or deepened so it could take the weight of the feeling running in the story. After a first draft I realized that all the language I had used was too light. So there was another draft and then another one. And as I worked on it, it turned into a process of more and more simplifying, or in a way limiting the language. I ended up with something like three hundred words, the smallest vocabulary Gielgud had ever worked with. And that ran straight into *Crow*. However, it was a way of concentrating my actual writing rather than of bringing me to any language that was then useful in *Crow*. It simply concentrated me. That was probably its main use. It gave me a very clear job to work on continually, at top pressure. You knew when you had got it and when you hadn't and it was lots of hours you could put into it. And all that momentum and fitness I got from it, I could then use on those shorter sprints.

Faas: Your writing of the actual Crow poems began in 1966 with Baskin asking you to write poems for his Crow drawings, I gather.

HUGHES: Yes. But the actual way of writing was really the way I wrote for a while when I was about nineteen. In other words, it's the way I should have written all along. So, it wasn't an arrival at a style. It was just simply picking up a style that I had neglected earlier.

Faas: Are there any poems left from that period?

HUGHES: No, because I never used them then either. They just seemed irrelevant to all the things that I was trying to do in a more deliberate way.

Faas: But did you practise that other style for a certain length of time?

HUGHES: Yes, for a while. When I wasn't trying to write like Yeats or Eliot.

Faas: Were they pseudo-theological lectures like "Theology" and that kind of thing?

HUGHES: No, just little fables and anecdotes interpreting this, that and the other in a sort of plain, rough, almost flat way of going on.

Faas: Solving little problems.

HUGHES: Yes, rather than creating a colored substance. And not a poetry of observation either.

Faas: Like in *The Hawk in the Rain* and *Lupercal*.

HUGHES: That was obviously what I wanted to get. But that other was a particularly natural and easy way of writing I simply abandoned.

Faas: The mythic folktale behind *Crow* starting with God's nightmare's attempt to improve on creation etc., seems to have been like a quarry for your poetic creativity ever since the mid-sixties.

HUGHES: It is a quarry in that it is a way of getting the poems. So it is not the story that I am interested in but the poems. In other words, the whole narrative is just a way of getting a big body of ideas and energy moving on a track. For when this energy connects with a possibility for a poem, there is a lot more material and pressure in it than you could ever get into a poem just written out of the air or out of a special occasion. Poems come to you much more naturally and accumulate more life when they are part of a connected flow of real narrative that you've got yourself involved in.

Faas: So the underlying story would be some kind of autobiographical myth.

HUGHES: Why autobiographical? It's just a way of getting the poems.

Faas: In some poems the distance from the quarry seems to be a lot shorter than in others. Parts of *Gaudete*, for instance, obviously seem to reflect the story almost directly. So does "Crow's Song About God."

HUGHES: Yes. About man coming up to the gate of heaven and asking God to take back life. That's a direct episode from it.

Faas: Or "Bride and groom lie hidden for three days" about the two lovers reassembling each other's bodies.

HUGHES: That's right at the end of the story, when Crow is crossing the river and has the seven questions put to him by the Ogress he carries across. His answers move from one pole of total disaster in the relationship between him and the female to the opposite pole of totally successful, blissful union. And meanwhile, this Ogress on his back turns into a beauty, before she escapes into the oak forest on the other side of the river. And there are many more episodes in this happy land until the Ogress eventually becomes his bride.

Faas: The Ogress in *Crow* seems to resemble the Lady of the *Gaudete* poems. Both are frequently associated with horrific elements.

HUGHES: The Tiger, yes. She is the whole works. [Both laughing]

Faas: Are critics aware of the extent to which the name Lumb is associated with your life? Your house in Yorkshire is called Lumb Bank.

HUGHES: It's a fairly common West Yorkshire name. It means chimney, the tall factory chimney.

Faas: What type of baboon inspired the "baboon woman" in *Gaudete*?

HUGHES: The sacred Thoth baboon of the upper Nile. It's a peculiar breed amongst baboons. The male has a very stocky body, a beautiful peppery green fur, a long thick tail, an enormous head and extraordinary eyes. They were the sacred baboons in Egypt.

Faas: In the original Crow story the protagonist was to save a desecrated female in the underworld who then becomes his bride. In *Gaudete* the baboon woman with her "face as if sown together from several faces" is given rebirth through Lumb. The sudden reemergence of this theme was my most striking experience in reading the book.

HUGHES: But in *Gaudete* the women are being put together in a mistaken, wrong and limited way.

Faas: When did the underworld plot of *Gaudete* begin to evolve in your imagination?

HUGHES: It tied itself all together in 1971 or so when I began to look at the *Gaudete* material again. Then I realized that that was the more interesting part of the story. And my first hope was that I'd somehow or other manage to do it all together. But then I became more interested in doing a headlong narrative. Something like a Kleist story that would go from beginning to end in some forceful way pushing the reader through some kind of tunnel while being written in the kind of verse that would stop you dead at every moment. A great driving force meeting solid resistance. And in order to manage that I had to enclose myself within a very narrow tone, almost a monotone, so that the actual narrative trimmed itself down more and more. The original story was much more complicated in detail and had many more characters and irrelevant novelistic digressions.

Faas: What originally made you write the story?

HUGHES: I simply wanted to make a lot of money by writing film scripts. And that was the first one.

Faas: It is easy to misinterpret *Gaudete* because for a long time the reader is made to sympathize with Lumb until suddenly his whole scheme is described as an "error" caused by some sort of "ritualistic hocus pocus."

HUGHES: Various people in the book give their opinions, in various tones of voice, which I indicate. My own opinion I withhold. It's like a play—it contains no author's comments. As far as interpretation goes—I leave all options open.

Faas: Maud has a much deeper contact with the underworld than Lumb.

HUGHES: The idea is that she is the representative in this world of the woman that he is supposed to cure in the other world.

Faas: You mean the woman she follows in the cemetery who "walks to the far end of the path" and then disappears.

HUGHES: Yes, she is the buried real woman that has disappeared from this world. That's the general notion. Maud is her Doppelgänger and so in a way has control over Lumb to bring about this renovation of women and therefore of life in general in this world. But while she is inadequate to it he is even more so, the whole situation being impossibly crystallized in the immovable dead end forms of society and physical life.

Faas: At first I thought Hagen was to be the hero of the book.

HUGHES: In fact, I had originally planned to make it his story. A story of what's going on in his head.

Faas: Starting off with "Binoculars, powerful/Age-thickened hands."

HUGHES: So Hagen would discover everything through Garten, this little foxy character and general knockabout, who through his spying sets everything going. He is a sort of inverted child equivalent of Hagen, the ungrown element in him. So I was vaguely thinking of that kind of balance for a while. The balance also between German/Scandinavian, and ancient Britain/Celtic, between Puritanical suppressive and Catholic woman worshipping. And the whole thing just being the story of English Maytime. But I sacrificed most of that to make it work as a narrative that would be dramatic and readable, at every point, while at the same time being slightly puppet-like.

Faas: Seals in *Gaudete* seem to play the role of emissaries from the underworld.

HUGHES: All the forms of natural life are emissaries. The actual bodies of the people are emissaries.

Index

Printed May 1980 in Santa Barbara & Ann Arbor for the Black Sparrow
Press by Mackintosh and Young & Edwards Brothers Inc. This edition is
published in paper wrappers; there are 750 cloth trade copies; & 294
numbered copies have been handbound in boards by Earle Gray & are
signed by Ted Hughes & Ekbert Faas.

TED HUGHES

Born in Mytholmroyd, West Yorkshire, Ted Hughes attended Pembroke College in Cambridge where he first met Sylvia Plath. The two poets were married from 1956 till 1963, the year of Sylvia Plath's death at age 31. "A poet of the first importance" (Alfred Alvarez), Ted Hughes has won numerous prizes and awards since the publication of his first volume in 1957 (e.g., Guinness Poetry Award, 1957; John Simon Guggenheim Fellow, 1959–1960; Somerset Maugham Award, 1960; The Queen's Medal for Poetry, 1974). His reputation as a major poet so far rests on five volumes of poetry, *The Hawk in the Rain* (1957), *Lupercal* (1960), *Wodwo* (1967), *Crow* (1970) and *Gaudete* 1977). Besides these, Hughes has published numerous books of verse as well as plays, short stories and children's literature. He has edited and translated several other poets such as Keith Douglas and János Pilinszky. His adaptation of Seneca's *Oedipus* provided the basis for Peter Brook's celebrated theatre of violence production of the play at the Old Vic. Further collaboration between Hughes and Brook culminated in *Orghast*, a mythic play in a language of pure sound performed at the Fifth Arts Festival in Shiraz in 1971. Historically speaking, Hughes' primary importance may lie in his role as Britain's first major poet of global cultural dimensions. This achievement is well borne out by his various critical writings on other poets, shamanism, primitive poetry, etc., of which an important selection is here collected for the first time.

EKBERT FAAS

Ekbert Faas was born in 1938 in Berlin. He studied in Munich, Paris, Madrid and London and holds a Ph. D. (1965) and a Dr. habil. (1971) in English Literature. Besides articles, interviews and translations, he has published books on Renaissance literature, post-Romantic poetry, Modernist and non-Western aesthetics, and with Black Sparrow Press, *Towards a New American Poetics; Essays & Interviews. Charles Olson, Robert Duncan, Gary Snyder, Robert Creeley, Robert Bly, Allen Ginsberg*. At present he is writing a biography of Robert Duncan and a study of the transcendence of tragedy in Euripides, Shakespeare and Goethe. A writer as well as a teacher by profession, he has held appointments at European and North American universities and for the last few years has been teaching at York University in Toronto.